THE VISUAL EXPERIENCE

THE VISUAL EXPERIENCE

An Introduction to Art

BY *BATES LOWRY*

Chairman, Department of Art, Pomona College, Claremont, California

PRENTICE-HALL, INC., *Englewood Cliffs, N.J.*

and HARRY N. ABRAMS, INC., *New York*

Library of Congress Catalog Card Number: 61-10977
HARRY N. ABRAMS, INCORPORATED, New York, N.Y.
Printed in Holland

CONTENTS

THE CREATION OF A WORK OF ART and the perception and understanding of it, are two highly complex acts of the human spirit. No single way of describing either act can be completely satisfactory, for a work of art exists for each of us in many different ways. From this condition arises not only the power and fascination that a work of art exerts, but also the possibility of fashioning different approaches to help those who wish to become sensitive observers. The particular approach in this book is one that I have used with a wide variety of students and have found very often to accomplish what I believe to be the most desirable aim—that of giving the student the ability to see for himself, the capacity to enjoy and understand works of art on his own. In order to help the reader become independent in his experience of the visual arts, I have tried to discuss the works of art in such a way that he is constantly challenged, as his confidence and ability increase, by seeing further possibilities of visual expression and further levels of meaning. At the end, he should not be satisfied but should be anxious to see more works of art and to read more about them.

Three principal viewpoints are considered here. In the first, the work of art is looked at principally from the position of the observer; in the second, from the attitude of the artist; in the third, from the outlook of the critic. Naturally, none of these positions is totally exclusive of the others, and an equally logical order of this material might well call for a sequence different from mine. But, in this book, a psychological sequence seemed preferable—indeed necessary—if my primary aim was to be realized.

Within the different parts of the book, emphasis is invariably on the individual work of art—in the hope that its analysis will reveal something of the visual process without merely providing the reader with a formula to be applied to other works of art. The first two parts, which deal with the work of art in the most immediate sense, make up the bulk of the book because they seem to me to be the most necessary at this stage of the reader's development. The third part is in the nature of a postscript in which I seek to point out, in summary fashion, some of the possible directions in which the reader may now move with his newly gained ability to see.

Perhaps more than any other type, a book like this one owes a great deal of whatever value it has to the students, colleagues, and friends who, by their willingness to discuss these aspects of art, have helped to shape its substance. Over the years in which it has been developing, these discussions have been many. None have been more influential, however, than those which took place at the University of Chicago during the time I spent there as a student, under Professors Otto von Simson, Ulrich Middeldorf, and Peter von Blanckenhagen, and as a teacher on the Humanities Staff of the College, where I benefited particularly from working with Professor Joshua C. Taylor. To the Director of the Home-Study Program of the University of Chicago, Dr. Leonard Stein, I owe the very significant debt of my first opportunity to organize my ideas and put them into writing. The material upon which this book is based first appeared under the imprint of his organization in 1954 in a form greatly reduced and altered from its present state. At that time I was particularly fortunate in being able to discuss many of my ideas with Dr. Alan Fern, whose sensitive eye and perceptive mind did much to help that earlier version.

In the intervening years, I profited most from my association with the group of scholar-teachers brought to the then new University of California at Riverside, where an inquiring and sensitive mind in the arts was the possession of many, but particularly the mark of Professors William Sharp, Milton Miller, and Marshall van Deusen.

During the past year and a half, while this book has been in active preparation, I have again benefited from a number of people who were kind enough to read certain sections and discuss them with me. I should like to thank particularly Miss Ruth Butler, for her help on the first section; Mr. Warren Brown of the Print Room of the Baltimore Museum of Art, who read the chapter on Prints as well as the entire first section; and Mr. Richards Ruben of Pomona College, who so willingly gave me excellent criticism on the last two sections of the book when I most appreciated receiving it. In addition, I have been fortunate in having had at various times the counsel of Dr. H. W. Janson, the advice of Mrs. Kate T. Steinitz, the warm encouragement of Mrs. Clemencia Kessler, and the fine editing pen of Mr. Sam Cauman.

For the always enormous task of gathering photographs and securing permissions I am grateful to the Abrams editorial staff. I myself was the recipient of innumerable courtesies and advice from museums, private collectors, and dealers, specific acknowledgement of whose generosity in allowing their works to be reproduced may be found listed elsewhere. I am especially grateful to the Museum of Modern Art, where Mr. Willard Tangen aided me greatly, as did the members of other departments. For their help in typing the manuscript I should particularly like to thank Deirdre Toller and Dorothy Lovasy.

One debt that can never be sufficiently repaid in any form I owe my wife, who has been a continual helper, worker, and guide in every aspect of this book. I wish to dedicate it to her.

B. L.

PART ONE   *The Observer*

The Visual Experience

THE WALLS OF AN ART MUSEUM shelter many kinds of objects. Although the term "art museum" most frequently brings to our mind an image of lofty rooms with low benches on the floor and massively framed oil paintings on the wall, this mental picture actually corresponds to only a small number of the many rooms that make up the museums of Europe and America. If we reflect a moment about any one of these museums, we realize that our first impression of its contents must be expanded to include such other things as sculpture, prints, and drawings. But even these occupy only a minor part of the total space. The larger part is filled with collections of furniture, ceramics, textiles, metalwork, and the many other articles that man has made for his use or adornment. To the galleries of paintings that formed our original mental image we must add rooms for the display of silver teapots, Chippendale chairs, snuffboxes, Venetian glass, tapestries, and Chinese bronzes, if our concept of art museums is to be complete.

Expanding our concept of the art museum to include all of the articles housed within it may cause us to wonder just what determines whether an object is worthy of entering a museum devoted to the visual arts. What, we may ask, are the requirements that an object must meet in order to be admitted? What selective principles are applied to bring together two such dissimilar objects as a painting and a chair? Apparently, both have certain qualities that make their presence desirable in a museum devoted to art. We often tend, however, to see their differences rather than to see both as works of art. We may say of the painting that it is a higher type of art than the chair, or we may use the title of "artist" solely for the man who created the painting, and the term "artisan" for the man who created the chair. But how little these classifications have to do with determining whether an object is worthy of display in an art museum is made clear to us when we realize that such distinctions can be made without our ever seeing the painting or the chair. And surely this would seem an arbitrary method of selecting articles for an art museum.

That we should be reluctant to see a similarity between a chair and a painting is a result of our ordinary experience with these objects. We see each article primarily in terms of the purpose for which it was created; and for us, a painting serves a different and, perhaps, more exalted purpose than a chair. We know that the painting is more capable than a piece of furniture of inducing subtle or inspired thoughts in us. The painter may be striving to depict the mystery of the Nativity, the cabinetmaker to express solidity or elegance. But both the painter and the cabinetmaker are attempting to convey, through visual forms, an idea or an emotion. The procedures that these two men may follow in expressing their ideas visually are the same. Thus the chair and the painting are alike in how their purposes are achieved, and on this basis they may be judged as being worthy or unworthy of entering the museum. If a painting with a lofty subject is poorly conceived visually, it is less a work of art than a chair in which visual form has been perfected. Such a painting might well be denied admittance to the museum, whereas the piece of furniture would be welcomed.

Whether an object enters an art musuem depends, then, on the degree of success that the artist attains in visually expressing the purpose of his work. For, primarily and ultimately, the object—painting or chair—is what the artist has created. If he is a poor artist, without skill or imagination, his work will be poor. And it will remain so whether it was made in 1652 or today. Time cannot make a poor work better, although it may allow the work to acquire the fashionable name of antique and to be sought after simply because of its age. An object's value as a work of art—its claim to be considered a good work of art—is determined solely by the artist's ability in expressing his ideas or emotions in visual form.

To speak about art it is not necessary to stay within the confines of our imaginary museum. We find people everywhere who attempt to give visual expression to their ideas. The dress designer, the landscape gardener, the interior decorator are primarily concerned with visual forms. The products of their creativity may be bad or good, depending upon whether they are poor or excellent artists. The visual arts are very much a part of our daily lives. The clothes we wear, the chairs we sit on, the plates we eat from are all products of attempts to present ideas in visual form.

The way in which these ideas are presented is not the same in all of these activities. The designer of wallpaper has certain considerations and restrictions in presenting his concepts that do not exist for the sculptor. And the sculptor in turn is concerned with problems peculiar to his own work—problems that are different from those of the print maker. Yet, underlying these varied activities and their particular problems, there exists a certain unity that may allow a single artist to operate in a number of these fields, limited only by his own technical knowledge. During the Renaissance it often happened that one artist was active as architect, painter, sculptor, dress designer, and stage producer. Today, artists are equally versatile in their accomplishments; they work, as has Picasso, in sculpture, painting, prints, and ceramics. The foremost requirement of all these activities is the ability to work with the eye.

Being able to work with the eye is not something that one is born either with or without. Some people possess a natural feeling for the visual arts, but such persons are as rare as the

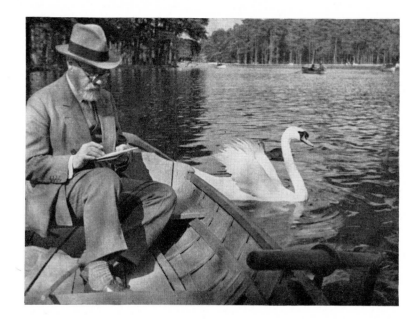

1. Henri Matisse sketching
in the Bois de Boulogne, Paris

natural-born composer. Visual sensitivity is not a mysterious talent inherited along with blue eyes or brown hair. We are not born with a knowledge of how to see, any more than we are born with a knowledge of how to speak English. We are born only with the ability to learn how to speak English. We are born also with an ability to learn how to see. We learn about English through training and study, but only rarely do we go through this same learning process, at home or at school, with the visual arts. Without this learning process in speaking, we would make only unintelligible noises, and would lack any ability to communicate orally. Our ability to communicate visually is equally affected by any neglect of training or study.

But what kind of training develops our inherent sensitivity to the visual arts? To begin with, we must learn how to see—not look, but see. Looking and seeing are as different as babbling and speaking. To look means that our eyes operate only to the extent that they keep us from being hit by a car, assist us in learning the news, or amuse us through television. To look means to walk down a street every day and yet be unable to recognize a photograph of it, or to know only the shop windows and not the entire buildings. That we generally look rather than see is obvious from how difficult it would be for us to describe our home so that a stranger might recognize it upon entering. Some type of description we could manage, since we are practically forced to know the location of certain items in our surroundings. And it also might be possible for us to make a numerical listing of objects in our home, but few of us can actually picture the shape of the legs on the desk, the arms of the chair, or the color of the floor where the light enters or the shadows fall. Most people only look and do not see. If looking were not different from seeing, then the best critic and warmest appreciator of a painting or statue would be the one who remained the longest before the work of art.

2. Henri Matisse
Le Cygne (The Swan),
etching for
Poésies de Stéphane Mallarmé
1930–32

Seeing is an act that occurs only with effort; we must train ourselves to see. We may begin simply by looking around us, studying the objects that we have with us every day. But, instead of merely looking at a table and automatically identifying it as such, substituting a word for an image, we should study its form—how the vertical legs join the flat plane of the top, how the corners meet, where the carving occurs. But to see is not simply a matter of opening our eyes wider. We must think about what meets our eyes. The eye and the mind must both work together if we are to see.

In learning how to see we cannot rely solely on reading books. We begin to see only when we

3. HENRI MATISSE
Le Cygne, II (The Swan, II),
preliminary drawing for
etching for
Poésies de Stéphane Mallarmé
1930–32

act for ourselves. For what we actually do in learning how to see is to build up our experience with visual forms—experience made up of continually renewed contacts with the numerous objects around us. Seeing by proxy, that is, through the eyes of a critic or teacher, will not make us acquire any experience to rely upon. Only from our own experience will we derive a knowledge that will enable us to act securely and confidently in the world of visual images.

This training in how to see is no different from the training that an artist undergoes. True, he may have been born with the faculty of acquiring this ability more readily than others, but he, too, must build up an experience with visual forms. The artist studies and observes constantly:

the many sketchbooks the artist fills are ample testimony to his practice. To be able to draw an apple in a few quick lines or to suggest the texture of a grape by a brush stroke is not an inherent trait. The good artist has drawn and studied the apple or grape until he knows intimately the peculiarities of its shape, color, texture, or mass. The very simple line etching of a swan by Matisse (fig. 2) was not achieved so quickly and easily as it may appear. Behind the simple, suggestive lines of the finished product lies the careful, detailed sketch made from nature (fig. 3). From his observation of the object Matisse became familiar with the characteristics of the swan, learned how to see it, so that he could translate it into such an elegant form.

In this way, an artist is enabled to present his idea clearly. By his past experience with the object, the artist learns not only those characteristics which are of importance visually, but learns how to use these elements in giving form to his ideas. This book attempts to discuss how to see by emphasizing what to see.

CHAPTER 1

The Visual Process

HOW MUCH WE ENJOY A WORK OF ART is an indication of our ability to see. The more our visual experience expands, the greater becomes the amount of pleasure we receive from the visual form that the artist has created. This pleasure should not be confused, however, with the response aroused in us by the idea that the artist is expressing. A painting that is a plea against destructive warfare may appeal to us because we share the same sentiments, or a painting of a certain type of countryside may cause us to think wistfully of our childhood surroundings. A particular statue may give us pleasure because it calls to mind the virtues of a favorite hero from history or a novel.

Such responses are a natural part of our reaction to a work of art. We must, however, be sufficiently alert and honest to recognize when our enjoyment results simply from a personal reaction to the idea without regard for the form in which the artist has clothed the idea. Such reactions do not come from our visual experience, but from the concepts we happen to hold with respect to various subjects. The stimulation that we receive from the idea of a work of art is conditioned by these concepts; we feel pleasure if the concept expressed is similar to our own, annoyance if it disagrees with one of ours, or we may experience the sensation of forming new concepts or altering old ones. But this type of reaction is the same regardless of the form of the object. It makes no difference whether the work of art is a painting, an opera, a symphony, or a novel.

Unless we experience an additional response based on the particular form of the object, we will remain indifferent to the expressive quality peculiar to each of the arts. We will fail to recognize what made one man express his ideas in painting, another in poetry or music. The fusion of idea and visual form—the genius of the artist and the source of the aesthetic experience—will not exist for us unless we learn to see. In learning how to see, the artist has come to recognize the particular contribution to our visual experience of such individual elements as line or color. He has become so sensitive to the effect of these elements that he finds them the natural and necessary means of expressing his ideas. To be able to share in this visual process we too must recognize these elements.

We can begin to acquire an understanding of the visual process if we observe the behavior of our eye when it is confronted by an object such as this Egyptian vase (fig. 4). As we examine this vase, we find our eye attracted primarily to the lines that make up its decoration. To describe what our eye does when concentrating on this decoration, we say that it follows the lines of the decoration. These lines appear to make our eye move in the same manner as our eye now follows this line of print. Thus, when drawing a line, the artist is providing a path along which our eye will travel.

Basically, there are two directions to which we relate the movement of our eye—horizontal and vertical. This movement may be simple, such as that of a straight line between two points, or it may be more complex, like the movement of the lines on the vase. Here, our eye moves horizontally through a series of wavy movements as it follows the lines describing their pattern across the surface. The regularity of these movements establishes a pattern, and we are quick to sense this quality of the line. If this pattern were continued indefinitely our eye would tire and lose interest in the lines. Because of their effect on the movement of our eye, we would describe the lines as being monotonous. A line, then, can not only induce our eye to move, but a certain type of line can evoke in us a particular sensation.

Our eye is extremely sensitive to even minor variations in the movements of a line. For example, one reason why we do not find the pattern of lines on this vase monotonous is that no one line is an exact duplicate of another. Also, if we try to describe the nature of these lines of decoration more accurately we find that we must differentiate between the lines on the upper part or neck of the vase and those on the body. For our eye, as it follows the lines on the neck, describes a jagged path in contrast to the smooth path offered by the lines on the body of the vase. We speak of the lines in this way because it seems physically easier for our eye to follow the curved lines than to follow the straighter lines that meet at more acute angles. Because of this sensitivity of our eye, we come to associate many different physical reactions with the movements of a line.

We may also note that our eye moves up and down more vigorously as it follows the lines on the neck in contrast with the meandering, lazy-like movement it goes through in following the lines on the body. We may even apply adjectives like "slow" to the lines on the body and "quick" to those on the neck. We attribute such qualities of time to the lines because our eye seems to take different amounts of time to follow different types of lines. All of the words that we use to describe a line are derived from the action that our eye appears to go through when confronted by a line. Our descriptions of lines as smooth or fast is simply a recognition on our part that they have the power to make us feel a certain way. Thus, the element of line, even as seen in this very simple example, can be a very effective means of expressing ideas or concepts visually.

If, in place of the simple pattern of lines of the Egyptian vase, we are confronted by a painting

4. EGYPTIAN. Glass Vase
1500–1200 B.C.

or drawing in which there occur a number of lines in various combinations, our reactions become more refined and are closer to what we might call an emotion. Such responses are evoked not only through identifying the lines with the actions of the eye but through relating these lines with our remembered responses to other feelings or emotions encountered in similar situations. Our memory of such situations enables us to make these relationships. Naturally, this further degree of association is made possible only by the extent of our visual experience. The more frequently and the more keenly we have observed the visual elements of a situation, the more refined and immediate will be our response.

When, for example, we look at this Japanese painting of a winter landscape (fig. 5), we are fully convinced that the terrain is harsh and the cold bitter. The extent of our experience of similar surroundings naturally conditions our response. But our response is not due solely to our own experience, for the artist must persuade us to make these associations. Our conviction about the character of this scene is aroused by more than the subject that the artist has depicted; our feelings are made intense by the manner in which the painting has been created. When we examine the painting, we find that the artist has used lines that are short, choppy, angular, and predominantly straight. Only with difficulty can we find a curved line in this painting. The lines that the artist has used are in themselves rigid and frozen, and thus characterize the scene clearly and forcefully.

5. SESSHU. *Winter Landscape*
Japanese, Muromachi Period,
late 15th century

6. MA YUAN. *Bare Willows and Distant Mountains*
Chinese, Sung Dynasty, early 13th century

What a different reaction we have when we turn to a landscape scene (fig. 6) painted by another artist! The harsh sense of icy winter climate that we received from the former painting is now replaced by a calm, almost serene feeling. Partly, this difference in feeling results, of course, from the fact that this artist depicts a scene without snow. But this landscape appears to us to be peaceful and gentle even though the terrain is still mountainous and the trees remain bare. Clearly the major difference between this work and the other rests in the type of line this artist uses to depict the natural objects in the landscape. The heavy, wide lines of the former are here transformed into thinner, lighter lines, and in place of the short, choppy lines of the other

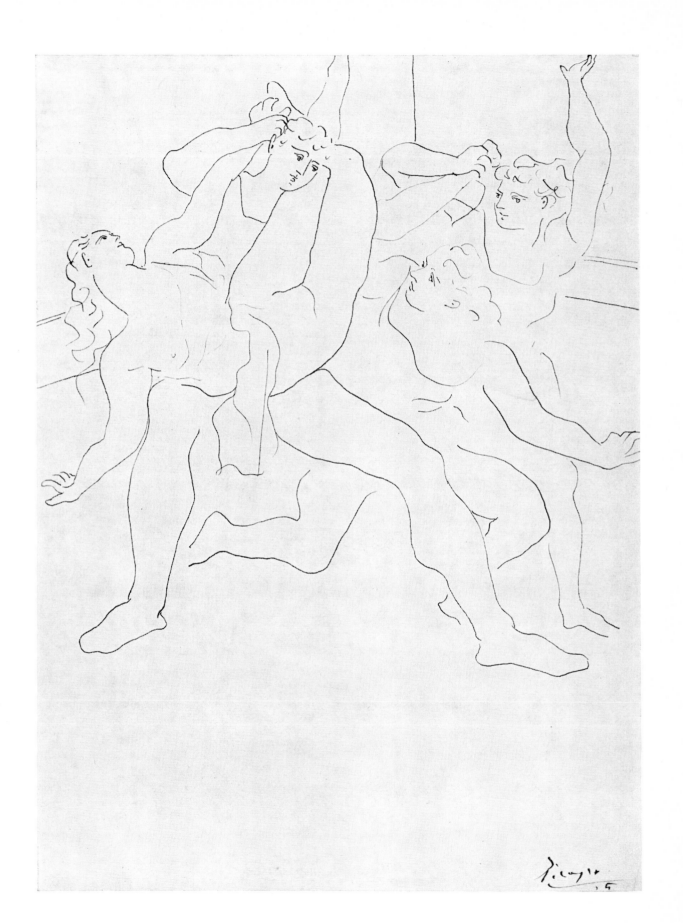

work, our eye is here given longer lines to follow. Too, these lines move in soft curves that are enjoyable to our eye after the rigid lines of the winter painting; the mountains, for example, do not end in jagged peaks but terminate in rounded summits. No harsh or angular line is allowed to detract from the tranquility the artist is endeavouring to depict.

Each of these paintings represents the use of a different type of line—a line similar to one of the two types that we first encountered on the vase. Through the more subtle use of one of these types of line, each artist has been able to produce in us more complex reactions than we experienced in viewing the same type of line when it was used simply as decoration. By their understanding of the expressive possibility of line, both artists have been able to convey to us their own feelings about the two scenes.

How only a few lines become a very sensitive means of expression in the hands of a capable artist can be seen in the drawing by Picasso (fig. 7). The drawing is made up primarily of the kind of simple outlines that we may make when we draw around our hand on a piece of paper to provide the eye with a record of what it has seen. But, by the subtle changes in the directions of these lines, Picasso makes each one express a slightly different character. Our eye moves quickly over some of the lines, slowly over others, is forced to make abrupt stops or to continue for a great length. In this way, Picasso is able to convey to us not only a picture of four dancers, but a very real sense of the motions that they are going through. He makes us aware of the individual actions that each figure must perform in order to carry out his assigned role in this dance. We see the dancers formed by the outline drawing, but we sense the nature of the dance from the character of the line itself. The artist's understanding of the expressive possibilities of line derives from his rich visual experience. To be fully comprehended, his work of art demands an awareness on our part of the visual process by which it has been created.

OPPOSITE PAGE

7. PABLO PICASSO. *Four Ballet Dancers* (drawing). 1925

CHAPTER 2

Line

8. *Father, Baby Sister, Self, Mother*
pencil drawing by a child of 5

WE HAVE SEEN THAT A LINE may be simply the record on paper of how our eye moves when it examines an object. We have also seen that by control of this line, the artist may produce varying sensations in us. These sensations range from the direct pleasure received from the movement of the eye when looking at the Egyptian vase to the more subtle and complex type of enjoyment that we received from the landscape paintings and the Picasso drawing. In each of these cases, the feelings evoked were related to lines drawn by the artist.

Drawing lines is one of the means that we use to record the appearance of objects in nature. A linear record of an object's appearance helps us to become familiar with the object itself, a purpose especially served by our childhood drawings. When we were children, we made drawings principally to satisfy a need for characterizing and classifying the increasing number of objects we encountered. Such a quest seems to underlie these two drawings (figs. 8 and 9) by children who, at the ages of four and five, recorded the appearance of members of their families. By these linear records they were assisted in comprehending the world around them.

In making linear records of how objects appear to us, we often reduce our total visual experience to very basic elements. We use a kind of linear shorthand that we have developed by an intuitive selection of that one aspect of our visual process which most readily enables us to perceive an object. For example, the five year old child distinguished between masculine and feminine figures through simple outline shapes representing clothing. A skirt can be represented by a few lines making a simple shape because quite frequently the first step in our perception of an object consists of an impression of its outline shape. When we draw such outline shapes we know, of course, that these lines do not exist physically as a part of the object, but we use them because they correspond to the way the object appears to us. Because our comprehension of the outline shape of an object is instantaneous, and because it is rarely the sole aspect of our visual

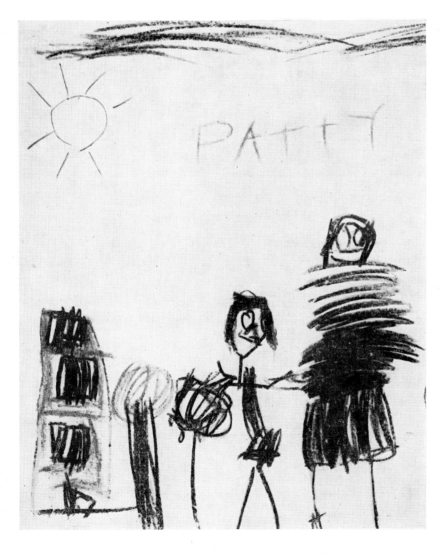

9. *Building, Tree, Grandmother, Grandfather* crayon drawing by a child of 4

10. TINTORETTO. *Christ Before Pilate.* 1566

experience of an object, we generally are not aware that we have first seen an object in this fashion. We did not realize, for example, that before we looked at the lines of decoration on the Egyptian vase, we already had received a visual impression of its outline shape. However, when we make a linear record of what we see we often do so according to only this one aspect of our visual experience.

To make a linear record of an object's appearance we may at times use only a single line instead of an outline shape. For another aspect of our visual experience is seeing objects in terms of a basic direction implicit in their form. For example, we may see a standing figure as a single, vertical line, or we may record a column, a tall building, or a tree in the same manner. When we use a line in this fashion, our record becomes a type of linear symbol for the object in the same way that the sign of an arrow is a symbol for a moving force. Both of the children's drawings show such lines combined to make "stick figures," a term that aptly describes how we may simplify our visual experience of an object. For the moment, we ignore the detailed appearance of an object in order to concentrate on its most basic aspects. We draw the major line implied by the nature of the object.

Representing an object in terms of an implied line encourages us to see a similarity between objects that actually are quite different. The tree, the tall building, the column, or the standing figure become connected in our mind by virtue of their verticality. The child who, at the age of four, drew such a series has expressed quite simply the basic verticality of all these kinds of objects. Not only may our eye see these various objects simply as vertical lines but, soon, we come to associate with verticality all of the qualities we have found to exist in them. A tree is firmly rooted, a building soars, a standing figure is erect; and all of these qualities may be expressed by a vertical line. As our experience increases we assign to these vertical forms qualities more difficult to define, such as honesty, righteousness, or superiority. We give expression to such associations by the figures of speech that we employ: "a tower of strength," "a pillar of the community," "a man with his feet on the ground," "a judgment firmly rooted in fact." Obviously, if the artist desires to impart similar qualities to his work, he will be led to the forms that engender such reactions and encourage us to make such associations.

The painting by Tintoretto *Christ Before Pilate* (fig. 10) offers us an example of how we may perceive an object by the line implied by its form. It is in this way that the artist clearly conveys to us the nature of the event taking place, for we are quite conscious of the fact that the man we see being brought to trial is not appearing before his superiors or even his peers. Christ is the dominant figure of this scene because the artist makes His figure appear to us as a single, strong vertical accent within the composition. And Tintoretto emphasizes this effect by relating the figure only to the architectural background, where the many pillars and columns of the buildings echo and reinforce the verticality of the figure of Christ. All of the figures surrounding Christ are depicted by a series of twisted, convoluted curves; no other figure possesses the verticality given to His figure, or shares any of His qualities. Christ remains the dominant figure, the one to which we devote our attention and feelings.

In the painting by Pollaiuolo (fig. 11), the implied lines of the combatants make us aware of the character of this battle. Attracted first to the lion skin, our eye travels down the arm of Hercules into the twisting curves of the Hydra, finally coming to a halt as it follows the similarly twisted path of the river into the distance. The swift and intricate movement of our eye, which causes us to sense the excitement of the battle, results from our following the directional lines of the lion skin, the arm, the Hydra, and the river; our eye did not follow the outside lines of the arm of Hercules but viewed it simply as a diagonal line. In the same manner, the body and necks of the Hydra were seen only as a combination of sinuous lines echoed by the

11. ANTONIO DEL POLLAIUOLO
Hercules Overcoming the Hydra
1460

12. GREEK. *Centaur and Lapith,*
metope from the Parthenon
447–442 B.C.

lines of the river. Whereas Tintoretto offered our eye a number of vertical elements in his picture, Pollaiuolo has repeated and emphasized a curving line and contrasted it with a diagonal line. Thus the tenor of the struggle has been heightened for us by the artist's emphasis on those lines which enable us to react swiftly to the painting, to react in a way that makes the transformation of his mental image into visual form successful.

Another struggle from the classical world is presented to us in a relief sculpture from the Parthenon (fig. 12) depicting an incident in the battle between the Lapiths and centaurs. Here our eye is confronted with a combination of strong, diagonal lines, often in opposition to one another, creating a feeling of conflict. We see the body of the centaur as one of these diagonals extending from the curve of the flanks to the bent forelegs. And, in the opposite direction, a violent diagonal line is seen in the arm of the Lapith as it forces the centaur to rear back. Our eye also senses the other diagonal lines which add to the violence of the conflict, as in the legs of the Lapith and the centaur, and in the right arm of the Lapith. Too, we sense the curved line of the cloak, which causes our eye to move rapidly from the left side of the sculpture along the arm of the Lapith, slipping up and over the shoulder, across the chest and down again to the knee. This movement of our eye allows us to encompass and grasp the figure of the Lapith easily, and this surge of movement make us sense the powerful thrust of the outstretched arm.

The line of the cloak may well remind us of the similar role played by the line of the lion skin in the previous painting. But, in comparing these two struggles we find that we are less positive about the outcome of the struggle between the Lapith and the centaur. At the moment, the Lapith appears to be the victor, but the artist has given the centaur the power to resist. No such suspense exists for us in the previous painting, where the curved lines of the Hydra add to the excitement of the struggle but cannot overcome the dominant diagonal lines given to the body of Hercules.

13. GREEK. *Perseus Slaying Medusa*,
metope from Temple C at Selinus
About 550 B.C.

The direction implied by a gesture or a glance creates another movement of our eye, which we speak of as a line. When a finger is pointed our eye moves from it to the object pointed to, thus creating a type of line. A similar line results when we follow the glance or stare of a person to the object of his attention. Thus, we may speak of yet another diagonal line as existing in the Parthenon sculpture, a line created between the eyes of the two contestants. And, in the painting, we are aware of a line running between the club of Hercules and the Hydra that defines for us the path of the movement to be taken by the raised club. In both cases, the violence of the struggle has been emphasized. The importance such lines have for our reaction to an event may be seen if we look at another representation of a conflict depicted in Greek sculpture (fig. 13). Here our eye is distracted from the bloody, final blow given to Medusa because Perseus does not look at his victim but, instead, stares out at us. This lack of contact between the two protagonists may lead us to see the work more as a symbolic representation of the deed than as a scene of action, unless we know the circumstances in which Perseus was acting. Only when we remember that to kill Medusa it was necessary to avoid her frightening and death-giving glance do we realize that the effect is deliberate, that in the direction given to Perseus' stare lies the essence of the story.

How sensitive we are to line and how readily we may see even three-dimensional objects in terms of line is evident if we compare two representations of the same character from the story of Queen Niobe (figs. 14 and 15). The pedagogue is a trusted slave who, along with Niobe and her children, was destroyed by the wrath of Apollo and Diana. In both statues he is shown leaning forward, glancing up fearfully at the pursuers and raising a hand in a protective gesture. But

14. ROMAN. *Niobid and Pedagogue*
Copy of a Greek statue of the 3rd century B.C.

15. ROMAN. *Pedagogue*
Copy of a Greek statue of the 3rd century B.C.

in the one statue he appears to have stopped to await his fate, while in the other statue he appears still to be fleeing. These differences allow us to see these two pieces either as representing the slave at different stages of his reaction to the impending doom, or as different conceptions of the way this figure might react to his fate.

Each artist shaped our conception of the character by arranging his piece of sculpture so that certain lines appear dominant. The artist of the fleeing figure presents to our eye as many strong diagonal lines as possible. These lines are not seen in opposition to one another, as in the struggle between centaur and Lapith, but as running parallel to one another in a way that suggests swift movement. The principal diagonal line runs from the outstretched left foot directly up and across the body, where it is enforced by the slanting fold of drapery, to the right shoulder. This line is echoed by the parallel lines of the garment and the strong line of the neck. The position of the arms, arranged so that our eye travels across them with the least possible interruption, effectively contributes to the mobile character of the statue.

These qualities of line are avoided by the artist of the other piece (fig. 16). Where the first piece presents to our eye clear, strong diagonal lines, this figure presents less definite, more broken and more vertical lines. The figure of the boy naturally introduces additional lines, which serve to interrupt the lines of the slave and cause our eye to take a longer time to grasp the figure. The diagonal lines that we perceive in this piece are sufficient only to convey the impression that the figure once was moving but now has stopped. Thus the diagonal line of the boy's leg is softened by the curve of the drapery, and the garment of the slave is made to fall from the shoulder in straight lines. Even such a small change as the way the cloth is arranged about the neck tends to make the figure more stationary. The upraised arm is seen at a slightly different angle, and our eye is confronted with a line that changes direction with every joint—the fingers, the palm of the hand, the lower and the upper arm all move in different directions. His other arm is not flung away from the body but rests quietly on the arm of the boy. And the boy's arm makes a horizontal line across the entire piece that divides it into almost equal halves, stressing the equilibrium of forces that makes the figures appear at rest. By their understanding of the power of line, the artists have been able to present to us two different interpretations of the same subject.

16. ROMAN. *Niobid and Pedagogue*
Copy of a Greek statue of the 3rd century B.C.

17. GIOVANNI BELLINI. *The Flight into Egypt.* About 1480

A final example of how line may be used to express a specific concept in visual form may be seen if we turn from scenes of antique mythology to a Renaissance painting of a biblical subject by Giovanni Bellini (fig. 17). Here the artist is dealing with a flight of a different kind. This group does not convey to us the urgency expressed by the fleeing slave, yet we are aware that these travelers are not taking a leisurely journey but need to proceed steadily to some appointed place. Naturally, we can learn this from the title, *The Flight into Egypt*, as the story is a familiar one. But, whether familiar or not, the story becomes meaningful and convincing here only because of the way in which the artist uses visual forms.

Our eye is led across the painting in an easy but purposeful manner by the way the artist has repeated several lines similar to one another in their general form: the line of the road, the line made by the grass, the line made by the river, and, finally, the line of the hills. And as our eye moves horizontally across the painting from left to right, we sense an increasing speed of movement. We recognize a distinct difference in how our eye is made to move in the right-hand side of the painting. If, to test this feeling, we divide the picture in half, we discover that

18. BELLINI
Detail of *The Flight into Egypt*

the Virgin and Child remain almost stationary, whereas Joseph continues his striding walk. In this truncated version the Virgin and Child are seen surrounded by curved lines, which contribute their grace and serenity to produce a tranquil scene of love between Mother and Child. These curved lines also are extended, however, to the right, where they pick up movement. As our eye travels along the reins of the donkey, for example, it picks up the sharper curve of the drapery along the right leg of Joseph and moves more quickly. Also, the road, that first follows a meandering curve, suddenly veers straight after it passes the Virgin and Child. Behind Joseph the movement is also increased by the sharply rising line of trees on the distant hill.

All of these increasingly rapid movements are brought to a climax in the figure of Joseph himself, whose clothing presents to our eye many straight lines that meet or cross one another

19. BELLINI
Detail of *The Flight into Egypt*

abruptly. A change of character in all these lines, however, might make our eye travel too quickly, and thus destroy the general peacefulness of the scene. This the artist has avoided by adroitly introducing other lines to contain and control the movement. Such is the effect, for example, of the line made by the staff held by Joseph, or by the tree whose branches point against this movement, by the group of trees forming a series of vertical lines between Joseph and his family, by the line of the halter ending in a long loop. Nor may we ignore the very important line made by the glance that Joseph directs back toward his family. The artist has been able to make us feel at once the necessity for speed that places Joseph under such strain and, also, the loving care that the Virgin is bestowing on the Christ Child. Such are the shades of emotion that line may express when an artist knows its capabilities.

CHAPTER 3

Light and Dark

20. KARL SCHMIDT-ROTTLUFF
Woman with Hat (woodcut). 1905

WHEN DISCUSSING HOW OUR EYE followed the lines of decoration on the Egyptian vase, we might have made the even more basic observation that these lines existed for us only by virtue of a contrast between light and dark. Without such a contrast we would be unable to see anything. Only by the contrast between the dark ink of the type and the lightness of the paper does this line of print become visible. The dark ink alone does not make the print visible to us, any more than does the lightness of the paper. This line of print would be equally visible if the ink were light and the paper dark. It is the contrast between them that enables us to see.

A line drawn by an artist is born, in a sense, from our need for a contrast between light and dark. When Picasso drew a line to indicate a leg or an arm of a dancer he knew we would recognize the dark line against the light background as a type of boundary existing between an object and the rest of the paper. By darkening the area between these lines, Picasso could present to us, if he so desired, the figures of the dancers as dark shapes silhouetted against the light area of the paper. Or by darkening the area around the figures he could present them to us as light areas against a dark background.

This is how the German artist Schmidt-Rottluff has conceived his woodcut representing a woman (fig. 20). For it is only through the contrast of light areas against a dark background that this figure exists for us. We have no difficulty in perceiving the form of this woman despite the almost abstract pattern of these areas of light and dark. In fact, we are so sensitive to these areas that merely by placing a light streak to either side of the figure the artist can make us see the woman as existing in some type of setting.

The opposite approach, of creating a figure out of dark areas seen against a light background, is followed by the artist of the Chinese painting representing a demon (fig. 21). What appear to be white lines within the figure are only the result of the spaces that occur between the dark areas. But the artist does not limit himself only to a single way of contrasting light and dark areas; he bounds a few of the light areas by dark lines. In doing so he clarifies certain areas of his work and also gains expressive power from this variety. Had he depicted, for example, either the cloth worn by the demon or the bag it is carrying as dark areas against a light background, the entire figure probably would have been difficult to comprehend. And, more important, there would be lost the peculiar stoop and gait of the demon that is so essential to the impression of fear that the artist is trying to convey.

21. KUNG K'AI. *A Frightened Demon* (detail of a scroll painting) Chinese, Sung Dynasty, 13th century

22. TORII KIYOMASU. *Woman Holding Comb* (woodcut)
Japanese, Edo Period, early 18th century

Varied contrasts between light and dark areas can make our eye move about a work of art in a way similar to what we have seen to be the effect of different kinds of lines. By this means the artist of the print *Woman Holding Comb* (fig. 22) creates for us a real sense of the graceful pose of this figure. As our eye tends to be attracted primarily to the sharpest contrasts of light and dark, we are led in this work to the brilliant dark-and-light decorative disks that the artist has placed on the train of the robe, at a point near the knee, and on the cuff of the sleeve. In picking up these points our eye moves from one to the other with a swaying motion that complements the curving lines of the robe. Our eye is then attracted to the similar decorative motif at the neckline of the garment, but we do not see it, like the other motifs, as a major focal point of the figure, because the artist has reversed the light-and-dark pattern of its design. Our eye picks up this motif with the others but does not pause here, being more attracted to the final dark area of the hair. Had the artist not reversed its light-and-dark pattern, this area would have competed for our attention with the hair and thus disrupted our impression of a sensitively constructed rhythm. The movement of our eye in response to this careful arrangement of areas of light and dark enhances and reinforces the graceful gesture of the figure.

In addition to the major focal points of light and dark there occur other ornamental motifs of lesser contrast, which play a secondary but supporting role in clarifying the action of this figure. The dark handle and rib lines of the fan, for example, link together two of the major points, creating a continuous diagonal movement across the figure. At the cuff of one of the sleeves and at the train of the robe, a shell-like ornament is added to the circular motif to form a larger, more intricate decorative pattern, breaking up the light area of the robe. The combining of the shell and the circular motifs at these two places makes us more conscious of the material of the robe here than anywhere else on the figure. We become aware of the robe as a physical object, with the result that it appears to be heavier at these points. We actually sense the weight of the garment and the way in which it pulls the body to one side. In contrast to these two points, the more delicate and less elaborate decoration on the other sleeve makes this part of the figure seem suddenly lighter, and we sense the lifting action made by the hand as it is raised to the hair. Thus, the variations in this light-and-dark pattern make us sense the movement of the figure even more precisely.

In the Japanese print, the shell ornament creates small areas whose complex pattern breaks up the sharp contrast between the lightest and darkest areas of the figure. In the etching by

Braque (fig. 23) the figure itself exists only because of the varying degrees of light and dark created by such areas of intricate pattern. By various combinations of lines crossing one another or running parallel to one another, the artist forms different patterns, which appear to us either as light areas divided by dark lines or as dark areas filled with light spots. In some sections, the lines and spaces of the pattern are so evenly distributed that we are unaware of the contrast in light and dark, and the area appears to our eye to be gray—a middle step between the extremes of light and dark. Others appear closer to one or the other of the two extremes, so that within the work we seem to see a whole range of distinct values between light and dark (fig. 24). By arranging these various values of light and dark the artist creates an always changing, constantly shifting image of the mythical earth goddess and her symbolic serpentine animals. The clear movement of the previous work is replaced here by a chaotic, undirected movement that is generated by and contained within the figure—contained within what is ultimately the extremely decorative pattern of the work.

The presence of several different values of light and dark in the Braque print reduces the amount of contrast that we see between the lightest and the darkest areas. Although within this work there occur areas as dark or as light as those of the Japanese print, here they are enmeshed in areas of gray, which soften the transition between the two extremes. The painting entitled

OPPOSITE PAGE

23. GEORGES BRAQUE. *Théogonie* (etching). 1934

24. Details of *Théogonie*

OPPOSITE PAGE

25. Mu-Ch'i. *Persimmons*. Chinese, Sung Dynasty, 13th century

Persimmons (fig. 25) is dependent for its effect upon an arrangement of different values in which our eye does not experience any abrupt change between light and dark. For example, the contrast implicit between the stem and body of the lightest persimmon is less striking than it might be because the entire fruit is seen in the context of the other slightly darker fruits. The placement of the lightest and darkest areas in the painting has also affected the degree of contrast we see between them. For the lightest and darkest pieces of fruit are kept far apart; to relate them our eye must travel through those of intermediate value. The way in which the areas of light and dark are defined also softens the contrast in values. Unlike the precise ornamental motifs of the print, which stand out so sharply, the areas of light and dark in the painting are set off less distinctly. The dividing line between the darkest fruit and its neighbor to the right, for example, is barely marked. By all of these subtle transitions between different values the artist concentrates our attention on distinguishing between the various pieces of fruit. According to its value, we see one fruit as smooth and firm, its skin shiny in the light; another piece, its skin darker and less firm, as mellower and riper. Thus, from these different values and the transitions between them, each fruit acquires distinctive qualities.

The infinite number of ways in which an artist may vary the contrasts between light and dark afford him the possibility of evoking in us an equally vast number of sensations, for we make many different associations in response to a change of values. A distinct contrast between pure black and white represents clarity, as expressed in the phrase, "Everything is as clear as black and white." Sharp contrasts in value can also suggest to us other qualities that we associate with clarity, such as precision, firmness, objectivity, alertness. Values which come in between the two extremes are less likely to arouse the same associations. The values that tend toward gray take on a different meaning for us as contrasts between them are reduced. Such areas are more apt to create for us a feeling of haziness or softness with which we may make an even further association of vagueness or indeterminacy. As we have already seen, our reaction depends upon the context in which we experience the different qualities of light and dark. In the instance of the Japanese print, the patterning of light and dark created for us a sense of movement and even of weight; with the painting *Persimmons*, it was our sense of touch that was aroused. Thus, light-and-dark is as expressive an element for the artist as we have seen line to be. By controlling the contrasts between the two he may give his visual forms particular meaning.

26. EDOUARD MANET. *The Dead Toreador.* 1864

By a stark, bold contrast of light and dark, Manet makes his painting *The Dead Toreador* (fig. 26) convey a striking effect of the finality of death. The contrasts throughout the work are so uniform, and the number of values so few, that we see the entire painting instantly, almost suddenly, as our eye is confronted by a scene of photographic reality. And the pattern made of the light-and-dark areas is so strong that we are denied the possibility of seeing this figure as surrounded by the same kind of space as that in which we exist. The slippers and socks, which the position of the toreador leads us to see as being farther away, are no less distinct, no less brilliantly contrasted, than the hair and the face. This contradiction of our experience with the appearance of objects in space creates a barrier between ourselves and the world into which death has just pushed this figure. The impact of these same areas of light and dark is so strong that they suggest to us the violent and abrupt death of this figure. Manet need not contort the face of the toreador into a grimace of pain or anguish to impress us with this reality, but is able to convey still another concept of death by the toreador's peaceful expression.

In contrast to our experience with the Manet painting, we are barely aware of the light and dark areas in the etching by Paul Klee (fig. 27). Yet the almost imperceptible changes in value that this artist creates by varying the space between the horizontal lines drawn across the figure are equally essential to the expressive content of the work. These irregularly spaced lines form light and dark areas that direct our interest to the figure's areas of sense perception, drawing our attention to the hands, the eyes, the ears, etc. And, unlike the treatment of the Manet, the subtle changes from dark to light encourage us to see this man as existing in a physical space similar to our own. The web of lines creates a kind of atmosphere around the figure through which our eye moves slowly, as if the space were difficult to penetrate. This weird atmosphere created by Klee might even be said to produce an effect of stillness, that emphasizes for us the concentration that this old man is devoting to his task. We seem almost capable of hearing his mind at work. What his thoughts may be we are not sure, but it is apparent that his plans are being laid with a deliberateness peculiar to the very young or the very old.

The light and dark areas in the works that we have seen so far were not created in response

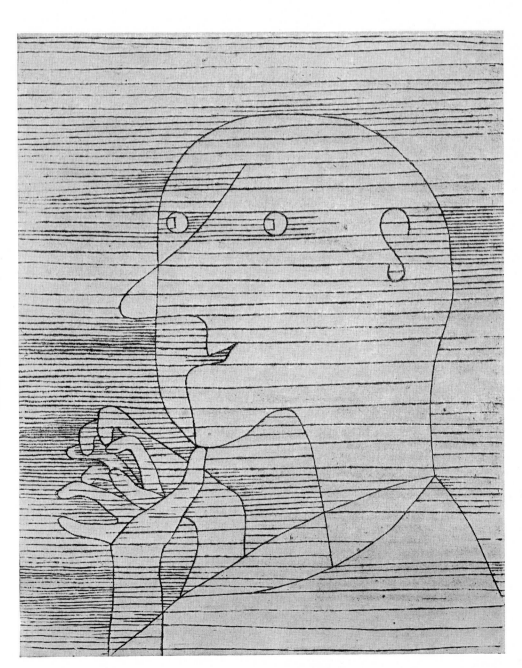

27. PAUL KLEE
Old Man Figuring (etching)
1929

to the artists' observations of how light, either natural or artificial, illuminates an object. These artists were not primarily interested in translating their ideas into visual form by reproducing the effect of light and shade. Naturally, however, the patterning of light-and-dark areas in a work of art may result from the artist's representing his subject as if it were being seen in a particular kind of light and shadow. In the painting by Titian, *St. Christopher* (fig. 28), various shadings within and about the figures create areas of light and dark that help convey the meaning. Here, for example, many changes in value give the appearance of space to the area surrounding the figures. We feel clearly that the figures are moving in a world so much like our own that we, too, could enter it and walk about in it. And the shadings within the figure of St. Christopher lead us to see some parts of his body as being farther away than others. For example, the white sleeve, which stands out so clearly, brings the shoulder of the saint forward, whereas the less distinct differences between the garment and his right leg make us see the leg as pushed back away from us. The arm and hand grasping the top of the pole are divided into several areas of light and dark, all of which define their position and movement in space. A gradual lightening which culminates in the fingers brings the arm forward.

By his concern for representing the effect of light and shade, Titian not only makes us conscious of the saint and the Christ Child as solid, three-dimensional figures moving in a world of space, but creates a pattern of light and dark that helps to convey the meaning of this scene. For we are convinced of the strength of St. Christopher, not by his size alone but by our awareness of the force with which he pushes the pole. We sense clearly the force exerted in this action because our attention is attracted to his right arm and shoulder by the white shirt—the lightest area in the painting. And, in turn, the arm is made to appear more powerful by being represented as a dark area against the light area of the sleeve. Similarly, the gradual change from the dark area of the saint to the much lighter area of the Christ Child is also important for our impression of this scene. If the change between these two highly contrasting areas were abrupt and clearly delineated, for example, the two figures would appear to us to be separated from one another. We would not feel that the position of the Christ Child on the shoulder of the saint was secure, and the meaning of the painting would be destroyed. Thus Titian has created, through the different effects of light and shade, an expressive pattern of light and dark that makes us feel confident that St. Christopher has the power and strength to cross the river, no matter how heavy his burden may become.

An artist may also utilize light and its effect on the appearance of different objects to create a pattern of light and dark that is primarily decorative. Light used in this way, for example, is

OPPOSITE PAGE
28. TITIAN. *St. Christopher*. About 1523

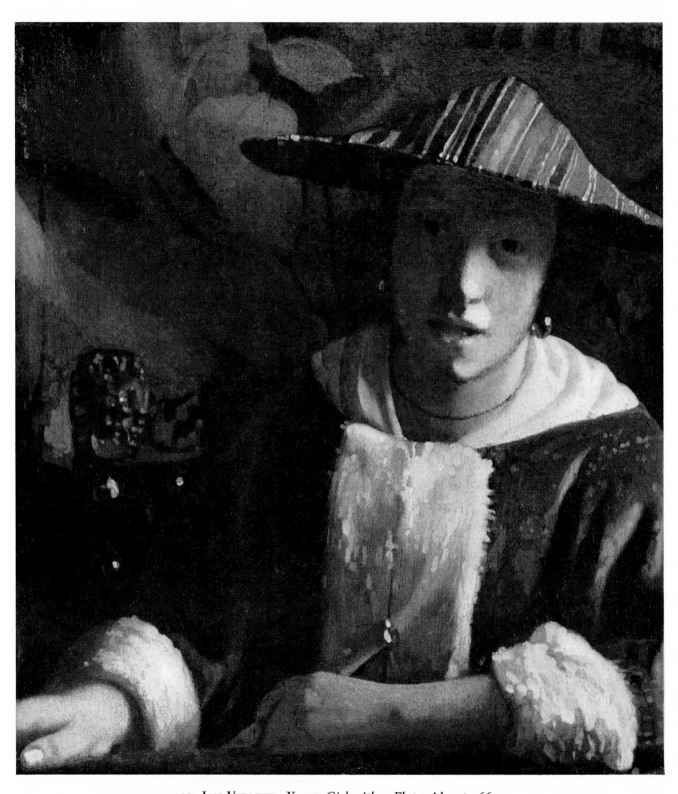

29. JAN VERMEER. *Young Girl with a Flute*. About 1664

the most important feature of the small painting by Vermeer of a young girl (fig. 29). The light, represented as entering from a point outside the painting, is directed to illuminate the left side of the girl. Within this luminous space Vermeer introduces various objects, which, because of their contrasting textures, reflect the light with different degrees of intensity and thus create areas of different values. The brass chair studs act in this way because their metallic surfaces reflect the light brightly and break up the solid dark of the velvet upholstery. Vermeer also creates contrasts in values through the positions he assigns to objects in relation to the constant light source. The position of the hat, for example, turns the strong design of the striped material into a series of varied contrasts between light and dark: the darkest and most brilliant stripes occur where the hat projects the farthest toward us and into the light. From this point, one side of the hat recedes into shadow, the stripes diminishing in contrasts of value, while the other side decreases equally in value contrast as it comes closer to the source of light. Vermeer also uses the shadow cast by the hat to create a middle value on the face, an area broken up by the light falling on the nose. Thus a judicious placement of objects within a particular type of light chosen and directed by the artist produces a light-and-dark pattern that delights us by its variety. And the pleasure afforded our eye by this pattern becomes a determining factor in our impression of the character of the woman portrayed.

Brilliant light and deep shadows are responsible for the strong emotional character of the painting by Rembrandt, *The Descent from the Cross* (figs. 30 and 31). To depict the lowering of an inanimate heavy weight so that we do not feel uneasy about its security, and yet maintain an

30. REMBRANDT. Detail of
The Descent from the Cross
(see fig. 31)

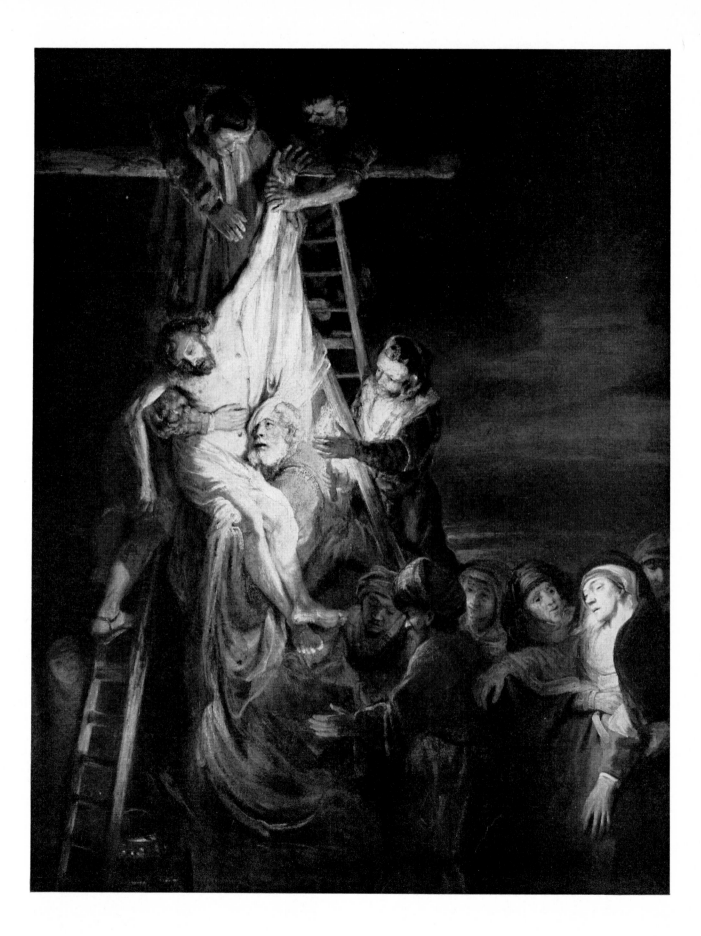

aura of reverence about the figure of Christ, is in itself a difficult task for the artist. In addition, the event requires that a large number of people and various pieces of equipment be introduced into the scene, thus creating the danger of overcrowding the canvas. Among such a crowd of people the poignant reactions of the principal characters in the story might easily be lost. Rembrandt has resolved these problems and gone on to tell us the story with passion and conviction, partly through his use of light and dark.

The body of Christ and the winding sheet form the lightest area in the painting—both brilliantly illuminated by the torch. This same light falls on the head and shoulders of Nicodemus as he receives the body of Christ. But the torch is shielded by the bearer with his hand in such a way that its light does not fall on the group of figures assisting in the descent. We are sufficiently aware of their presence to know that Nicodemus will have help in his task, but our eye is not required to examine each figure in detail. Instead, Rembrandt allows the light to pick out only those parts of the painting essential for our comprehension of the scene: a few rungs of the ladder are shown emerging from the shadow; the strain and power of the leg muscles of the man supporting the body are underlined by light; and the lines of the heavy, curved folds of the cloth, which emphasize both the weight of the body and the care with which it is being lowered, are stressed by having the edge of the cloth caught in the light. These spots of light are only minor accents, however, in comparison with the area of light about the head of the swooning Virgin (fig. 30). Within the nocturnal scene, this brilliant area encourages our eye to relate it to the light surrounding the body of Christ—the area of which it is the complement in both value and action. The very act of fainting, which causes her body to slump heavily into the arms of her attendants, reminds us of the body of Christ being lowered into the arms of Nicodemus. Her reaction to the event is a comment that emphasizes our own emotion toward the lowering of the body. Thus, by the element of light and dark, Rembrandt turns a complicated physical and psychological story into a simply expressed, powerful visual event.

OPPOSITE PAGE

31. REMBRANDT. *The Descent from the Cross.* 1650–51

CHAPTER 4

Color

WE HAVE SEEN THAT simply by contrasting light and dark areas, an artist may create a visual form that evokes a particular reaction from us. Our impressions of the paintings of Manet, Klee, and Titian were brought about primarily by the subtle and sophisticated use that these artists made of our sensitivity to distinctions between light and dark. The expressive content of the painting *Persimmons* was derived from the soft transitions among gray, black, and white. But if we turn from this still life of fruit to one painted by Courbet (page 57), we find that the light-and-dark areas in a painting can possess still another quality. For here our impression comes not only from the contrasts between light and dark areas of different values but from the color of these areas. This added quality of color offers the artist a powerful means of transforming his feelings or ideas into pictorial form.

The perception of color is the single most strongly emotional part of the visual process. Our reactions to color are often strong and immediate, and we associate the most diverse experiences and emotions with certain colors. Blue, for example, is a color that can cause us to feel wistful, sad, or lonely. It also has the ability to make us feel cool. Red, on the other hand, can give us the feeling of heat. We could describe the still life by Courbet, for example, as being a very warm painting. In another instance, red might create in us an impression of violence or destruction. And these same two colors may even effect our perception of depth. A red color generally appears to be closer to us than does a blue color; cooler colors appear to recede, warmer colors to advance toward us. These colors also have a purely sensuous appeal. The mass of red color in the Courbet painting, for example, is capable all by itself of giving us a great sense of delight. At other times this color, and others as well, may displease us or even appear revolting. The ease with which these varied associations can be provoked demonstrates the impact that color has on our visual experience.

Because the number of colors or hues is infinite, and the possible variations and combinations of these colors endless, the range of impressions that the artist is able to create through the use of color is equally vast. This very diversity of causes and effects, that makes color such a rich, expressive element, also makes it difficult, however, to describe precisely how we see and experience color. In order to do so, experiments with our perception of color have been made which have led to the establishment of systems in which the various qualities of color, and the relationships that we appear to perceive among the hues, are expressed in certain diagrammatic patterns. But our knowledge of the nature of color and of our perception of it has not passed far beyond the stage of collecting observations on our reactions. No single system has yet been established that successfully organizes the study of observable phenomena into an orderly science. How the hues relate to one another, and what reactions certain hues and their combinations may produce, still are questions for which no single answer exists. Ultimately each artist, on the basis of his experience, determines his own theory of the nature of color and its effects.

Certain observations of our experience with color are so frequently made, however, that the majority of those concerned with perception accept them as being valid. One such observation, for example, comes from our experience in looking at a variety of hues. Some appear dominant over others. We discover our eye to be strongly attracted to the hues red, blue, and yellow, a reaction that we recognize by calling these hues "primary colors." Our attraction to these colors obviously is taken into account by the artist when he creates his work. In the painting *El Espolio* by El Greco (page 59), for example, the principal figures, both with respect to the composition and the event portrayed, are depicted in primary colors. The figure of Christ is enveloped in a robe of red, the foreground figures clothed in garments of blue and yellow. Although equal in size to some of the areas of primary color, the green garment worn by the man to the right of Christ does not strike our eye with the same force. It is the primary colors red, blue, and yellow, that attract our eye and initiate our impression of this scene.

Identifying three hues as those for which we have a special affinity leads to a further observation of how our eye behaves when looking at color. With the three primary colors fixed in our mind as points of reference, we become aware that we tend to see all other colors in terms of their relationship to these dominant hues. The other hues are characterized by us according to whether they are more or less closely associated with one of the primary colors. We do so partly because we have learned from our experience with paints that by mixing certain primary colors we may produce different hues. We know, for example, that green paint can be created by bringing together yellow and blue paint. Even without this knowledge, however, we actually see the color green as being more closely related to either yellow or blue than to red. Unlike green and yellow, the colors green and red do not appear to merge with one another. Similarly, an orange hue always appears to us in terms of yellow and red, never calling to our mind the color blue.

That we see different hues as either closely or distantly related to one of the primary colors is an observation that the artist may use to create different effects. Courbet, for example, places in the center of his canvas the single, most brilliant piece of red fruit. All of the surrounding red pieces are markedly duller; the only pieces depicted with the same degree of brilliance are those of a dominantly green color. Together with the central red fruit they create a large bright area in the foreground which makes us see this part of the scene as caught in a strong light. Combined with the effect the red areas create of advancing toward us, this impression makes us feel that it is we ourselves who are holding the light that illuminates the scene. Courbet is able to convey this impression primarily because of the way our eye reacts to the combination of red and green. Without the presence of the color green, for example, the central area might well become a blinding spot of red before our eyes, might appear almost to jump out of the painting toward us. By placing green ones of similar brilliance next to this red area, Courbet anchors the red area within the composition while still creating the effect of distance and light that he apparently desires. The natural opposition we see between these two hues creates a balance of color that does not reduce the impact of the central area but allows it to function as an expressive element essential for the total effect.

The jockey scene by Degas (page 60) is another painting in which the relationships that we sense among different hues determine our impression of the work. As in the painting by Courbet, the most brilliant area of color is located at the center of the canvas. Degas gives to the silks of the jockey occupying this spot the colors yellow and blue. Our eye immediately is drawn to this area, the only one in which these two primary colors are to be found. Almost instantaneously, our eye also picks up three dots of red, nearly all we see of the racing colors worn by an adjacent jockey. The way in which Degas introduces the red color breaks up the sense of balance that we might otherwise associate with an area made up of all three of the primary colors. These small dabs of red literally make our eye jump. We move quickly, for example, to the red jockey cap in the upper right-hand corner of the canvas—an area that most nearly matches in brilliance and size the central area of yellow and blue. And from the bright spot of the jockey cap our eye moves among the colored silks of the other jockeys.

The movement that our eye makes in response to color reinforces the disorganized, candid snapshot appearance that Degas wishes to convey of this concentrated group of horses and riders. By attracting our eye first to the blue and yellow area, Degas moves us back into the midst of the crowd, but the red dots send our eye forward again where we continue to move in and out among the figures. All of these movements are intensified because the dark areas and relative absence of brilliant hues in the foreground keep our eye within a compact area surrounding the central blue and yellow combination. And the nature of this movement is controlled by the three small dots of pure red. They deny our eye a resting place. We never experience a sense of a regular flow of movement or of completing the motion. No sooner does our eye return to this point than it is once more set into motion. Thus, the hues that Degas has chosen and the way he has arranged them, visually express the constant shifting, restless actions that characterize this group gathering for the race.

In addition to revealing the distinctions that our eye makes between the colors, as well as the way in which it groups them, observations on our perception of color also show that our eye is sensitive to differences within the appearance of a single hue. We are aware of changes in both the value and the intensity of a hue. Within a painting, for example, we may distinguish between both lighter and darker, as well as brighter or duller, areas of the same hue. In the still life by Courbet, the color of the central piece of fruit appears to be so brilliant that we think of it as being as red as red can possibly be. It is the red of the greatest intensity, whereas the fruit above it is of the same value of red but diminished in intensity, a change that emphasizes the projecting appearance of the central area. The piece of fruit farthest to the left is almost the same in intensity as the central red area, but is different in value, thus continuing the effect of an illumination over only a small, immediate area. Varying the value and intensity of the color red is another way in which Courbet uses color to create the effect that he wants to achieve in this painting.

By varying the value and intensity of certain colors in his watercolor *Subtropical Landscape* (page 58), Paul Klee is able to convey a particular aspect of this type of scene. Initially our eye is confused by the many hues and different shapes that Klee uses to represent the profusion and variety that characterize luxuriant tropical flora. By breaking up the hues into many small areas Klee prevents one hue from becoming dominant and allows a sense of liveliness to pervade the work. But, since so many of the areas of different hue appear to rise from the bottom of this painting toward the top, we also sense an organic logic existing beneath the surface confusion. Our feeling of an upward growth of plant life is also stimulated by the large pink triangular form in the center. The great intensity of the pink areas makes this triangle stand out clearly as a shape that points upward, even though its form is partly made up of hues similar to others of the lower section. The upward movement is reinforced and carried to the topmost part of the painting by the triangular form in the upper right-hand corner, suggestive of a palm tree. By all of these methods Klee gives a rising direction to the closely massed shapes of different hues, visually recreating the struggle for light that must occur when the number of plants rising from the soil is so great.

To give us this impression of a struggle for light, the painting apparently is able to recall to our mind what occurs when taller foliage blocks out the light. Klee does so by making us sense that the rising forms are hindered in their upward movement—an effect he achieves simply by changing the values of the hues. For Klee has made the entire upper portion of his painting darker in value than the lower section, thus grouping the many hues and various shapes within this painting into two large areas. The slanting sides of the central triangle define precisely the change in value between the two areas. The uniformly light value of the hues in the lower section forms a wedge that pushes up against the darker values which act as a barrier to this movement. The opposition of these two areas is given its strongest expression in the center of the painting, where the apex of the triangle, which is flanked by the lightest and most brilliant areas of the scene, meets a triangular form of the darkest, dullest hue, which points downward. The impact of these two conflicting movements is aptly symbolized by the black exclamation point— a visual aside made by the artist to the viewer. This mark of exclamation not only serves as a comment on what occurs at this point, but by its function as a symbol of a sudden burst of emotion, it also gives an additional meaning to the large triangular shape. For, finally, we cannot help but see that the intensely brilliant colors here also appear to radiate away from the central point; as representing, in fact, the light that has filtered through the heavy mass of foliage, catching the plants below in its sparkle.

When we turn from the Klee watercolor to the oil painting by El Greco, we are immediately struck by the similar color pattern that each work presents, and by the similar movements that our eye is induced to make in experiencing the two works. Although radically different in content, size, and intent, each of these paintings is broken up into a great number of variously shaped areas of contrasting hues. And both artists rely upon the movements that our eye will make among these areas in order to convey the expressive content of their work.

The rising forms in the Klee painting move away from the round black dot in the foreground in three principal directions: straight up to the apex of the triangle, and off to either side up and away from the center. In the El Greco painting, we find these same three directions given to the forms rising from the center point of the lower edge of the canvas: two diagonal movements created through the color combinations and lines of the garments go off to the sides of a vertical movement centered in the figure of Christ. Of the two lateral movements, that on the right impresses us as being the stronger, because this area of the painting is the brightest in intensity, an emphasis Klee gives to the same side of his work through the form suggestive of a palm tree.

In both paintings this added force makes us see the movement on the right as rising continuously from bottom to top in a diagonal direction. But, at the same time, the entire ascending movement of the lower section of each work meets a barrier in the central area that brings it to at least a momentary halt. We have seen how Klee achieves this effect by changing the valus of the hues at this point. A similar use of color is followed by El Greco in providing on either side of the upper portion of the figure of Christ large areas of color that are dark in value. The bluish armor of the knight on the left acts to absorb the movement, as does the green garment of the figure on the right. Together with the figure of Christ they form a horizontal barrier of color that is knit more closely by the many stitch-like diagonal lines made by the bent and outstretched arms, the rope, and the rose-colored reflection of the sleeve of Christ's robe in the metal breastplate. Thus, El Greco also effectively separates the lower and upper portions of his canvas.

But, unlike Klee, El Greco divides his painting not only into a lower and upper section but into a foreground and background. Our eye not only moves over the surface of the canvas but back into depth. As the large central area of red advances toward us, the rising movements generated by the arrangement of colors and lines in the lower section of the canvas appear to go back into space. The two principal diagonal movements seem to be deflected to either side by the figure of Christ. In establishing this feeling of depth, El Greco has again emphasized the movement on the right-hand side of the painting, for on this side is placed the figure who, by leaning over toward us, gives us the strongest sensation of depth. And the emphasis given to this side by the intensity of the colors is also reinforced by the relationship in depth that the hand and arm of one of the Marys in the lower left-hand corner establishes with the arm of the man in

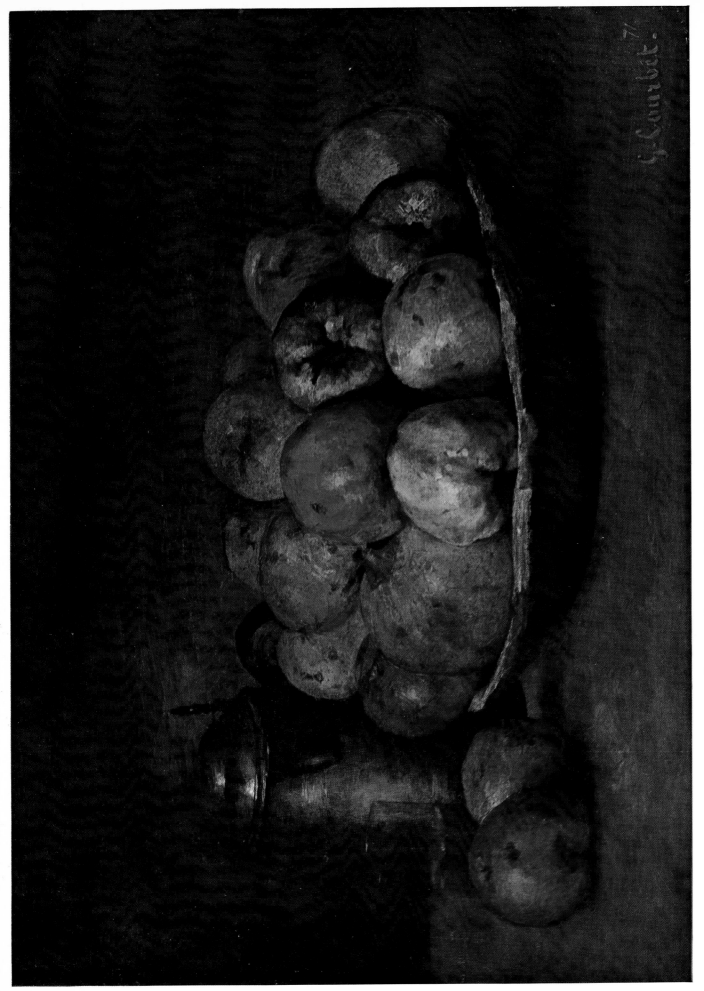

GUSTAVE COURBET. *Still Life: Apples and Pomegranates.* 1871

PAUL KLEE. *Subtropical Landscape.* 1918

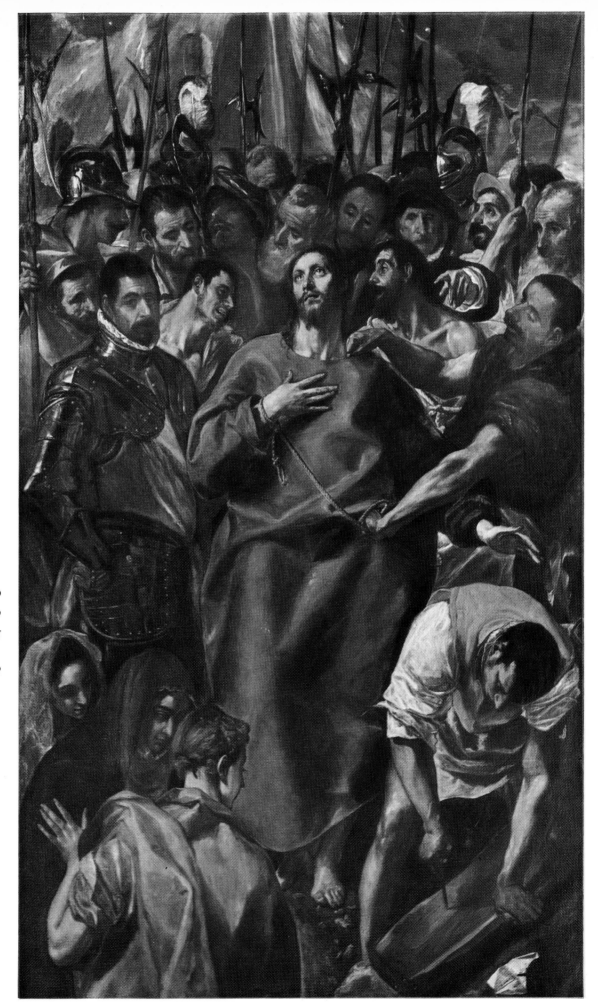

EL GRECO
El Espolio
(The Disrobing
of Christ)
1579?

EDGAR DEGAS. *Jockeys*. About 1881–85

green. All of these movements back into space are halted, however, by the darker and duller hues of the figures on either side of Christ.

Behind these two figures the movements become more chaotic as the number of figures is increased, the gestures and actions less completely seen, and the colors broken up into more numerous and smaller areas. We see these figures, then, not only as stopping the strong receding movements, but as holding back the swirl of confused movement coming from behind. Thus, we are made to feel quite clearly the emotion and excitement about to break around the figure of Christ; we are given a very real sense of the action taking place. And El Greco makes the meaning of this action clear—makes us feel the enormity of the act about to be committed—by his vertical division of the canvas. In emphasizing the right-hand side of the canvas through the different intensity of the colors, El Greco makes the left a quieter and less powerful area, a distinction that divides the commentators on the action from the participants in it. In this way, the anachronistic figure of the knight is removed as a participant in the actual event, an effect supported by the fact that he does not look at anyone or anything within the scene. We are to see him not as a defender of Christ the man, but as a defender of what Christ represents.

What Christ represents is clarified by two gestures, which by being isolated from their surroundings by both color and position in depth, stand out amid the actions on the right-hand side of the painting. Between the yellow and green areas, in the pocket of space created there, the hand of Christ is seen extended in a forgiving gesture. And it is almost with a feeling of shock that our eye finally takes in the most brilliant area of yellow in the painting, the area around the sleeve of the outstretched arm of the man in the upper right section of the canvas. His arm projects boldly from the canvas and he stares directly at us. We now understand that he does not point at Christ but accuses us. We are made to comprehend the meaning of this painting, then, primarily because of El Greco's knowledge of the expressive power of color.

CHAPTER 5

Pictorial Space

32. REMBRANDT. *A Winter Landscape.* About 1647

IN DISCUSSING COLOR WE NOTICED that we tend to relate certain hues with certain distances, that red and other warm colors appear closer to us than blue and the cooler colors. And we have seen previously that by contrasting light and dark an artist may evoke in us certain sensations of depth. The drawing by Rembrandt, *A Winter Landscape* (fig. 32), shows us that line, too, possesses the power to give us an impression of depth. A few heavy strokes of the pen, a diagonal direction to a line in one area, and several faint lines are all Rembrandt needs to be able to depict a countryside that appears to us to stretch far back into the distance. Our sensitivity to depth is apparently very great, for we receive impressions of depth from the simplest combinations of lines, colors or light and dark.

Our tendency to perceive depth in these ways furnishes an effective means of expression to the artist. As with any of the other elements we have considered, the artist may either encourage or discourage our natural bent. He may, for example, create a work that provokes only a slight impression of depth, as in the painting by Pisanello, *The Vision of St. Eustace* (fig. 34). Or, on the contrary, the artist may choose to open up the flat surface of his paper or canvas. Instead of preserving the natural two dimensional state of his work, he may encourage us to see the work in three dimensions, as does Antonello da Messina in his painting, *St. Jerome in His Study* (fig. 33).

With this new dimension the artist creates an imaginary space, a space that may be similar to or different from what we ordinarily experience. Into this space the artist introduces whatever objects he desires and places them within this space as he chooses. The world that he creates is one in which the laws governing the relationship of objects to one another, to the space they are in, and to us, are determined solely by the effect the artist wishes to produce. Like Antonello, he may create a space and a relationship between objects that seem to parallel the experiences we have within our own world. Or he may depict a world in which our experience of space and of objects is challenged, as in De Chirico's painting, *Evil Genius of a King* (fig. 35). The powerful impact of this work is due largely to the way in which the artist on

ABOVE LEFT

33. ANTONELLO DA MESSINA
St. Jerome in His Study. About 1475

ABOVE RIGHT

34. PISANELLO. *The Vision of St. Eustace.* About 1438

RIGHT

35. GIORGIO DE CHIRICO. *The Evil Genius of a King (Toys of a Prince).* 1914–15

the one hand encourages, and on the other denies the possibility of our relating this scene to customary spatial experiences. In abetting this willingness of ours to perceive depth, an artist is governed by only two factors: one, his knowledge of how we will react to certain spatial arrangements, and two, the idea or feeling he wishes to produce.

On first impression, Pisanello's work (fig. 36) does not arouse in us a strong feeling of depth. We tend to be more aware of the surface of the painting than we are of any space that might be behind it. This reaction dominates our impression of the work, even though the artist has depicted his figures in a manner that normally would encourage us to see them as three-dimensional objects. For example, the shading within the figures gives them a certain solidity; they do not appear simply as shapes seen against a uniform background, like a wallpaper design or a pattern similar to that on the Egyptian vase. There are other aspects of this painting that may also be comprehended in a way that makes the figures appear to exist in depth. The fact that portions of the figures cut across one another, for example, may make us see the one whose outline is intact as being in front of the partially eclipsed figure. Also, the fact that the figures appear smaller in the upper portion of the painting may make us see them as being farther away from us. This conclusion is possible, however, only after we realize that the rabbit in the lower right-hand corner is depicted as being larger than the bear found in the upper section of the painting. It is actually our knowledge of the relative sizes of animals that forces us to see the bear as being farther away than the rabbit.

All of these factors may lead us to a new understanding of the pictorial space that Pisanello has created; but this intellectual process does not alter our original impression of this painting. Our feeling for depth remains only slightly aroused; we remain more conscious of the multitude of figures than of their particular position in space. Although we may eventually comprehend the figures in the top part of the painting as being farther away from us than those in the bottom, we continue to be more sensitive to the over-all pattern of the work. The value of the upper portion of the painting, in comparison with the bottom, may be closer to gray, but we are not led to see the top area as being less distinct or more distant, for the contrasts between values remain nearly uniform throughout the work. The degree of contrast between the herons and the water, for example, is approximately the same as that between the dogs and the ground in the left-hand corner. This uniformity encourages us to relate one area of the surface to another on the basis of their correspondence in value and size. We disregard what actually makes up this area. Since our knowledge of the relative sizes of animals does not intrude, we may visually equate a rabbit with an animal that we know to be larger. We relate the different areas in terms of their role in a visual pattern, not in terms of their content. In moving about the entire surface of the painting, we sense the decorative pattern and unity that this movement creates. However, we also are conscious of the two principal figures. As our eye explores the decorative pattern it encircles the two largest areas and isolates the figures that compose them. Within the forest, amid the activity of the chase, Christ appears to St. Eustace alone.

As we turn from the work by Pisanello to that by Antonello (fig. 37), we suddenly feel a

36. PISANELLO. *The Vision of St. Eustace.* About 1438

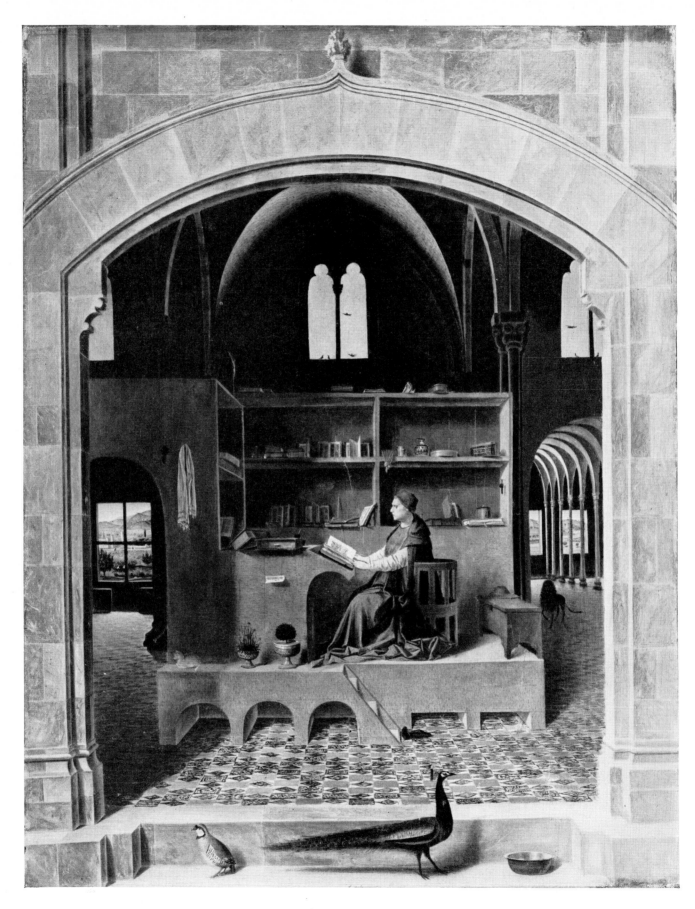

37. ANTONELLO DA MESSINA. *St. Jerome in His Study*. About 1475

sense of freedom. Our eye is invited to explore the world behind the surface of the painting. The sweeping movement our eye makes in the space delights us. We begin to experience the ample world the artist has laid out before us: a vast and vaulted room with windows opening out to a distant countryside. Our eye takes in at a glance the seated figure of St. Jerome and the size of the room, and we are conscious of the additional space beyond the windows. We look through the windows at the hills and houses caught in the sparkling light but we do not find ourselves tempted to move into this space out and beyond the room. Our curiosity is not aroused by what exists outside of the room itself. In fact we seem to feel a definite preference for staying within the room, to examine its contents more carefully.

Our spatial experience with this work is initiated by the open doorway the artist has constructed in the stone wall that otherwise occupies the surface of this painting. We look through the doorway into the room itself. Our attention is immediately caught by one of the objects closest to us: the large bird on the doorstep. The other objects here receive only a cursory glance as our eye, now attracted by the intricate pattern of the floor, moves into the room itself, and our eye follows the pattern to its conclusion at the farthermost walls and windows on either side of the painting. As we have seen earlier, we do not feel an urge to pass beyond this point. On the contrary, our desire is to return to the main part of the room itself, an area through which our eye traveled so quickly that we have the impression of having only partially experienced its contents. Thus, once we have glimpsed the view beyond, this point of the painting holds no interest for us and our eye returns to the front of the room.

Having returned to this area we begin to explore the room more carefully, led by what appears to be a strong compulsion to examine each object minutely. In doing so, we become thoroughly familiar with the position that each object occupies, and the definition of space becomes very clear. Why we feel so compelled and why the space seems so clearly defined are explained in part by the care that the artist has taken to accent the edges of his forms. Each form within the painting is precise, from the edge of the doorstep to the edges of the shelves. And once our attention is called to this factor, we notice that not only the edges but the corners of objects have been stressed. By emphasizing the meeting point of two surfaces, the artist persuades us to see the work in terms of these surfaces or planes. We become sensitive to every change in direction that these planes may undergo and, as we concentrate on this movement, there emerges a clear definition of the space within the entire painting.

This impression is different, however, from the feeling of vast and limitless space that is evoked from us by the Rembrandt drawing. This emotion is based on an impression of distance rather than an impression of clearly defined space. Naturally Rembrandt also uses planes to create this effect, but they are not so clearly defined. In contrast to the precise and elaborate planes used by Antonello, the planes in the drawing are merely indicated or suggested. How different this is from the method of Antonello can be seen if we notice the details of the doorway by which the artist invites us to look into the room. This opening has been carefully framed by the artist with a molding in which each break is emphasized, making the stone wall appear to be made of layers that were gradually cut away to reveal the room. And at the point where our eye first enters, the painting is even more minutely detailed than elsewhere. The molding of the doorway rises from bases with many carefully articulated divisions to capitals that are relatively flat and undefined. Thus, the initial attraction of our eye to this part of the painting by the shape of the dark bird is reinforced by the stress given to the varied planes of the doorsill and the bases of the moldings. At this point, our sensitivity to the movement of the planes is aroused, and we then proceed to examine each object in the room by interrelating its various planes, always remaining conscious of and sensitive to each change in direction. As we move from one object to another, we have an impression of actually building up the space, of re-creating the space made by the artist. This space finally becomes so clear and familiar to us that we feel we could easily make a ground plan or build a model of this room. By this emphasis on planes, the artist has been able to make us very aware of a particular kind of space. We sense quite clearly the effect of being enclosed within the space, and it is this feeling that makes our

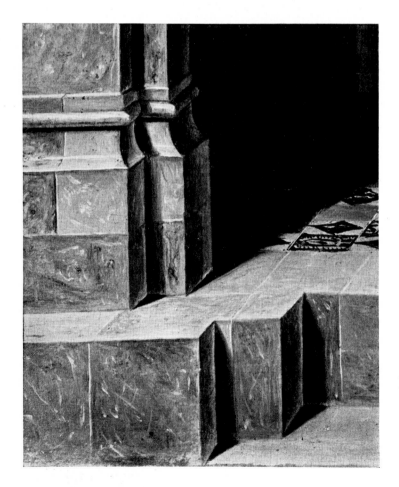

38. ANTONELLO
Detail of *St. Jerome in His Study*

39. CANALETTO
Courtyard of a Building in Ruins
About 1760

spatial experience in this work so different from what we experienced in the line drawing by Rembrandt.

If we look at a drawing by Canaletto of a courtyard (fig. 39), we encounter planes used in quite another fashion. Here our impression is similar to the feeling of distance that we received from the Rembrandt drawing, for our eye travels quickly to the distant skyline. And, although our eye returns from this point to examine other parts of the courtyard in a manner similar to its action in the painting by Antonello, here it constantly goes back to the most distant section in the work. Canaletto achieves this effect by not allowing any protruding planes to interrupt the surface of the wall placed on the left. Those few that do exist in the form of cornices are not emphasized. Instead, the stress is laid on the unity of this plane, with a result that is quite apparent if we compare it with the effect given by the wall on the right. Here the unity of the plane is broken up by the colonnade, the buttresses, and a type of balcony, all of which impede the movement of our eye along this wall. As our eye examines the different elements that make up this plane, we also discover that we tend constantly to return to the plane on the left, a movement that Canaletto encourages in different ways. The plane of the balcony, the span of the arch, and the line of the roof all divert our eye from receding along the wall on the right, and

40. Antonello da Messina
St. Jerome in His Study. About 1475

transfer our attention to the left. By directing our movement in this way, Canaletto gives us a feeling of great distance but also breaks up the tunnel-like appearance that such a composition might easily present.

The possibility of such an appearance also is diminished by the two archways that span the courtyard and divide its vast space into smaller areas. This division helps to define the space more clearly, but the spatial articulation and definition in this work obviously are different from what we have seen in the painting by Antonello. The enclosed space sensed in this work is replaced in the Canaletto drawing by a sense of open space. Antonello at first encourages us to experience the possible distance in his work by the vast plane of the floor, and then, by the multiplication of planes, induces us to explore the room slowly until we gain a very definite idea of its spatial quality. By keeping the number of planes to a minimum, Canaletto directs all of our attention to an immediate experience of the entire scene placed before us. In the Canaletto work we find ourselves content to look at the view through the courtyard, whereas in the Antonello painting we find it necessary to examine more completely the space that the artist has created.

A great deal of the difference in our feeling for these two works may be traced to the initial concept that we form of our relation to the pictorial space. The portion of roof that Canaletto introduces in the upper left-hand corner of his work not only directs our attention to the left but places us in a definite setting. We comprehend our own position as being fixed beneath this roof. For, although the physical space of our own surroundings appears to us as a continuation of the space in the courtyard, the enclosing roof defines our position more specifically. From this position we look into the courtyard and we admire the vista that extends before us. In the

41. CANALETTO. *Courtyard of a Building in Ruins.* About 1760

42. HENRI DE TOULOUSE-LAUTREC
Monsieur Boileau au Café. 1893

Antonello work, our position in relation to the space in the painting is also defined for us by the artist, but in this case, we do not feel our space to be a continuation of that in the painting. Here the artist makes us locate ourselves completely outside the scene. We never step beyond the doorway, but remain fixed there, looking into St. Jerome's cell. Where the artist places us in relation to the world he creates is, therefore, an important factor in how we react to the spatial arrangement of a work of art.

How this factor relates to the total impression we form of a work may be seen if we compare the painting by Antonello with Toulouse-Lautrec's gouache, *Monsieur Boileau* (fig. 42). The man in the café appears to be very close to us, as if we, too, were in the café. Our impression is similar to what we would receive from the Antonello painting if we were suddenly to leave the doorway of the Antonello painting and walk toward St. Jerome's desk. In coming closer to the figure of St. Jerome we would become less aware of the entire room; our attention would center on him, and the rest of the room would be cut out of our vision. This is, in a sense, what

Toulouse-Lautrec has done to bring us into contact with his central figure. He both moves us into the room and limits the amount of space that we experience. On the basis of what we have seen in the previous works, we easily recognize the importance of the table top in effecting this movement. The table, cut off by the frame of the picture in such a way that it appears to jut out of the pictorial space into our own, acts as a bridge across which our eye travels to the central figure.

As our eye moves across the plane of the table top, it is brought into contact with other planes in the painting: first, the plane of the other table top; then with the plane made by the back of the nearest man; thereafter, with the planes of the buffet, the screen, and the patterned floor. Enumerating these planes makes us realize that our eye encircles the central figure, and thus creates a pocket of space in which this figure is set. This is the only space in the painting with which we associate a strong feeling of depth, and the figure of the man is the most solid object in the work. Thus, by severely limiting the amount of depth to which we respond, the artist effectively isolates for our attention the person of M. Boileau. Naturally, Toulouse-Lautrec also uses other ways to draw our interest to this figure. He is not only the largest and the most central figure, but he is also the only one who looks in our direction. Still, these devices are only complementary to the way the artist uses our reaction to planes in order to limit our experience of space, and thus make us particularly aware of this isolated figure.

"Isolated figure" is a descriptive term that we have also applied to the painting by Pisanello, where the central figure is seen in the midst of many other objects. Recalling the primarily decorative effect of this painting may make us aware of a similar element in the work by Toulouse-Lautrec. For this artist not only stresses the spatial qualities of his work, but its surface pattern as well. We experience a certain amount of space within this painting but we are also aware of its over-all decorative effect. The planes that surround the central figure serve in both of these capacities, for not only do their forms define the space within the painting, but their surface areas give an ornamental pattern to the work. Our eye relates these planes of various colors and decorative designs to one another and to other sections of the painting in the same way that it related the various areas of the Pisanello work. The surface pattern of shapes and colors gives a flat quality to these parts of the painting, but in this case the fact that these areas are seen as planes makes us feel all the more strongly the concentrated space occupied by the figure.

We might at this point return once again to the painting of St. Jerome, for although we have discussed the particular feeling of space the artist creates through his use of planes, we have not yet seen how this impression contributes to our final understanding of this work. Both the clear spatial definition we have formed of this room and the sense of physical reality that we have come to associate with the many objects in the painting are impressions that relate to the total expressive content of the work. For the artist builds upon these impressions in a way that leads us closer to an understanding of what he is trying to say about the personality and character of St. Jerome.

Because both of these impressions have already been conveyed to us, our eye does not wander aimlessly about the room, but follows a path leading directly to the reading figure of the saint. Our sensitivity to space and our awareness of three-dimensional objects have been so stimulated by what we have earlier experienced that the artist may change the emphasis he gives to this characteristic of his work in order to achieve another purpose. We are not aware, for example, that as we are led from one object to another, the distance that our eye moves into depth is constantly decreasing, and that the number of defining planes is reduced as we approach the figure of the saint. The impressions already built up are so strong that we even attribute solidity to forms represented simply as flat surfaces. The archway on the left side of the painting, for example, gives no indication of the thickness of the surface that it pierces, yet we see this surface as a wall of a certain solidity. We do so because we associate the shape of this archway with the three completely defined, similarly shaped openings in the front of the platform. Thus, without disturbing what is by now our expectation of encountering only objects that seem real, the artist subtly shifts our attention to the entire surface of this plane and stops our movement back into the painting. As the surface of this wall flows without a break into the plane of the desk, our eye also moves in this direction and arrives at the figure seated before the desk.

Exactly at this point the artist introduces another arched form, which, because of its shape and apparent thickness, echoes and completes the archway to the left. This device induces in us a feeling of having arrived at a destination, and our eye feels content now to remain in this area.

As our eye centers on this area of the painting, our attention also is called to the many objects collected here. The various books, plants, utensils, and other items depicted here present to us a miniature still life which begins to divert our interest. But these articles are so arranged that we find ourselves always brought back to the figure of St. Jerome by way of the slant of the reading shelf, or the vertical line of the central support of the bookshelves, or the diagonal line of the stairway. And, each time that our eye is brought back from examining the tiny objects of the surrounding still life which occupy such a minute quantity of space, we are more impressed by the amount of space taken up by the figure of St. Jerome. His form appears so large and massive that for us he dominates the platform completely. And, since we have a clear idea of the relation of this one section of the room to the entire space of the painting, we also see this figure either as the point from which all the movement within the work emanates or the point at which it culminates. In this room, so isolated both from us and from the surrounding countryside, the presence of St. Jerome is felt strongly. This room is his world, and he remains oblivious to our presence.

Antonello has presented to us a figure on which our attention ultimately centers, but, unlike Pisanello and Toulouse-Lautrec, he never allows the figure to become isolated from its surroundings. As we have seen, the figure of St. Jerome is fixed within the many planes of the room and its contents, and he becomes defined for us by the sensitive way in which the artist

 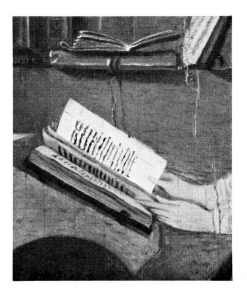

44. ANTONELLO. Details of *St. Jerome in His Study*

has caused us to experience these planes. Toulouse-Lautrec uses the same means, but in a different way, to convey the character of the man depicted in the café. The first impression we have of him is that he probably is a lover of good food, a man with a certain elegance of manner, a man of supreme confidence. That we feel so positive about this man's character results from many of the descriptive elements that the artist has included, but the one characteristic which most strongly influences our impression is his posture. He holds himself erect, as if this were a very necessary act. We have the distinct feeling that an act of balance is required, and when we sense the reason for his posture, we are amused, for it becomes apparent that the man must be sitting on a small and probably insecure chair. Despite this situation, however, nothing in the expression of his face or his body suggests alarm. This is an act that, having been performed countless times, has given him confidence in his actions. As a lover of good food must, he has learned how to distribute his weight evenly. All of these associations come to our mind solely because of the impression we have of this man's carriage. The artist has engendered in us such a sense of positive knowledge that we even find it possible to imagine the position of his legs—spread apart but with feet together. The reason our impression of this man is related to his posture, even when a part of his body is hidden by the table top, is that the artist fashions the planes of his work into expressive elements.

The plane of the very table top that hides the figure is responsible for our feeling about this man's position, for Toulouse-Lautrec has shaped the plane so that it suggests this posture to us. At the point where the table top is closest to the figure of the man, the movement of the plane slopes away from his body to either side, continuing the planes of his body and emphasizing the force of his weight. As this plane spreads out and away from the man, our eye is led toward the corners of the table top, where a reverse direction is initiated. The other two sides of the plane now move toward one another, and our eye is led down to the point where we would expect the two sides to meet. The point at which the plane completes itself exists, however, only outside the picture frame. This point is the very one that we have already seen to be responsible for fixing our location with respect to this scene. Thus, from the moment of our initial contact with this work, the movement of our eye back and forth across the plane has built up the impression that we receive of the man's posture.

The table top as a real object is much less important to Lautrec than the expressive power of the plane by which it is formed. Clearly, the shape of the table top is not what we might normally expect to encounter, but Toulouse-Lautrec has so impressed us by the expressive power of this plane that we ignore or fail to notice the disparity. The form of the plane has been dictated solely by what Lautrec wished to express. The table top has been made subordinate to the idea and has been transformed into a plane capable of evoking various reactions. We concentrate entirely on the figure of this man with whom we have been brought into contact, and we begin to sense at least a part of his personality.

HENRI DE TOULOUSE-LAUTREC. *Monsieur Boileau au Café.* 1893

HENRI MATISSE. *Piano Lesson*. 1916

PIETER DE HOOCH. *A Dutch Courtyard*. About 1656

JOHN CONSTABLE. *Barges on the Stour.* About 1811

CHAPTER 6

Objects
in Space

45. REMBRANDT. *Self-Portrait.* 1658

MAN'S SENSITIVITY TO PICTORIAL SPACE determines to a great extent the way Toulouse-Lautrec, Antonello da Messina, and Pisanello conceived of their paintings. To transform into a visual image the feelings or ideas that he wished to convey, each of these artists sought to make us respond to pictorial space in a different way: Antonello, by encouraging us to explore carefully a small amount of precisely defined space, Pisanello, by denying our feeling for depth. Our sense of the movement of planes in space was used by Antonello to lead our eye toward the figure of Saint Jerome; by Toulouse-Lautrec to isolate the figure of M. Boileau and to imply

46. Rembrandt. *Self-Portrait*. 1658

something of his personality. The paintings that we have seen by these artists all have a single figure in a particular setting as their subject. Although each artist treats space differently, all encourage us to see the figure in relation to the setting. Our idea of the solidity and real appearance of the figures is formed more by the way in which the artist conceives the setting than by the way in which he depicts the individual figure.

How important the setting is for our understanding of the figure in each of these works is evident if we compare the painting by Toulouse-Lautrec with a self-portrait by Rembrandt (fig. 46). Although we first may be struck by the fact that the figure is seen in a position similar to that of M. Boileau, we soon realize that the paintings are otherwise quite different in appearance. The carefully arranged planes that create the space around the figure, and, in addition, characterize the setting of the Toulouse-Lautrec painting, are without parallels in the work by Rembrandt. The artist has depicted himself in surroundings that are not detailed or precise. But the absence of these space-defining elements in no way diminishes the sense that we have of the massive bulk and weight of the figure. Rembrandt is able to create an effect similar to, and even more pronounced than, the effect of the work by Toulouse-Lautrec, but without depending upon a similar clear definition of space. Obviously, Rembrandt uses different means to convince us of the three-dimensional quality of this figure.

What first encourages us to see this figure as a solid body is the fact that we consider the area surrounding the figure as representing space. This section of the canvas appears to recede in depth because of the effect of the varying contrasts of light and dark. The subtle, blurred shifts of value in this area impart to the entire canvas the appearance of an undefined amount of space and atmosphere, a part of which is occupied by the figure of the artist. As an object seen in space, the figure immediately takes on a certain tangible existence for us, but the impression of solidity given by it arises primarily from the way in which Rembrandt emphasizes the planes of the figure itself.

Each of the light and dark areas of the garments acts as a plane whose movement describes the character of the body underneath. The enveloping cloak, the broad plane of the shirred blouse, and the expanse of robe falling from the waist, convey to us immediately the basic form of the body. At the same time, the downward thrust of the cloak and robe, and the horizontal spread of the blouse stimulate a strong feeling for the power and mass of this figure, an impression further strengthened by the repetition of the basic movements of these planes in the walking stick, the sash at the waist, and the scarf at the neck.

The same three elements also call to our attention those parts of the figure so crucial for establishing the personality of the subject: the hands and the face. By the time our interest centers here, our impression of the figure's strength and mass already has established for us a concept of this man. So swiftly have we been brought into contact with this figure, and so keenly do we sense his immediate presence, that the personality and character expressed through the face and the hands become intensely real to us. We feel that we are being offered an opportunity to acquire an intimate knowledge and understanding of this man.

The bold, clear way in which Rembrandt gives an appearance of solidity to his portrait is closely related to the way Barlach conceives of the sculpture *Man Drawing a Sword* (fig. 47). In his painting Rembrandt makes more emphatic the feeling of solidity we are apt to attribute to the figure because we see it as existing in pictorial space. Similarly, Barlach heightens our feeling for the solidity and mass of a figure that, because it is a piece of sculpture, we naturally see as a tangible solid object in real space. In the Barlach sculpture the essential characteristics of the figure are again revealed to us through the relationship of a few broad planes. The robe stretched between the legs of the figure, the breadth of this garment as it moves away from the knees, and the unbroken expanse of the cloak falling from the shoulders, all are planes that act to move our eye swiftly over the figure and to form an idea for us of a man of great strength.

Like Rembrandt, Barlach arranges the garments to create simple and powerful planes that encourage us to think of the underlying figure as a solid body. However, in the piece of sculpture, such planes do not just indicate a possible solidity; they actually define forms of different shapes and volumes. From the different points of view that we obtain by walking about this piece of sculpture, the individual planes fall into place as parts of whole solid objects. The upper portion of the figure takes on more clearly the appearance of a bell-like form coming down over the short cylinder of the middle section—a section that in itself constitutes a cylinder rising from the rectilinear form that the encompassing robe creates out of the lower part of the figure. The concept we form of this figure is built, then, on the relationships we see existing between these forms of different shape and volume.

In contrast to our impression of the Rembrandt self-portrait, that of the Barlach figure is strong in movement. One reason for this difference is the way each artist treats the cloaks. Rembrandt completely encompasses the figure within the outline of the cape, emphasizing the downward thrust of the figure's static weight. In the Barlach piece, the large, enveloping form of the cloak also weighs down upon the body, but in the course of its fall it is lifted and spread out by the action of the arms coming from beneath its folds to grasp the sword. As this action deflects the cloak to the side, its downward thrust is also countered by the upward push of the figure's center section. These two opposing forces do not meet, however, for the narrow, cylindrical form of the body, as it ascends, appears to pass underneath the bell-shaped cloak.

In the actual piece of sculpture, of course, one form does not physically pass beneath another form, but, nevertheless, these two forms appear related to one another, like the stem and cap of a button mushroom. The two forms appear to us to fit within one another, the one disappearing beneath the other lowered over it. This interpenetration of the forms makes us conscious of them as both hollow and solid forms and, thus, creates for us a new way of looking at this figure. We now are aware of both the amount of space enclosed by the shell of the garment and how much of this space is occupied by the solid figure. We see the garments as a volumetric envelope of space within which exists the body of the man, an impression reinforced for us by the way in which the artist accents the feet protruding from beneath the robe and the head projecting from the collar.

47. ERNST BARLACH
Man Drawing a Sword. 1911

The impression built up of this man by means of a subtle relationship of solid and hollow forms makes us sense the nature of the action he is about to take. The sword and hands merging with the broad, sweeping line of the cape suggest the motion that the man will make in wielding the sword. The central point, to which our attention is fixed by the hands and the sword, is also the point where our awareness of the interpenetration of the forms of this figure is the greatest. Our concept of this figure's being made up of an object within an object is established for us at the same moment that we are shown the one hand of the figure grasping the hilt of the sword and the other the sheath. The artist conveys to us a precise knowledge of exactly what will occur when the sword is drawn. And, by the sharp twist of the head in this otherwise frontally developed figure, Barlach hints at the force about to be unleashed.

Both Rembrandt and Barlach have used their knowledge of how we perceive objects in space to make us acutely aware of the physical existence of a single figure. Each artist has appealed to this part of our perceptual sensitivity by giving to the figure a self-contained shape within which the relationships of planes or forms can be keenly sensed. In both instances, the associations we made on the basis of our response to planes and volumes were directed at characterizing a single figure. That these same means may be used with equal effect to convey the expressive content of a work involving several figures within a setting can be seen in a fresco painted by Giotto (fig. 48).

This fresco, one of a series depicting the life of Christ and the Virgin Mary, shows the High Priest receiving Mary into the temple. We see her being presented by her mother, Anne, in a ceremony witnessed by several groups of spectators. All of these figures have been grouped by Giotto in a way that enables us to encompass the entire scene by only a few movements of our eye. We appear to follow an established path through this work, leading from the lower left-hand corner to the figure of Anne, to the Virgin, along the outstretched arms of the priest, to the apex of the pyramidal roof. At this point we are aware of the possibility of moving in either one of two directions, but, being attracted by the dark edge of the corner of the roof, we follow in its direction, dropping down to the two figures in the lower right-hand corner. From here our eye crosses the front of the platform, returning to the point where it originally entered the scene. As our eye completes this movement, we become aware that in following this path our eye has created the outline of a triangle, a shape that binds both figures and architecture into a unified visual image.

However, we understand this essentially linear movement of our eye not as simply defining a triangular shape on the surface of the fresco, but as creating a completely solid object, a pyramidal form of which the temple roof is the capstone. The two planes that make up this roof give to the triangular movement of our eye another dimension, one which we are led to associate with the entire fresco because Giotto continues to make us aware of that side of the pyramid which recedes from us. One way he reinforces our feeling for the solid form is by giving emphasis to the planes of the stairway and archway. But a more important way in which he continues our awareness is his treatment of the two standing figures in the right foreground.

Of the two men seen here, one looks away from the ceremony itself to address a remark to his companion, and, by this casual action, directs our attention to the right. But, since in addition to turning his head toward his companion this man also gestures toward the ceremony, our attention is equally attracted to the left. Thus this single figure indicates two possible directions of movement to us in a manner not unlike that of a crossroads marker. Both of these directions are expressed in the planes by which Giotto has depicted the robe of this figure. Seen from the back, the broad surface of the robe is formed into two clearly defined planes by being divided directly down the center into a light and a dark area. The line made by this division is, by virtue of its position and of its function, the counterpart of the dark descending line of the roof. This figure, then, performs a role identical to the temple roof in creating our impression of the

48. GIOTTO. *The Presentation of the Virgin.* 1303–6

pyramidal form. Figures and architecture are merged within the over-all shape—both are subordinated to the single pyramidal shape of which they are parts.

By making us see the figures and architecture of this painting in terms of this single shape, Giotto makes us very much aware of the three-dimensional quality of each. As these figures become fixed in our mind as parts of the larger, solid form, they themselves become endowed with solidity and massiveness. We feel keenly the existence of these figures as objects that must occupy and displace a certain amount of space. Our feeling is stronger for these figures as tangible objects with a specific location in space and a particular volume than it is for the figures in the works by Antonello or Toulouse-Lautrec. In them, the solidity of the figures is conveyed by the way the artist uses planes to define the setting of the painting and the location of the

49. GIOTTO. Detail of
The Presentation of the Virgin

figures within this space. But in the Giotto fresco, as in the work by Rembrandt, the planes of the painting are not used to define pictorial space but to define the figure as a volumetric object. Although Giotto provides us with a setting in the form of symbolic architecture, there is in fact no setting like that of St. Jerome in his cell, only a dark background against which we see the single pyramidal form of figures and architecture combined. The temple does not place and define the figures, but is seen by us as a part of an indivisible whole.

Once we are aware of the solid geometrical form implied in this painting, we see and comprehend the individual figures in terms of their relations with it. Except for the two men in the right foreground, whom we see more as part of the setting than of the ceremony, the bystanders are excluded from a place within the pyramidal form. The diagonal line from the left-hand corner to the apex of the roof divides the spectators from the participants. Within the form itself our attention appears to be brought to bear solely on the ceremony. We are made to concentrate on the actions of Anne, Mary, and the priest because Giotto, like Rembrandt and Barlach, links the expressive content of his work with the movements of planes within the total form. By this movement, Giotto makes us experience the solid form of architecture and figures

50. GIOTTO. Detail of
The Presentation of the Virgin

in still another way—we are given a sense of actually penetrating the form. We see this pyramidal form as being cut into by the shape that Giotto has given to the front plane of the temple platform. Our eye moves from the lightest plane of the robe in the right-hand corner to that of the temple platform, a plane which grows markedly narrower as it approaches the steps. Its pointed shape accentuates a direction back into space that was begun by the plane of the robe. This movement in depth makes us particularly aware of the area cut out of the pyramid by this plane and the one formed by the side of the stairway. Immediately above the point where these two planes meet occurs the ceremony, a point on which our interest remains fixed.

The impression that we receive from this work and the adjectives that we may choose to describe our feelings about this event are a result of the solidity we associate with these figures. They present a contained appearance, the majority seen cloaked in robes, with their arms close to their bodies. Their gestures are few and never agitated, making the depicted actions particularly meaningful. The ponderous movements of the figures give a slow and measured pace to their actions, which thus attain an importance adding to the emotional effect of the event. Perhaps from this very sense of immobility arises the sincerity that we associate with this work.

The particular character and effect of these figures by Giotto are made more apparent if we look from this fresco to one by Masaccio titled *The Tribute Money* (fig. 51). This scene of the toll collector requesting payment from Christ and the Disciples presents a group of figures who, because of their different gestures and stances, are immediately seen as more lifelike than the cloak-enveloped figures by Giotto. In place of immobile figures that impress us as solid objects occupying or displacing a very definite amount of space, we now see more animated figures related to one another through their movements. The curving lines of the draperies and the implied lines of the outstretched arms weave the four central figures into a harmonious and rhythmic unit. But this linear quality does not make us less aware of these figures as three-dimensional objects. For although we do not think primarily of the solidity of these figures, we are keenly aware of them as objects existing in space. The different actions of the figures make us aware of the individual, articulated parts of the body, and we identify ourselves with these figures. Because of this response we attribute to them the same physical qualities we know ourselves to possess, and they become corporeal forms of a definite weight and life.

Our response to the movements of these figures is initiated by the toll collector, a figure that we see from the back and which, like the bystander in the right foreground of the Giotto fresco, indicates two possible directions of movement. But rather than sensing this movement because of the planes of the garment, we are sensitive here to how each movement of the body necessarily gives rise to a complementary movement. The one foot raised off the ground makes us feel how the weight of the body must be shifted to the other leg, and the outstretched arms, one slightly back, the other forward, make us feel the gentle twist of the body at the waist and the movement of the shoulders. And we respond also to the turn of the head as it moves our eye in still another direction, sending our glance to the figure of Christ, whose movements, both those depicted and those only indicated by the drapery, are to some extent a mirror image of the figure of the toll collector. As our eye records these various motions, we not only imbue the figures with a plastic existence but see the area between them as space filled with an air of a measurable density. We are not, as with the work by Giotto, reacting to the amount of space occupied by a figure, but to the amount of space that such a figure activates or creates by its movements.

The incident enacted by the three foreground figures is dramatized for us within a pocket of space that they create by their gestures and movements. Masaccio increases the effect of this space by containing it within a small area not dissimilar from the wedge of space cut into the pyramidal form in the work by Giotto. Here, however, the pocket of space is roughly semi-circular in shape, a shape described by the placement of the figures and reinforced by the ring of Disciples standing behind them. At either end of this group stand two figures whose voluminous robes and motionless posture give them a massive appearance that stops and contains the movements of the other figures. The group of the Disciples also serves to separate the foreground area from the vaguely defined landscape in which the scene is set. Because the mountainous landscape rises to the top of the fresco, little emphasis is given to the skyline, with the

51. MASACCIO. *The Tribute Money.* 1427

52. MASACCIO
Detail of *The Tribute Money*

result that we are aware of the bulk and mass of these natural features without determining their forms precisely. Thus, although they contribute to the space of the entire painting, their role is not unlike that of the flat, dark background in the Giotto fresco. They create an atmospheric space in which the entire group of figures is seen as a single form—a form within which the smaller area of concentrated space is contained. Within this small but powerful area of space Masaccio has also concentrated the most detailed studies of human character. By depicting their reaction to this event, he turns these physically palpable figures into emotional beings.

The way in which Masaccio endows his figures with the qualities of plastic forms by emphasizing the articulation of the human body is essentially a sculptural approach. Just as Rembrandt and Barlach both used similar means in creating their figures, so, too, the boxwood statuette by Francesco da Sant'Agata (fig. 53) is closely related to figures by Masaccio, particularly that of the toll collector. To create the image of the athletic body of Hercules, Francesco, too, has chosen to show the figure in a stance that demands a play of muscles and makes us conscious of the figure's tension. The slightly raised leg, its movement back and to the side, and the position of the arms and hands grasping the club make us feel the pull exerted on the entire

53. Francesco da Sant' Agata. *Hercules*. 1520

body from toe to neck. And, since we know that this is a pose impossible to hold over a long period of time, we also anticipate the sweeping movement that this action will create. The feeling that we have for this figure is more powerful than that evoked by the less actively moving figures of Masaccio, and our impression of the space created by this figure is also stronger. By his actions and by the movements we foresee, the figure activates the space around him, and we recognize how large an amount of space is needed to contain his actions.

The fresco by Giotto, too, has its counterpart in the way in which a sculptor may conceive his work, for Giotto has convinced us of the solidity of his figures in a way similar to that used by Michelangelo in creating the marble group, *Pietà* (fig. 54). The individual figures composing this group are seen within an encompassing pyramidal form. No figure, or any part of one, protrudes outside of the over-all form that the group creates. The arrangement of arms and legs that binds these figures together concentrates our attention on the figures and their relation to one another. Our eye is caught first by the unsupported arm of Christ, which slants down the center of this group to display immediately before us His hand and wound. The position of this arm makes a dividing line between the movements of the two side figures coming forward toward it. The extended arm of the figure to the left moves toward the leg and hand of Christ, the same point from which the draped leg of the figure to the right recedes. And we are also directed to the hand of Christ by the position of the bent leg and by the pronounced fold of drapery immediately beneath it.

Away from this point, toward the upper portion of the group, the movement is made more complex by the twisted body of Christ. The arm falling back and around the left-hand figure creates, within the group, an open space that accents the impression of depth. Because we see this side as receding into depth, the other side appears to come forward. In part, this feeling is produced because the open space on the left has no counterpart on the right-hand side. The corresponding place where such space might exist on the right is closed by the figure of the Virgin as she leans toward the body to receive it in her arms. And the intimate relationship of Mother and Son is expressed again in the way the head of Christ is made to fall toward the Virgin. Yet all these varied actions, which subtly express the relationships among the figures, also combine to create a continuous line of movement around the group. For our eye can travel without interruption from Christ's hand on the left, along his arm, and across the band of cloth on his chest to the hand and arm of the Vigin. This movement binds the figures into a closely linked group and forms a base below the apex of the piece.

Towering above, and leaning over from the back, is the final figure of this group, who gazes

54. MICHELANGELO. *Pietà*. About 1550–56

down upon the Virgin and Christ. Because of his position and because no continuous movement of our eye connects him with the other figures, this man is set apart from the rest. His hooded and swathed figure presents a spectral appearance that makes his identity difficult to ascertain. He seems too important and imposing a figure to represent Nicodemus, the man who helped take down the body, but to see this figure as an image of God is equally difficult, for the features are those of Michelangelo himself. No matter how we may interpret the meaning of this enigmatic figure, we cannot help but be aware of his position within this group, for he is placed along the direct line of our vision. Our eye travels from the hand of Christ displaying the wound, to the face motionless in death, and finally to the head of the mysterious figure whose saddened gaze spreads out over the entire piece, investing it with a compelling pathos.

55. Giovanni Battista Moroni
"Titian's Schoolmaster." About 1575

An example of the two different ways in which the artist may make us conscious of the plastic quality of an object can be found in contrasting the portrait by Rembrandt with one by Moroni (fig. 55). Unlike the immobile frontal figure painted by Rembrandt, which impresses us with its mass, the figure by Moroni is alive with a movement which both endows it with a physical reality and helps establish its personality. By its actions and gestures this figure presents to us a variety of different views of the human body, as if the several views we could obtain by walking around a piece of sculpture were merged into one. Seen primarily from the side, the figure turns toward us, as if our presence had disturbed him in his reading. The actual movements of the figure are not the only ones, however, that define it, for the angular shapes of the collar and hat are equally effective as planes seen in space. The pattern of light and dark about the face recreates and continues the movements of the body, giving the figure a vitality it would not otherwise have.

The relationship that Moroni suggests between the hat and collar of the sitter, on the one hand, and the body movements, on the other, makes us see the entire figure in terms of the various movements of these planes. It is this quality that gives rise most directly to the impression we have of seeing the figure from more than one point of view. Our eye is fascinated by the various possibilities of movement and by the relationships that emerge between objects otherwise not related. For example, the shape of the book with the sitter's finger placed as a marker echoes the area of the painting made up of the hat, face, and collar of the sitter. We are made to see them as somewhat similar objects seen from different angles. Thus, by stressing these different planes, Moroni creates a work whose unity lies in the movements of our eye in response to the planes. The figure itself is an indivisible part of the forms of which it is made up, a union of the subject with the sheer delight of forms moving in space, a concept of visual experience that is also reflected in the way that Lipchitz has conceived his figure, *Seated Guitar Player* (fig. 56). Here the distinction between visual form and figure is harder to make, for the sculptor merges the man and the guitar into a single object whose existence derives only from the movements of the planes. The strings of the guitar are likened to the fingers of the hand; the bent knee echoes the body of the instrument; and as we move about the piece these elements seem to exchange their roles and meaning. The piece becomes an ever-moving, mercurial work whose meaning is dependent solely on our conception of how we see objects in space.

56. JACQUES LIPCHITZ
Seated Guitar Player. 1918

CHAPTER 7

Visual Order

57. MA YUAN
Bare Willows and Distant Mountains
Chinese, Sung Dynasty, early 13th century

IN THE PREVIOUS CHAPTERS, our attention has been concentrated primarily on the expressive role of the elements of line or color in a work of art. The artist, however, conceives his work not only in terms of these elements but of their organization into a unified work as well. Similarly, the impressions that we receive from any single element within a work are tempered by the context in which the artist places them. Therefore, the way in which the artist combines the various parts of his work is another expressive element by which he may convey a feeling or idea.

All of the works that we have seen are composed and organized by the artist in a manner that complements and extends the impression induced by any individual element. The over-all shape, for example, of the painting *Bare Willows and Distant Mountains* (fig. 57) is intimately allied with the curved lines and gentle contrasts in values that the artist has used to convey to us his concept of this scene. So, too, the drawing by Picasso (fig. 58) has a necessary relationship to the sheet of paper on which it is drawn. Picasso may have chosen a sheet of paper of this size and shape because it suited the idea he wished to express, or perhaps the character of the drawing was determined in response to the size of the paper. Whatever the sequence of events may have been, the placement and arrangement of the figures within the area is as responsible as the artist's use of line for our impression of the rhythm and grace of the dance.

The organization of a work of art may simply emerge in the actual process of creation, the total form taking final shape only as the artist works upon it. Or the work may have been conceived initially in terms of a particular organization. In either case, the organization of every work of art is necessarily unique, for the compositional problem that each work poses can be solved only in terms of the effect that the artist wishes to convey in this one work. In resolving his own particular problem, however, an artist is often guided by certain widely followed principles or methods. These fundamental rules of composition, as they are often called, owe their formulation to the artist's experience with our reactions to certain types of organization. Therefore, the artist determines the principles to be followed in organizing his work solely on the basis of what expressive possibilities any one of these methods offers.

One way in which the artist may unify and organize his work is by making us believe that we see the work from a specific point in space. For example, we have seen that in the painting by Toulouse-Lautrec of Monsieur Boileau the fact that the table top extends to the very edge of the painting made us feel that we were both inside the café and located a certain distance away from the central figure. This distance was essential for our experience of the painting, for it not only made us sense the play that Toulouse-Lautrec established between surface pattern and objects in space, but helped to knit them together into an ordered whole. We also saw that establishing a point of view was a critical factor for our impression of the drawing by Canaletto

58. Pablo Picasso
Four Ballet Dancers (drawing). 1925

59. CANALETTO
Courtyard of a Building in Ruins
About 1760

(fig. 59), and the quite different use that he makes of this same factor accounts in part for the very different effects of each work. For unlike Toulouse-Lautrec, Canaletto has made our position in relation to the work much more precise by following a method for representing objects in space that requires all of the lines that would be parallel in nature to be represented pointing to the same place. We see this area in the drawing as the point where all of these lines would meet if extended. As our experience with the appearance in nature of parallel lines has been that they appear to converge as they recede from us, we see the point of convergence established in the drawing as being the point farthest removed from us. As it represents for us, then, the point beyond which we cannot perceive objects, we identify it as a "vanishing point." The effect of this vanishing point is immediate, for, when viewing such a work, we place ourselves in a position opposite it. This point, then, exercises a control over all parts of the work, binding them into a unified whole.

Where this vanishing point is placed within the work depends only on the desire of the artist. A central vanishing point is, however, one of the most commonly used. For example, in the painting *Oath of the Horatii* (fig. 60) by David, the lines bounding the planes of the walls and the floor are all directed toward a single point in the center of the canvas. In placing the vanishing point here, David helps to create a static quality about this scene that complements the statuesque appearance of the figures. But the effect that a central vanishing point may produce also depends upon the emphasis an artist may choose to give it. For example, in David's work, we are not actually shown the point where the lines might meet; we simply have had suggested to us the point where such a convergence would take place. By playing down the actual vanishing point, David encourages us to concentrate on the space within the planes. Had our eye been able to move directly to a vanishing point, the feeling of distance aroused would have disrupted the intimate and domestic spatial experience that David wishes to convey. As our eye is led by the lines in the direction of the vanishing point, we also become aware that David has not located an object *on* the vanishing point, but rather has placed an object *in front* of it. Our eye is first attracted to the swords, and is constantly brought back to them. By their position before the vanishing point these objects control the entire canvas visually, just as at the moment of the oath-taking they are the instruments that control the responses of all the figures. The conviction of the soldiers, forcefully conveyed by their stance and outstretched arms, is an emotion stimulated by the raised swords. And the swords are also the cause of the grief and despair expressed by the twisted lines of the swooning women.

A different use of the central vanishing point may lead to a work of quite different expressive content, as can be seen in the drawing by Jacopo Bellini, *Christ Taken Before Pilate* (fig. 61).

60. JACQUES-LOUIS DAVID. *Oath of the Horatii.* 1784

Unlike David, Bellini shows the point where the lines and planes converge, and as we move toward this point, we have the impression of going far back into space. The Bellini drawing gives us a feeling of vast distance, whereas the David work gives us a sense of enclosed space. The comparative sizes of the three arches that both these works depict might be said to represent the difference in the amount of distance we experience in each work. Only if we placed ourselves at a point as far away from the David painting as we feel we have penetrated into the Bellini scene would the three arches in the David work appear as small as those in the background of the Bellini. Because the figure of Pilate is placed on the exact point where all the lines converge, our attention is immediately drawn to him, even though he is the smallest figure in the entire scene. All of our movements are so channeled toward this figure—even the foreground figures form two diagonal sections pointing in this direction—that we must search out the figure of Christ among the crowd. Thus, Bellini effectively and ironically characterizes this event as being no more than a minor and very ordinary trial of one of the many cases that came before a Roman tribunal. The vast distance and enormous buildings dwarf all of the human figures except that of Pilate.

The expressive possibilities that other types of vanishing points offer the artist may be seen in Mantegna's fresco *St. James Led to Execution* (fig. 62). Looking from the drawing by Bellini to the fresco by Mantegna, we find we must shift our gaze sharply upward. Our eye

61. JACOPO BELLINI
Christ Taken Before Pilate (drawing)
About 1450

62. ANDREA MANTEGNA
St. James Led to Execution
About 1455

suddenly has been shifted to a new point of view. In place of a scene opening out directly in front of us, we now are presented with a scene enacted above us. Mantegna makes us look up simply by placing the point where the receding lines converge below the bottom edge of the painting. The diagonal path that our eye must follow toward this scene increases the effect already suggested by the similar lines within the painting. The many diagonal lines implied in the positions of the figures and objects are given an added force by the direction of our vision, which heightens the intense activity of the scene. So, too, the vertical lines appear stronger by virtue of their resistance to this movement, and we see the dominantly vertical figure of St. James as a man of power and strength undisturbed by the excitement around him.

Another way an artist organizes and unifies his work is through the creation of a sense of balance. Of the many approaches that artists have devised for achieving a sense of balance, the simplest method involves placing an equal emphasis on each side of a central axis. This arrangement, which we identify as symmetry, need not present an absolutely equal division of forms to

63. PAOLO VERONESE. *The Feast in the House of Levi.* About 1573

satisfy our feeling for balance so long as we sense a similar emphasis on each side of a clearly depicted axis. The drawing by Bellini is an example of this use of symmetry. The architectural forms are divided into equal parts by a central axis, and on either side are grouped figures and objects that, although not absolutely identical, we sense to be the same with respect to balance.

The painting by Veronese, *The Feast in the House of Levi* (fig. 63), is an enormous canvas filled with a multitude of figures and objects, but the organization given to this work by the artist enables us to comprehend the entire scene easily. Veronese has provided for the many figures an architectural setting that both divides the total canvas into smaller areas and provides a means of uniting them. Like the drawing by Bellini, Veronese's painting has a central vanishing point, but Veronese has expanded the single enframing arch of the Bellini design into a series of three openings of equal size. Within this setting, Veronese encourages us to concentrate on the entire central area rather than emphasizing only the central axis on which the figure of Christ is placed. The area itself is given dominance in the painting by the two columns that frame it and by the sloping lines of the balustrade on either side, which lead us toward the center area but stop short of entering this section. Thus, within the uniform, over-all framework, Veronese establishes a balance between the entire central area and the two side areas.

In organizing his work, an artist may make us aware not only of the existence of a balance between certain areas or objects but also of the way in which this balance is accomplished. He may induce us to see how the balance is built up as one form is related to the other. Our eye re-creates for us, as it were, the process that the artist went through in establishing the balance. As it does, we perceive a sense of order in our movements that we associate with the sensation of rhythm produced for us by music. This experience can be initiated for us simply by a repetition or variation of the shapes within a work of art. We have a tendency to see as related those objects which are similar in shape, color, value, or subject. Our eye, for example, when attracted by one yellow object, moves at once to any other yellow area in the painting. Or a round object set within a work made up of primarily angular forms can become a focal point for us and induce our eye to move about the work in a certain way.

Depending on the effect that he wishes to achieve, an artist emphasizes in different ways the rhythm inherent in the organization of his work. For example, although both David and Veronese organize their paintings partly by relying upon the unifying effect of three arched openings, each work possesses a markedly different rhythm. We do not receive a sense of flowing rhythm from the Veronese work because the way in which the artist has framed the three archways effectively breaks up the movement of our eye from one arch to another. The arch of each opening is contained within an architectural unit of supporting piers and larger flanking columns, thus clearly separating each section from the other. As we are brought to a full stop on either side of each area, the rhythm created by the repetition of the similar frames of the archways is restricted to a steady, unvarying beat.

A distinctly different rhythm exists in the painting by David—a more flowing one with an alternation of strong and weak accents (fig. 64). In part, this rhythm is set up by the architectural details that David has chosen to give to the three archways. Rather than separate the archways from one another by flanking columns, as Veronese has done, David connects all three by allowing two arches to spring from a single supporting column. No sooner has our eye followed the rise and fall of one arch than it is moved immediately to the next. Thus, our movement from one side to the other across the canvas is continuous, for our eye is led without stop along the molding on the two side walls and around all three of the openings. The movement and rhythm induced by the architecture echo a similar movement which David has introduced between the groups of figures by his use of a strong pattern of light and dark. These two horizontal and parallel lines of movement are woven together into a more complex rhythm by our movement back and forth in depth between the two, a relationship that David facilitates by establishing a numerical correspondence between the three groups of figures in the foreground and the archways. The sense of rhythm engendered by the David painting emphasizes

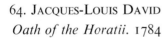

64. JACQUES-LOUIS DAVID
Oath of the Horatii. 1784

the intimate relationship existing between architecture and figures, while at the same time creating a unified work. In the painting by Veronese, the rhythm of the architectural forms contrasts with the movements of the figures, and so provides the artist with an opportunity to control his enormous canvas. The architectural framework allows Veronese to depict a rich assortment of individual actions and gestures within a vast amount of space while still presenting to us a work that, because of its basically simple organization, our eye can embrace easily.

Since the organization of a work of art is necessarily a part of its expressive content, each work has its own unique composition. Certain arrangements, however, of colors, lines, or shapes are more pleasing and satisfying to us than others. It is not surprising to find, therefore, that one artist may produce a work with a composition quite similar to that of a work by another artist. These two works need not be at all similar in appearance, however, for each composition may have been achieved through very different means. Thus the painting *Piano Lesson* (page 78) by Matisse bears little or no resemblance to the painting *A Dutch Courtyard* (page 79) by De Hooch, even though both are works organized in the same way.

The similar way in which these two paintings are organized may result in part from the common interest that these two artists share. Not only have Matisse and De Hooch chosen to depict a simple, domestic scene, but in neither instance is the subject matter itself the principal concern of the artist. De Hooch is less interested in depicting a family scene in a convincing setting than in presenting to us a pleasing arrangement of the shapes, colors, and textures of certain objects as they may exist in a physical world of space and light. Similarly, the primary interest of Matisse also rests in the arrangement of areas of certain colors and shapes, although without reference to a physical light or space. This difference of interest is to a large extent responsible for the difference in appearance of these two works, but the ultimate goal of both artists is similar. Both Matisse and De Hooch present to us, on canvases of similar proportions, balanced arrangements of objects that create tranquil and elegant paintings whose primary appeal and interest lie in the sheer beauty and sensual pleasure to be derived from the juxtaposition of certain colors, shapes, and textures.

The balance arrived at in both these paintings is basically a simple one. In the De Hooch painting, for example, the figure of the little girl with the starched white cap is balanced by the tower seen in the distance beyond the fence in the upper left-hand corner. The group of figures around the table in the lower left-hand corner is balanced on the upper right by the vertical line of the brick building, the dark area of the window, and the blue of the sky. Thus, De Hooch has organized his painting by creating four areas approximately equal in size which balance one another in a crisscross arrangement on the surface of the canvas. The painting *Piano Lesson* is similarly organized by Matisse. The small metronome in the lower right-hand corner is balanced in the upper left-hand corner by a much larger but similarly shaped area of green. The curved lines of the statuette in the lower left-hand corner, as well as the area where several different hues are brought together, are balanced by the strong vertical forms and the sharp pattern of light and dark in the upper right-hand corner.

65. MATISSE. Detail
of *Piano Lesson* (see fig. 67)

66. DE HOOCH. Detail of
A Dutch Courtyard (see fig. 68)

These two paintings display not only a similarity in over-all organization and balance but also in the detailed arrangement of objects within their four major areas. The lower right-hand corner of the Matisse, for example, is quite similar to the corresponding area of the De Hooch. The sculptural figure of the small girl placed on the flat plane of the brick floor corresponds to the sharply defined metronome placed on the flat, fuchsia-colored plane in the Matisse painting. Another similarity between the objects of this area rests in the way in which the projecting edge of the steps (seen to the left of the little girl) and the white vertical line (made by the simulated scaling of the brick) are echoed in the Matisse work by the vertical, light-blue area and the dark shape of the solid part of the music rack. The importance of the steps as a three-dimensional object in the De Hooch is matched by the striking shape and the dark value of the music rack in the Matisse.

Similar relationships between the two paintings may be seen if we compare the lower left-hand sections. De Hooch arranges his figures in a close-knit group around a table, where they present a lively area of interest both in activity and in visual pattern. The figures are related to one another by a number of means: the direction of the glances, the balance of light and dark, the line of the woman's glass, and the man's pipe. All of these elements are concentrated about the table top, an area to which we are also led either by the flowing lines of the man's arm or by the post of the wooden fence. It is an intense and active area in this otherwise tranquil painting. The same impression is given by Matisse to this area of his painting by the concentration there of a number of various shapes and different hues. The points of the triangular forms of different hues brought into conjunction with one another in this section create a sharp note of excitement. The small but intricately shaped vase placed within the otherwise angular shapes of this area stands out as clearly as does the red skirt of the woman in the De Hooch painting. And the curved lines of the female statue in the corner of the Matisse introduce a note of languid grace that is echoed in the De Hooch scene by the soft arrangement of drapery.

67. Henri Matisse
Piano Lesson. 1916

That De Hooch represents a three-dimensional and Matisse only a two-dimensional world is not so critical a difference for our experience of these works as we might expect. De Hooch does balance his work by a contrast between the presumed position certain objects occupy in depth, but, as we have seen, he does not encourage us to penetrate the pictorial space. He does not excite but rather stills our tendency to experience objects and places in terms of three dimensions. Nevertheless, the relationship between objects that De Hooch is able to suggest through the use of space is a means that Matisse denies himself. This remains a crucial difference between the two works.

What De Hooch gains in arranging his objects in depth, Matisse partially compensates for by using a canvas over three and one-half times as large ($96 \times 84''$ to $27 \times 23''$) but at the same time maintaining the proportions of the objects depicted. Since the relation between the size of the object and the size of the canvas is similar to that of the De Hooch, the larger size of the Matisse makes it appear a magnified version of the De Hooch painting. By this increase in size, certain flat areas of color in the Matisse gain an importance they would not have in a work of smaller format. For example, that the strongly three-dimensional metronome can be balanced by the flat, triangular wedge of green in the upper left depends to a great extent upon both the real and the apparent size of this latter form. The importance gained by the metronome's being one of the few plastic elements within the painting is countered by the importance that the green area attains because of its hue, shape and, most important, size. The balance of these two objects corresponds in the De Hooch to the balance of the figure of the girl in the foreground and

68. Pieter de Hooch
A Dutch Courtyard. About 1656

the tower in the background. Despite their difference in size, we see these two objects as balancing one another because we are aware of the distance in depth that separates them. De Hooch relates these two areas of his painting by placing in one the object closest to us, and in the other, the object farthest away. Matisse relates the same two areas in his painting by placing in one the most clearly three-dimensional object, and in the other, the largest area of a single hue. Throughout the two canvases we may discover other examples of how the radical difference in the way these artists depict individual objects resolves itself to satisfy a commonly shared desire for the effect of the over-all composition.

The simple balance of large areas within these works makes us aware of their equilibrium, but in neither work do we sense a static balance, for our eye moves back and forth from one area to the other. Our eye is made to shift in this manner partly because both Matisse and De Hooch have avoided making the center of their composition into a point of interest. They do not provide us with a single focal point to draw our attention. The rhythm and movement we experience because of this constitutes the principal effect of both these works. But despite the striking similarity in the organization of these two paintings, each work creates for us a distinctive impression. The strong palette and bold forms used by Matisse provoke a response different from that produced by the deep space and warm colors used by De Hooch. As individual as these impressions may be, basically they are only different aspects of the same kind of visual experience. The expressive content of each work is imbedded in the sensitivity that each artist displays for the organization of a work of art.

CHAPTER 8

Unity of Expression

TO UNDERSTAND HOW WE SEE A WORK OF ART we have taken up, one by one, a number of the visual elements that an artist may rely upon to convey an idea to us in visual form. Isolating each of these elements has served to emphasize their particular nature and expressive possibilities; we must recognize, however, that this analytical method breaks up into parts what is essentially a unity. Line or color or light and dark do not exist apart from one another in a work of art. Nor does the artist conceive his work in a series of steps, such as first in line, then space, then color. These elements exist for the artist only in the context of the whole work that he is creating. Although one artist may create a work primarily in terms of color, because he finds this to be his most satisfying means of expression, and for similar reasons another artist may conceive of his work solely in terms of spatial arrangements, any single work of art necessarily includes other visual elements. Each of these elements contributes to the achievement of a unity of expression for the thought or feeling that the artist is attempting to present in visual form.

How an artist uses various elements in such a way that each reinforces, rather than disrupts, his desired effect can be seen in a comparison of two very similar paintings. Perugino and

LEFT

69. RAPHAEL
The Marriage of the Virgin
1504

70. PERUGINO
The Marriage of the Virgin
About 1500

Raphael both have depicted the marriage of the Virgin (figs. 69 and 70) as taking place in almost identical settings. Both paintings are set within an arched frame, their space divided into a foreground, middleground, and background. In each painting, the foreground is made up of three groups of people, the middleground is devoted to the pavement in front of the temple and a few groups of figures, and the background contains the temple. The three groups of figures in the foreground are divided into a central group composed of Mary, Joseph, and the priest, and into two lateral groups of spectators. Of these two groups, the one beside Joseph is made up completely of men; the one next to Mary, of women. Yet, as we enumerate the similarities existing in the two paintings, we become aware that our impressions of these two works are far from being the same. Despite their apparent similarities, we find that it is their differences to which we are increasingly sensitive.

The two paintings depicting the same event in such similar settings present, nevertheless, two different interpretations of this ceremony. Our relation to the scene as painted by Perugino is like that of spectators at a theater to the stage performance. At the same time, we consider ourselves privileged to watch this event, for, even if we should not be familiar with the story being portrayed, this marriage impresses us as being a significant occasion. As Perugino has depicted it, the scene of two people about to be joined by the priest inspires in us a feeling of awe. We sense a certain mystery about this union. Before the Raphael painting our concept of being spectators at a performance vanishes. We are encouraged to feel as if we could become members of the group surrounding the bridal couple. An invitation to join in the ceremony and share directly in the emotion of the event seems to be extended to us. Our impression is of a warm, pleasing environment, and we sense a bond between ourselves and the principals of this marriage.

These distinctly different impressions arise directly from the opposite ways in which each artist has used various visual elements to convey his particular conception of this event. Within a basically similar framework, the artists have handled space and line and light and dark so that they complement and extend one another in achieving the desired effect. How the artists have used these elements to create paintings of a very different nature can be seen from a more detailed analysis of how we see these works.

Our impression of Perugino's painting depends initially upon the way in which the artist has arranged the figures so that they stretch across the foreground in a row. By this arrangement, Perugino immediately sets up a barrier between us and the space in the painting, an effect that he reinforces by creating a straight, horizontal line out of the head-level of the figures. Within this tightly grouped mass of figures, some minor variation occurs in the distance between ourselves and a particular figure, but without arousing a strong feeling of depth. The two figures on either side of the painting are closer to us than any other members of this group, but, since they are seen in the uninviting gesture of presenting their backs to us, we are not inclined to see them as in any way existing in our space. From this arrangement of the figures in the foreground we derive our impression of witnessing an event taking place on a stage.

Within this unified group, the figures of Mary, the priest, and Joseph stand out and claim our attention. Naturally, their central position within the painting assures them of that, but this alone is not sufficient to account for our impression of this group. For an important quality of this central group is their apparent obliviousness to the figures on either side. Although we see the wedding spectators gather around the bridal couple, the latter present an appearance of being isolated and apart that emphasizes their importance and uniqueness. Perugino endows the couple with this quality partly by the way in which he depicts the two groups on either side of Mary and Joseph.

The attention of the members of these two groups is directed primarily at the two figures who turn their backs to us. By fixing these subsidiary focal points Perugino both pulls the figures away from the central group and gives unity and independence to each of these two groups. Within these groups, the figures are shown in a variety of postures, their glances made to stray from one another, to us, to the ceremony itself. We find our eye unable to concentrate on any one figure in these groups, for the rich profusion of visually stimulating detail constantly attracts us from one figure to another. The variety of gestures, the different textures and

71. PERUGINO. Detail of *The Marriage of the Virgin*

designs of the costumes, the linear grace of the women's coiffures and veiling, the sharp and intricate silhouettes of the men's headgear, all contrast sharply with the simple and quiet forms of the central group.

The arrangement of the figures within this central group also contributes to the total impression that we finally form of the event taking place. On either side of the priest, whose upright posture emphasizes the fact that he is the focal point of the action, is one of the two principals of the ceremony. As the fulcrum of this balance, the priest is represented as an absolutely symmetrical figure; even the part in his beard and the belt of his vestments emphasize this arrangement. By depicting the upper portion of his body in a clear silhouette against the pavement, Perugino underlines the symmetry of this group once more, and focuses our attention on the action about to take place. The figures of Joseph and Mary are connected to this central figure by two curved lines made by the folds of their robes. In keeping with the symmetry of this group, the two lines are almost identical, and the two figures are seen as equal in importance.

72. PERUGINO. *The Marriage of the Virgin.* About 1500

This balance receives further emphasis from the arrangement of light and dark within this central group. On either side of the central dark area of the priest, the figures of Joseph and Mary make up a complementary division of light and dark. Perugino balances the dark robe of Joseph by the light robe of Mary and treats the cloaks in a similar fashion. By these means Perugino achieves for this group a simplicity and a static quality that distinguish them from all the other figures in the foreground. Within this group of balanced and quiet forms, the only movements of which we are aware are those of the facial expressions and those of the action about to be taken.

As we concentrate on this foreground group we are at the same time conscious of the temple and of its intimate connection with the scene. Although through the diminished size of the figures scattered in the distance and the receding lines of the pavement Perugino physically locates the temple in the background, its form appears far more dominant than we might expect from a background object. Instead of the great distance that Perugino apparently intends us to see separating foreground and temple, we are more aware of a close relationship between the two. Thus, the space in this painting appears to us as vast and yet curiously limited. It is a type of space that does not correspond to what we normally experience, and its presence here contributes to this scene an unreal character which is a crucial part of the effect that the artist desires to convey.

Perugino encourages us to form this concept of the space in the painting beginning with our initial experience of the foreground figures. Stretched directly across the painting and occupying almost all of the available space in this area, the figures form a horizontal barrier between us and the space beyond. The horizontality established by these figures is an element that Perugino continues to emphasize, even though at the same time he induces us to move back into the painting by having the lines recede to a vanishing point. The consistency with which the effect of horizontality is stressed is evident simply from the shape that Perugino gives to the divisions of the pavement. They are markedly wide in relation to their depth. And as they lead back to the temple, the horizontal effect is again enhanced by the way in which the steps are divided into banks whose width is even greater than the pavement divisions. In moving farther back from the stairs to the temple we discover that it is the breadth of the temple that Perugino stresses. We are far more sensitive, for example, to the distance that separates the two side porches than we are to their position in depth. We tend to ignore the fact that the central porch is closer to us, that the side walls of the octagonal temple cut back into space. The pattern made by the side porches against the sky distracts our eye from the central vanishing point framed by the doorway.

The space that opens up behind the temple is recognized and even sensed by us, but we are more sensitive to the width or expanse of this space than to its depth. Instead of receding into the distant hills of the picture, our eye moves more persistently from one side of the picture to the other, as if intent on seeing everything within the entire scene. Stimulating us to act in this way are the trees whose pattern, etched against the sky, draws our attention out to the very limits of the width of the canvas. Thus, we are made to experience in the background a visual field as wide as the foreground. And Perugino uses this pattern of the trees against the sky to insist once again on the parallel nature of background to foreground by linking it with the staff held by Joseph. This sharp and accented form, similar in both design and value to the trees, always returns our attention to the foreground, so that our sense of moving back into space is neutralized.

The spatial experience that Perugino creates for us has the effect of keeping us constantly aware of the presence of the temple in this scene. This effect is equally conveyed by the quality of light within the painting. A strong, clear light pervades the scene, casting only small shadows and illuminating the temple as sharply as the foreground. The uniform light throughout the painting helps to keep us aware of the presence of the temple, and our attention is also drawn to it simply by the fact that Perugino does not depict the entire building. By omitting the dome and terminating the temple with a balustrade, he exaggerates the breadth of the temple and stresses the horizontality of the painting. If Perugino had depicted the dome of the temple, it would have become a separate and distinct object firmly planted in the background, thus clearly destroying the spatial effect that he wished to create. In its incomplete form, the temple bulks even larger in this scene, and finds its completion only in the foreground, where the hat of the priest suggests the form of the dome that we cannot see.

Basically, the setting of the painting is a very simple one: a square before a temple. But we have seen that Perugino does not evoke from us so simple an impression—our impression is of a very unreal and unfamiliar place. The scene takes place not simply in a square before the temple, but in a space created by, and existing for, this particular temple. This temple does not exist merely as a background for the scene, but makes its presence felt so strongly that we cannot help recognizing that our interpretation of this event must be made in relation to it. The wedding we see taking place is cast over with an air of awe and uniqueness because of the majestic presence of the temple.

To create a painting whose figures are so similar and setting so nearly identical, Raphael necessarily makes use of the same visual elements. But, as we have seen, his version of the scene creates a very different impression: it makes us aware of another aspect of the meaning embodied in this symbolic ceremony. What is responsible for this difference rests, then, solely in which of the different expressive possibilities of space, line or light-and-dark that Raphael has chosen to emphasize.

That Raphael is working in terms quite opposed to those of Perugino is made immediately apparent by the arrangement of the foreground figures. The solid block of figures stretched across the Perugino canvas is transformed by Raphael into a group arranged in a semicircle. The pocket of space now left vacant in the foreground encourages us to relate it to our own space. We can easily imagine that the group of spectators moves out into our space to form a complete ring before the principal figures, a group that we can readily join. A relationship between ourselves and the figures in the painting also is established by the action of the youth

73. RAPHAEL. Detail of *The Marriage of the Virgin*

on the right, who, in breaking the rod, bends over into what we identify as our own space. He invites us into the painting by this action in the same way that the side figures of the work by Perugino keep us out of the painting with their turned backs.

Just as we are no longer restricted to being spectators of an event on a stage, so, too, the principal figures are no longer treated as an isolated group. Not only do Joseph, Mary, and the priest become more intimate parts of the entire foreground group, but each of the principals also becomes more of an individual. For Raphael breaks up the rigid symmetry that binds the central figures into a single group in the Perugino painting. Through the different stances and the compensating movements that each figure must make to maintain its balance, Raphael makes us aware of them as plastic forms separated from one another by the space they create. And Raphael uses the light-and-dark pattern of this group to achieve the same effect. The contrast in values between Joseph's cloak and robe is balanced not as it was in the Perugino painting, by a similar contrast in Mary's garments, but by the garments of the closest figure in the left foreground. In establishing this relationship, our eye once more moves within the foreground space and makes us conscious again of the continuous circle formed by the participants, the spectators, and ourselves.

But our attention also has a clear, single focal point within this area. The glances of many of the spectators and of Mary herself are directed at the ring. It is on this one object that Raphael finally fixes our attention. No similar point of concentrated interest appears in the painting by Perugino, where Mary is seen with eyes cast down, not looking at the ring. In this scene the priest holds up Mary's and Joseph's hands before us—a symbolic representation of the act that is about to be performed. Raphael's concept is very different, for he makes us see the ring at the very moment that it is being placed on Mary's finger. Raphael replaces the symbol with the act itself.

Our attention, however, is not restricted to the foreground of this painting. As in the Perugino painting, the figures are seen in the context of a specific setting, and in both, the figure of the priest is used to relate the foreground group to the temple. Through the sharp

74. PERUGINO
Detail of *The Marriage of the Virgin*

75. RAPHAEL
Detail of *The Marriage of the Virgin*

76. RAPHAEL
Detail of *The Marriage of the Virgin*

77. PERUGINO
Detail of *The Marriage of the Virgin*

contrast in light and dark of the brocaded belt against the robe of the priest, Raphael introduces a vertical accent within the foreground figures. Our eye is carried farther in this direction by the tilt of the priest's hand and the line of his hat. This movement unites the group to the temple in the same way that the staff carried by the Joseph of the Perugino version directs our eye to the background. We also relate these two sections of the painting to each other because of the association that Raphael sets up between the form and value of the priest's hat and the dome of the temple. An association between the two which was only suggested in the Perugino, here is made specific.

The differences we have noted already between these two paintings are pointed up and, in a sense, exemplified, by the way in which each artist has depicted the temple. In place of the centralized building by Perugino, which impresses us more by its separate, clearly defined, and sharply articulated parts than by its existence as a three-dimensional object, Raphael creates a temple in which every architectural feature contributes to making us aware of the building as a physical entity. The protruding porches of the Perugino temple are absorbed by a continuous arcade; the pronounced octagonal shape is softened to an almost circular form; the horizontal balustrade disappears; and the crowning feature of the building, the dome, becomes visible. Each one of these changes helps to create a building whose existence as a tangible object is clearly felt. Thus, we see the temple depicted by Raphael as an independent, self-sufficient unit placed within the space of the painting. And the distance between temple and figures is not negated, as in the Perugino painting, but emphasized by the pattern of the pavement. The temple becomes much more isolated from the figures and its presence no longer dominates the scene.

78. RAPHAEL. *The Marriage of the Virgin.* 1504

But at the same time the temple does not become simply an accessory in an appropriate background. For some reason we realize that the temple and the foreground figures are equally important parts of this scene. We cannot help receiving this impression as our eye constantly moves between the temple and the figures, crossing with what seems to be an amazing speed the distance between the temple door and the ring. It becomes apparent to us that within this painting there exist two vanishing points, one centered at the open door of the temple, the other at the wedding ring.

Although this organization makes the two sections of the painting virtually independent of each other, Raphael creates a bond between them by placing the two vanishing points on the same line, the vertical line initiated by the belt of the priest's robe. Our eye moves from the one section to the other along this line and by this movement brings the ceremony and the temple into a relationship distinctly different from the one suggested by Perugino. Through a sensitive and subtle use of the vanishing point, Raphael has implied that the nature of what takes place in the moment the ring is placed on Mary's finger is essentially different from, and to a degree independent of, the nature of what is signified by the temple. The relationship that binds these two together, the dependence of the ceremony for its very existence on the existence of the temple—the concept so persuasively conveyed by Perugino—is not actually depicted by Raphael. He prefers to create the relationship by establishing the movements that we must make when viewing this scene. Again Raphael replaces a symbol with an act.

The differences that we have discovered between the two concepts conveyed by these similar paintings emphasize the interdependent role that the different elements play within a total work. To give visual form to an idea, an artist uses all of the means at his disposal. Working from both his experience and his intuition, he creates a work in which the various elements contribute to the unity of expression, the characteristic of his work that makes it a unique and original work of art.

PART TWO *The Artist*

CHAPTER 9

Materials

IN THE PROCESS OF ANALYZING various works of art, we have become aware of how we respond to different visual elements such as line, color, and space. Gradually, we have grown familiar with the visual language that the artist uses to express himself, and we have come to recognize that this language is based on the artist's visual sensitivity and experience. Also, we have found that this language becomes more intelligible to us as our own visual experience increases. The more the language of visual forms becomes our own, the closer we approach the point where the very idea of the artist can also be said to become our own.

To approach this point, however, we must also recognize that an artist speaks to us through a specific work of art—a work made of paint and canvas, or of ink and paper, or of wood, stone, metal, etc. For the visual elements in the works of art that we have discussed have no existence apart from the material of these works; visual forms come into being only through the brush, pen, or chisel of the artist. Thus our response to visual elements is related necessarily to the physical materials from which a work is created. And, because different materials have

79. JACQUES CALLOT
Ballet Dancer (drawing)
About 1620

80. PICASSO
Detail of *Four Ballet Dancers*

distinctive properties that affect the appearance of a work in different ways, our experience of the work is directly conditioned by the kind of material the artist uses. Just as the particular expressive nature of a line or a color depends upon the context in which the artist places it, so, too, the expressive content of an entire work depends upon the medium in which it is created.

Originally, we had to recognize that to fully appreciate the expressive quality peculiar to each of the arts we must take into account the fact that one man chose to create a painting, another a poem, and still another an opera. Similarly, we must be aware that one painter chose oil and another watercolor, or that one sculptor created a piece in stone, another, in clay.

Easy availability is not the primary reason an artist chooses to express himself in a certain medium. He chooses oil rather than watercolor because oil paint has qualities that make it a better medium to convey his thought. The choice of the material is a part of the fusion between the idea and the form—not an afterthought, but a fundamental part of the work. Idea, form, medium are indistinguishable parts of the creative act.

To see how important medium can be for our understanding of a work of art, let us look again at Picasso's simple line drawing of four dancers (fig. 81). As we have seen, because of the artist's very subtle use of line we receive from this work not just a view of four dancers, but also an idea of the actions that each dancer must perform to fulfill her role in the dance. We sense the character of the dance so clearly because we respond to the nature of each line in the drawing. In part, we do so because there are so few lines in the drawing, but primarily we are sensitive to each of the lines because Picasso has made all of them of the same thickness and of the same tonal value. There is no contrast between thick and thin lines, nor between light and dark lines. Their uniform quality makes them all equally attractive to our eye, and because each line is

81. PABLO PICASSO
Four Ballet Dancers (drawing)
1925

drawn precisely, we are quick to sense its character. Following the individual line, we become sensitive to its many changes of direction and to its abrupt ending. In experiencing these different linear movements, we realize how responsible they are for our original impression of this drawing. Obviously our experience with this work is affected by the medium that Picasso has chosen, for the character of the lines is due largely to the qualities of the medium.

The effect achieved in the drawing is the result of the way Picasso himself responded to the nature of the medium: pen and ink. As an instrument that may be controlled precisely, the pen enabled Picasso to give the lines their minute changes in direction and abrupt endings, and thus allowed him to endow a single line with a maximum of expression. The uniform width—so important for our being able to see each line—is a result of the type of pen that Picasso chose for his tool. For this drawing he elected to use a stiff pen rather than a flexible one, a type which would have produced a greater variation in the width of the lines. But it is the ink which gives the drawing its even tonal quality, for unless the artist varies the width of his lines or uses different kinds of ink, the tonal value of the inked line will remain constant. Picasso makes this quality of the ink—like the stiffness of the pen—operate as a positive factor in his drawing.

The drawing by Picasso is the happy product of a union of artist and medium. The artist has taken advantage of the natural characteristics of this particular pen and ink in achieving his effect. It would not be absolutely impossible to make a drawing like Picasso's with a different kind of pen, but to do so, the artist would have to overcome the natural tendency of this medium. Success in producing the same type of line by using a less stiff pen, for example, could be gained only by a great effort to maintain a constant pressure. And to what avail? In itself such skill may be of great fascination, but the end result would not contribute either to the artist's or to the spectator's visual experience.

Good artists cannot help responding to the nature of the medium. Thus, when Romney uses

82. GEORGE ROMNEY
Dancing Figures (drawing)
About 1775

a soft pen to make a sketch of four dancers (fig. 82), he produces a drawing with characteristics markedly different from those of the Picasso drawing. In the Romney sketch, the bold, swift strokes of the pen force our eye to move swiftly about the group, paying little attention to individual lines. The occasional wider lines and the few dark areas of ink help to set up a strong rhythm among the dancers. That these drawings are by two different men from different periods in time is not a sufficient reason to account for the differences between them. In each case, the artist responded to the feel of the pen. Romney, like Picasso, allowed the qualities of the pen to determine the content of his drawing.

The role that the medium plays in forming our reaction to a work may become even more clearly apparent if we try to imagine what the Picasso or Romney pen-and-ink drawings would look like if translated into a very different medium—a crayon drawing, for example. How waxy lines made with a crayon differ from the more solid, even lines of ink can be seen in a red crayon sketch by Callot (fig. 79). Like pens, crayons may be either hard or soft, but the distinguishing feature of the crayon line derives from the fact that the crayon is made up of ground pigments compressed with gum or wax. As the crayon is drawn across a piece of paper, the artist feels that its movement is sticky. In response to this feeling, he may vary the amount of pressure he places on the crayon or he may change the position of the crayon in his hand. In doing so, he produces lines of varying thickness and value. Thus, to use crayon to give an impression of the dance similar to that created by the Picasso drawing would necessitate a completely new statement of the idea. The idea would have to be conceived in terms of the new material.

83. JEAN-AUGUSTE DOMINIQUE INGRES. *The Golden Age,*
study for the fresco in the Château de Dampierre. About 1845

The various other materials that artists use to draw with, such as pencil, charcoal, pastel, chalk, and silverpoint, all have distinct properties that make each a medium of individual expressive possibilities. In these drawing media, however, the relation between the material used and the content of the work is always very close, primarily because the pen, pencil, or stick of material permits the artist to be in intimate contact with his work. The pen or pencil transfers the gesture of his hand onto paper directly and immediately. Because of this, many painters and sculptors first put their ideas into sketches, changing and perfecting them in this manner before they achieve their final work in a different medium. As an example, this drawing by Ingres (fig. 83) is only one of many such studies he made for different figures and groups that he intended to use in a fresco entitled *The Golden Age.* This method of working reveals why some collectors and connoisseurs prize the drawings of a painter more than his actual paintings. They feel that such sketches preserve the real genius of the artist, his finished work displaying more craftsmanship than creativity. But it is very rare for an artist not to continue to develop his ideas as he works with the actual material of his final product. Thus, although an artist may make many preparatory pencil sketches for an oil painting, it is infrequent for such sketches to correspond exactly to the finished painting. For example, in an oil painting by Ingres (fig. 84) of the same subject as his fresco—a work that was unfinished—we can see that the sketch contains only glimpses of what the group of dancing figures would eventually look like. Although such a re-working of the subject normally occurs between an artist's initial studies and his finished work, this change is also due to differences in the medium employed. The nature of oil paint itself becomes the final determining factor in the creation of the painting, the qualities of the material affect the form. For this reason many contemporary painters prefer working directly on the canvas without preliminary sketches or studies. When the painter works in this way, the idea is conceived in the same material as the final work, and the initial expression of the idea is shaped by the qualities of the material.

Of the many materials with which an artist may paint, oil paint has dominated Western painting for the last four hundred years. This fact alone indicates what a flexible medium oil paint is, a substance whose properties make it so susceptible to individual exploitation that it can be

84. JEAN-AUGUSTE DOMINIQUE INGRES. *The Golden Age* (detail). 1862

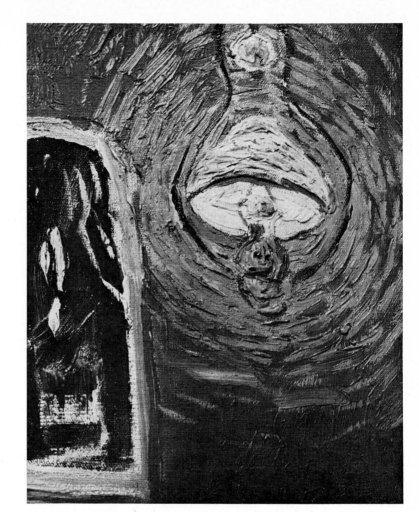

85. VINCENT VAN GOGH
Night Café (and detail). 1888

the common vehicle for the most diverse visual expression. In the details from two oil paintings, *Night Café* by Van Gogh (fig. 85), and *The Ecstasy of St. Francis* by La Tour (fig. 86), we can see two strongly opposed ways in which the medium can be used. The most immediate and startling difference rests in the surface texture of the two paintings. The rough surface of the Van Gogh painting, so obviously built up by the strokes of the brush, is completely different in appearance from the smooth, polished surface of the La Tour painting, a surface that almost seems to deny its origin in the brush. This difference, basic for the expressive character of each of these works, is simply a result of the physical properties of oil paint, which allow it to be used either in a very thick state or in a more fluid one.

Between these two extremes of oil paint there exists a wide range of possible consistencies, as we can see in the oil sketch by Constable (page 80). Each of the different consistencies used here affected the way Constable moved the paint about on the surface—sweeping broadly across one area, piling up the paint by short strokes in another, and elsewhere, dabbing it on by single isolated flicks of the brush. These different actions necessarily affected the character of the forms that Constable has created upon the surface of the painting. Ultimately, this landscape owes its form and its effect to the possibilities inherent in the physical substance of oil paint.

In the work by Van Gogh, as in the sketch by Constable, the brush stroke itself has a life as an expressive visual element. The thickness of the paint and the clearly separated strokes create the effect of the raw, powerful impact of artificial light. In the painting by La Tour the thinner paint has encouraged the artist to think in terms of larger areas and allowed him, as well, to separate these areas precisely. The enamel-like finish binds the separate parts together in such a way that we seem to see these areas of paint as lying beneath a transparent film, rather than as laid onto a flat surface. The light appears to reach us through several of these films, as if the very atmosphere in which the candle burns had melted upon the canvas. We experience the pulsing light and heat of the candle flame, not because of an imitation of the object but because its effects have been re-created. As in the painting by Van Gogh, this impression is intimately connected with the character of the material. La Tour's thin applications of oil paint have been placed over one another, the translucent quality of the oil allowing one color to exist beneath another. The mingling of tones and fine gradations of light and dark that this method makes possible, create rich, luminous hues, so that the darkest parts of the La Tour painting glow in a way that creates the effect of a shifting light. It is as if a real flame somehow were imbedded in the structure of the painting, a flame caught between the different layers of the paint.

86. GEORGES DE LA TOUR (?)
The Ecstasy of St. Francis (and detail). 1640–45

87. ANDREA MANTEGNA
St. Jerome (and detail). About 1470

The many ways in which oil can be used offer the artist a rich source of expressive power, but oil is only one of the numerous materials from which a painter may choose. Of these, the most commonly used media after oil paint are watercolor and tempera. Physically these three media differ from one another only in that the dry, powdered pigments, which constitute the "colors" for each of them, are mixed with different liquids: with an oil to produce oil paint, with egg fluids to obtain tempera, with gum arabic and glue for watercolor. How each of these liquid media—metaphorically referred to as "vehicles" because when mixed with a solvent they carry the pigments—is applied to the painting surface by the brush (oil may be applied also with a knife) accounts for many of the differences among the effects produced by these media. For, just as the various drawing media feel different when they are pushed or pulled across a surface, so, too, the feel of a brush loaded with tempera is a different sensation from the feel of one loaded with oil or of one saturated with watercolor. The way in which each must be handled to bring a form into being on the canvas necessarily affects the ways in which the artist conceives of his painting.

The detail of *St. Jerome* (fig. 87), painted by Mantegna in tempera, conveys some of the aspects of this medium. The precise outlines and intricate detailing of the robe and the rocks indicate how delicately form can be delineated with a tempera-laden brush. Although its surface is completely smooth, we are, as with the Van Gogh, very conscious of the paint's having been applied to a surface. In the Mantegna, however, rather than being aware of forms built up through the brush strokes, we feel that the forms came into existence by virtue of their outlines having been filled in with paint. This is a result not only of a difference in viscosity between the two media but of the fact that tempera does not fuse and blend as easily as oil to produce a variety of values. Consequently, the distinctions between areas of color and value in the tempera painting are marked. In comparison with the painting by La Tour, the less translucent quality of tempera with respect to oil is made apparent by the way in which Mantegna must rely primarily on shading to create effects of light, and by the presence of only very small areas of reflected light. Thus, from this painting by Mantegna, we can see that in its manner of application and in the effects that it produces, the tempera medium directs the artist toward a statement that is both microscopic and highly sculptural.

The very fluid character of the watercolor medium is immediately apparent in the detail from a landscape scene by John Sell Cotman (fig. 88). Here, the surface of the rocks and the details of their shapes are not described by the paint so much as their form is suggested or intimated by broad areas of subtly varied tonal values. The form of the rocks is an indistinguishable part of the form of the watercolor wash that floats upon the paper. Yet the paper is not merely a flat surface on which the paint is placed, for the artist has made equal use of the grain and value of the paper in creating this image—so much so that the surface seemingly is dissolved into a shifting, transient arrangement of transparent areas of color. The concrete reality of tempera landscape is exchanged, in the watercolor scene, for one of suggestion and mood.

In responding to the natural character of the medium he has chosen, the painter exercises a particular sensitivity to material that is a part of his natural talent. Whether he chooses the material to give form to a preconceived idea or whether the idea grows out of the material is

88. JOHN SELL COTMAN
Greta Bridge (and detail). 1805

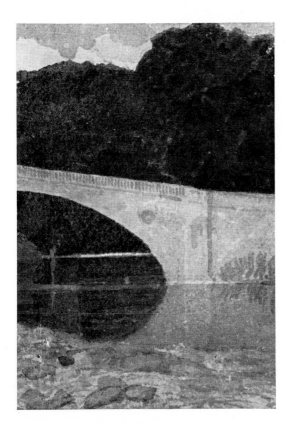

not a question that we should be able to answer from the work itself. If the painter has been in sympathy with the material, a distinction between idea and medium should not be discernible. In contemporary art, however, the artist has been especially conscious of the way in which materials give birth to forms. This is one reason why recent artists have welcomed so enthusiastically the many new materials available to them, such as lacquers, encaustics, enamels, vinyls, etc. The same attitude also accounts for the increasingly prevalent combinations of several different media in one work. This sentiment is found at its purest in the *collage*, a work that owes its form to the stimulation received by the artist from pre-existing material such as newspaper clippings, textiles, railroad tickets, sandpaper, buttons, etc. The work created in this fashion, such as the piece by Kurt Schwitters (fig. 89), has been shaped purely by the artist's sensitivity to the different shapes, textures, and colors of the different objects, and to the effects to be achieved by their arrangement.

When we look at sculpture we are generally more conscious of the material of which it is made, primarily because its material is simply more tangible and more obviously present than it is in painting. Normally, we are aware of whether a piece of sculpture is made of bronze, stone, or wood, and, without being overly conscious of the fact, we respond to the different surfaces and colors of these materials. To a large extent our impression of the sculpture by Maillol, for example, is formed by the rich, glowing patina of its bronze surface (fig. 90).

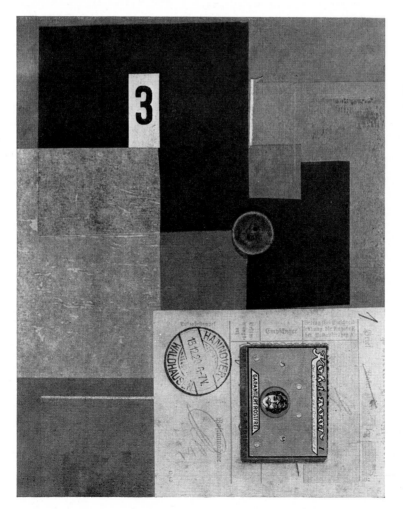

89. KURT SCHWITTERS
"*Merz*" *Drawing* (collage)
1924

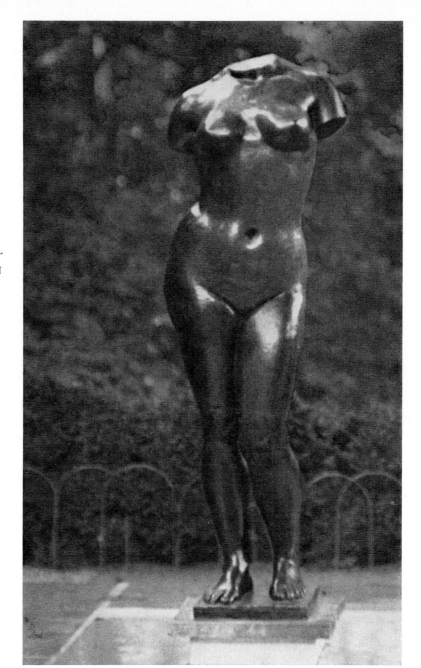

90. ARISTIDE MAILLOL
Study for "Summer." 1910–11

Through the pose and the subtly achieved balance of the figure, Maillol has created a rhythmic and expressive statement of the beauty of the human body, but the content of the work rests only partially in this aspect of its creation. For Maillol's statement about the human body takes on additional meaning for us precisely because it is a metal object. The transmutation of the body into bronze converts it into a work of art whose effect depends not only on our recognition of its descriptive aspects but on our sensitivity to the play of light upon the metallic surface, to our enjoyment of the beauty of the material itself. Yet in addition to playing this important role of stimulating our feeling for the sensuous quality of beauty, material plays an

91. ERNST BARLACH
Man Drawing a Sword. 1911

92. MICHELANGELO
Pietà. About 1550–56

even greater part in the creation of a piece of sculpture, for it determines to a significant degree the visual form that the sculptor creates.

Like the various painting and drawing media, the different kinds of material available to the sculptor affect the form of his work because of their physical properties. For instance, whether the stone yields easily to the cutting edge of the carver's chisel is a tangible characteristic inevitably influencing the appearance of the finished work. But how the artist must work with his material to transform it into a work of art is only one aspect of the influence of the material of sculpture over form. A far more important determinant is the kind of form that the material itself possesses before the sculptor begins to work on it. A block of stone or a piece of wood, for example, is a piece of material that in its original state, possesses a specific volume and shape. The natural shape and mass of the wood or stone becomes the framework within which the *carver* conceives the work that he wishes to create. In contrast, the material of the *modeler* is not embodied in a form of a specific mass and volume. The modeler works without a pre-existing form for inspiration, shaping the plaster, clay, or wax to build up an image that from the outset exists only in the mind of the artist.

The wooden figure by Barlach (fig. 91) and the marble group of figures by Michelangelo (fig. 92) are sculptures created by having been cut out of a larger piece of the material. To create the form the artist had to remove a portion of the original stone or wood. In doing so, the artist was able to free the form—a phrase descriptive of how the carver intuitively works in terms of the pre-existent form of his material. He sees the image that he wishes to create as lying within the particular size and shape of the stone or wood and, because of the nature of such material, he is led most naturally to conceive his form in terms of the material's basic volumetric properties. The volume and mass of the material become basic visual elements of his work and thus determine our own experience of the piece of sculpture.

For the carver, then, the block of stone or piece of wood lies between his concept of his work and its existence as a piece of sculpture. The degree to which it affects the individual work depends upon the inclination of the carver. He may, for example, draw his inspiration almost totally from the natural character and shape of a particular piece of material. Brancusi's work *Fish* (fig. 93) owes its definition of form not only to the veins of the marble but to the original shape of the stone as well. The sculpture has the appearance of being an almost untouched piece of marble, as if it were an object accidentally created by the action of time and weather. Material and form are in such harmony that the work appears not to be simply descriptive of the natural object but to have an existence of its own. For other sculptors the effect of the material's original form need not be so direct as it apparently was for Brancusi. Yet, unless the carver disregards completely the nature of his medium or seeks to overcome its inherent properties by virtuosity, he instinctively creates a work whose effect derives in part from the character of the particular piece of material. We do not know, for example, exactly how Michelangelo proceeded when carving the *Pietà*, but the arrangement of the figures within an enclosing pyramidal form indicates that the relations among the individual figures were determined primarily with reference to a desired over-all shape for the group. And this shape would appear to have been determined by Michelangelo's decision to make the piece in marble. If Michelangelo had chosen bronze instead of marble he undoubtedly would have created a *Pietà* of a very different appearance and content.

93. CONSTANTIN BRANCUSI
Fish. 1930

94. SIENESE. *Adam*
About 1485

We can see some of the different qualities a bronze figure may have if we turn to a Sienese statuette of Adam (fig. 94). Here the relations of the different parts of the piece do not suggest that the figure was conceived in terms of a simple, encompassing shape. As a piece modeled in wax before it was transformed into bronze, the figure of Adam was built up by the artist's adding and shaping soft, pliable material with his fingers or tools. Unlike an object freed from its material, the figure of Adam grew before the eyes of the sculptor. In shaping the formless wax into an image the sculptor sensed, as he worked, the position of the different parts in relation to one another and to the surrounding space. The object and the space that its movements define were created simultaneously, the sculptor responding to the constantly changing form that he was creating in space rather than to the changing aspects of a form being created within a given shape.

In the bronze figure of a girl by Butler (fig. 96) the textured surface points to its origin in a clay model, but its form indicates this evolution even more strongly. Less concerned with the relation of the object to the surrounding space than the Sienese artist, Butler gives us a figure equally in motion, although its movement is more from within. For we can sense the building up of this form by an additive process; wet clay has been packed and molded about the metal core needed for its support. The figure has been built from the inside out to the surface, each part of its solid form having been shaped by the sculptor to express the inner tensions and movements of this body engaged in a specific action.

How definite a role the material and the means of shaping it has for our experience of the Butler sculpture can be appreciated if we look at a work with a similar subject by Hayes (fig. 95)

95. DAVID HAYES
Woman Dressing. 1958

96. REGINALD BUTLER
Girl. 1956–57

executed in sheet metal with a welding torch. Instead of building up a form by molding solid material about a metal support, the artist here creates the form by enfolding the material about a void. This way of creating the form appears to make the sculptor think of the figure in much the same way as the carver—in terms of its volume. But because here the sculptor is aware of the space that he is enclosing, no sense of mass pervades the work. This volumetric figure of a woman undressing is curiously weightless. We are conscious only of the movement of the figure, a movement not explicit in itself but implied as the body rises into the descending hollow of the robe. In its subject the work by Hayes is similar to the Butler; in the movement of its forms it is reminiscent of the Barlach. That it is a work to which our reaction is different from our reaction to the other pieces is, to a great extent, due to the differences in material among these three.

The sculptor, like the painter, has a great many materials to choose from, each with its own characteristics and all demanding different tools and approaches if they are to be shaped into works of art. Each of the different types of stone, of wood, and of metal offers to the sculptor yet another possibility of expression. As with the painter, whether the sculptor is inspired by the material itself, or chooses the material because it fits his idea, is not a distinction that should be obvious from his work. And contemporary sculptors also give particular stress to the role of the material in determining the nature of their work. Like the collage makers, they too have created works whose forms depend solely upon what is suggested to them by the shapes and materials of pre-existing objects which they have found: metal pipes, springs, clockworks. As we can see in the work by Stankiewicz, *Bird Lover in the Grass* (fig. 97), their statement is frequently witty, the material gaining in meaning by being transmuted into a work of art from an object whose meaning as a form was once quite different. Such a change of meaning, which involves both the original quality of the material and the mind of the artist, is at the very center of the creative act.

97. RICHARD STANKIEWICZ
Bird Lover in the Grass. 1957

CHAPTER 10

Techniques

THE ARTIST'S CHOICE OF MATERIAL and the use he chooses to make of its natural properties have been seen to be acts clearly affecting the expressive content of the final work. The way in which Picasso and Romney use pen and ink, and the way in which La Tour and Van Gogh use oils, are indications of how intimately the artist and his material are allied. Our enjoyment and understanding of his work results, then, not only from the artist's visual experience but from his sensitivity to the characteristics of his material. The important part that this sensitivity plays in the creation of a work of art can be seen even more readily if we look at prints, such as woodcuts, engravings, etchings, or lithographs, where the immediate contact between the artist and his work is necessarily interrupted by the intervention of a technical and mechanical process. Prints, therefore, provide a clear example of how the technique that the artist uses to bring a work of art into existence both shapes and, at times, inspires his conception.

To create a print, an artist must be concerned not only with the materials that he works with, but also with the mechanics of printing. Instead of directly creating a work of art by using a pen to put ink on paper or a brush to put paint on canvas, the artist must employ a technique that will transfer ink from one surface to another surface. And, since the artist wishes to present a particular image through the appearance of lines or areas in a print, he naturally must be able to have exact control over where the ink will be placed on the paper. The printmaker's quest to obtain this control has led to the various methods now employed, each of which offers the artist different expressive possibilities rooted in the particular way in which each is carried out.

Actually, the many processes differ from one another only in the method by which each process retains the ink in a specified part of the printing block or plate. All the other differences among the processes are subordinate to this one factor. It is on this principle that the expressive possibilities of each process rest and it is this one factor with which both the artist and we ourselves are most directly concerned.

The direct relation between the way in which the artist controls the placing of ink on his

98. KARL SCHMIDT-ROTTLUFF
Woman with Hat (woodcut). 1905

printing surface and the way in which we experience the print can be seen in the woodcut by Schmidt-Rottluff (fig. 98). In this case, it is the light areas that did not print. When the paper was placed over the wooden printing block it came into contact with ink everywhere except in those areas. To be able to control the appearance of these two areas in the print, the artist cut out of his block of wood the areas that he did not want to print, so that these areas became lower than the printing surface of the block. Thus, when the ink was placed on the block it could be limited to that portion of the block which had been left at the height of the original surface.

Because the process is dependent upon cutting away areas of the block surface, the artist tends to conceive his work in areas of light and dark rather than in lines. The woodcut by Schmidt-Rottluff is made up of only such areas, the figure being defined through the juxtaposition of areas of particular shapes. The figure in the woodcut by Heckel (fig. 99) is more linearly conceived, but the character of the entire woodcut remains the result of the artist's working in large areas of light and dark. As is quite evident in the Heckel woodcut, the artist must use a knife or similar tool to cut away the areas which are to print light. The dark lines and shapes in the Heckel print result from the wood's having been cut away between them—on the wooden block they would appear as ridges of wood standing above the carved-out areas. That the cutting away of wood to give form to an image is not the same as passing a pencil or crayon over a piece of paper is clear from the character of these lines. The angularity and thickness of the lines in the Heckel woodcut speak clearly of the method by which they were produced and show how this method was a positive factor in forming the artist's concept. The character of the figure is derived both from the quality of the lines and from the boldness and sharpness of the decorative pattern created by the areas of light and dark. Both of these expressive features are inherent in the nature of the technical process by which the woodcut came into being. The differences between the woodcut by Heckel and the one by Schmidt-Rottluff result from the different way in which each of these artists took advantage of the characteristics offered by the process.

The nature of the woodcut process is so evident in these two works because they have been conceived in terms of the properties of that process. But, as we can see in this woodcut by

99. ERICH HECKEL
Woman on the Shore (woodcut). 1914

100. CHRISTOFFEL JEGHER (after Rubens)
Hercules Fighting Envy and Deception
(woodcut). About 1635

Jegher (fig. 100), it is possible to create by this process a print that does not present any of these properties. Although Jegher cut away large areas of the block to produce the light background, this print obviously was not conceived in terms of contrasting areas. In this case, there is no direct link between the concept of the artist and the process itself, because the design being reproduced was not made specifically as a woodcut. Jegher is translating into a woodcut a figure created by Rubens in oil. The effect and quality of this print rests, then, in the sensitivity of Jegher as an interpreter of Rubens and most particularly in Jegher's skill as a carver. It is his ability in minute and elaborate carving that enables him to convey to us the dynamic power and movement with which Rubens imbued this figure of Hercules. The flowing line and luminous shadows Rubens created with oil had to be brought to life in the woodcut by a more laborious process. To capture the movement of the figure and the force of the action, Jegher had to carve a multitude of closely spaced small lines. The intricacy of the carving not only produced the light-and-dark patterning so critical for the effect of this work, but also gave the woodcut a textured quality reminiscent of the oil sketch. Thus, the effect of the woodcut by Jegher is not related to those expressive possibilities most inherent in this process, but derived from the way in which Jegher uses his superior control over the material to extend the natural limits of the process.

In the actual inking and printing phases of making a woodcut, other considerations emerge that also affect the appearance of the print. For example, the uniform tonality of the Heckel print is an effect of these phases of the process. As in the Picasso drawing (fig. 81), the contrast in the print between the whiteness of the paper and the darkness of the ink is the same throughout. Although there are areas more dark than white, the contrast between the two is always constant. The brilliance and power of these contrasts derives indirectly from the difficulty of varying the amount of ink to be transferred from the block to the paper. Heckel has made a positive and creative factor of the need for spreading the ink uniformly over the surface if the woodblock is to be printed successfully. A gradation of dark and light values within a woodcut cannot generally be achieved by inking one area more heavily than another, for, when the block is put under pressure to print, either the excess ink will smear or the ink will not be picked up from the more lightly inked ridges. Thus, gradation in a woodcut is the result of varying the number and size of the lines in different areas of the print. As we can see in an enlarged detail of the Hercules woodcut (fig. 101), the scale of values results from massing many small lines in certain areas. By these numerous small ridges, each bearing the same amount of ink, Jegher is able to concentrate the ink in certain areas and so produce the dark values in the print while still spreading the ink uniformly. Jegher could not leave large

101. Detail of
Hercules Fighting Envy and Deception

102. Edvard Munch. *The Kiss* (woodcut). 1902

areas of wood standing to produce dark areas because of the difficulty in controlling the pressure necessary to print both large areas and small lines. Thus, in each of these three woodcuts there exists a uniformity in the size of the ink-bearing parts of the woodblock. Each artist has had to take this quality of the process into account when conceiving his work.

But another artist may choose to turn this characteristic of the woodcut process from a limitation into an expressive possibility. For example, the woodcut by Munch (fig. 102) is very similar to the print by Schmidt-Rottluff in the way in which the figures are created by simple outline areas. The figures in *The Kiss* are contained within a single area of solid dark, broken only by the few light lines and areas needed to clarify the group. By his sensitive use of areas of light and dark, Munch conveys clearly the embrace of the two figures, but Munch's ability to set this couple into an atmosphere that seems to cast a spell over the lovers, as well as over us, is due to the particular use he has made of the woodcut's limitation. The impression of space and atmosphere in the print derives from the grayed values of the vertical-grain lines that run across the surface of the print. Munch creates this effect by the simple expedient of using two woodblocks to achieve the final print. The dark area of the two figures, as well as the light areas within it, was produced from one block. After this impression was made, another block with a very coarse grain was inked more lightly and then printed over the impression of the two figures obtained from the first block. Thus Munch takes advantage of the single contrasts in value in the woodcut in a very different way from Heckel or Schmidt-Rottluff. And it is through this combination of values that our impression of the print is derived. Seen apart from the grained setting, the figures would exist in a less magical world.

Engravings and etchings are produced by a process that is in many ways the opposite of the woodcut process. The ink, instead of being placed on the raised portions of the printing block, is, in these processes, placed into grooves cut or bitten into a metal plate. Whereas the woodcut came into existence when the ink adhering to the raised surface of the block was transferred, by slight pressure, onto the paper, the etching or engraving came into existence when the paper was forced by great pressure into the ink-filled hollows of the plate. Unlike the maker of the woodcut, who must cut away areas of his block to allow a line to be seen, the etcher or engraver may place the lines of his print directly on the plate. Thus, it is not surprising that line is as dominant a feature in an engraving or etching as it is in a drawing.

What distinguishes an etching from an engraving is the method by which parts of the metal plate are removed to make the troughs that will hold the ink. In the engraving, the artist cuts directly into the metal plate, using tools specifically invented for this purpose. One of the most commonly used instruments is the *burin*, a sharp, pointed tool of very hard metal. To make what will appear in the engraving as a line, the artist pushes this tool against the plate, removing a slender curl of the metal. No matter how soft the plate may be or how hard the tool, cutting into the plate is a difficult task. The resistance that the artist feels between the metal plate and the metal tool naturally affects the character of the individual line and the appearance of the entire print. The nature of the line produced through engraving can be seen in a print by Pierre Millan

103. PIERRE MILLAN (after Rosso Fiorentino). *Dance of the Dryads* (engraving). About 1550

of a design by Rosso (fig. 103). Our impression of the movements of these dancing figures is, to a large extent, derived from the nature of the technical process used to make the print. Just as the type of pen Romney chose for his sketch of a group of dancers is largely responsible for the sense of movement we attribute to these dancers, so too, the burin and metal plate of the engraving have a prominent role for our impression of the Rosso work. The swift-flowing, darting pen line of Romney (fig. 82) is replaced in the engraving by one that is even, precise and angular. We sense the resistance met by the engraving tool as it cut these lines into the metal plate.

The disciplined character of the engraved line is due not only to the resistance between tool and plate, but also to the requirement that the artist control precisely the amount of pressure that he exerts on the tool. In his skill at controlling pressure on the burin rests the artist's ability to create the light and dark areas of his work, for the deeper and the wider the trough the more ink it will hold. Thus, the darker the line it will print in comparison with a line from a trough that is only lightly gouged. Although this characteristic of the process offers the artist the possibility of using a wide variety of values in his print, the difficulty of exerting exactly the right amount of pressure on the tool adds to the effort of making a line and thus also affects its character.

In the engraving by Millan the light and dark areas are not due to deeper or wider lines, but, as in the woodcut by Jegher, are the result of the massing of many small lines. An idea can be gained of the intricacy of this method and of the amount of effort needed to achieve it by looking at an enlarged detail of the print by Millan. We can see that the shadows cast on the ground are made up of a number of lines that cross one another to make tiny diamond areas of white within the dark. The luminous effect of these shadows is distinguished from the light-reflecting surface of the dancers' robes through the use of a different kind of cross-hatching and a slight variation in the pressure placed on the tool. The very dark areas among the distant trees are the result of cutting the lines so closely together that the ink has blurred in the printing process. By such various means, a narrow scale of light and dark can be achieved in an engraving, thus providing another expressive possibility to the worker in this medium.

Evenness of tone, as well as clarity and precision of line, is a characteristic that the engraving process offers to the artist as a means of translating his idea into visual form. Although the engraver's work requires great care and effort, he is able to obtain effects not to be found through any other process. It is the quality of the engraved line, for example, that makes the Rosso dancers into impressive, statuesque figures engaged in a ritual more serious than playful. The impression of quick movements and flighty gestures created in the Romney sketch is replaced in the Rosso work by a study of each of the participants in this dance, as well as by a concern for the purpose of the dance. Through a detailed observation, which the precision of the engraved line has encouraged, each figure is carefully described in terms of movement, gesture, and emotion. The effect of each individual figure is so strong that our impression of this

104. Detail of *Dance of the Dryads*

work depends more upon the character of the individual members of this group than upon the movement that joins them. The fluttering drapery which, even in its angularity, is still the principal source of movement in this work, does not sweep these figures into a whirl of movement. The figures of the dryads impress us as powerful and evocative members of a mysterious sect.

In addition to its other qualities, the engraving process offers to the artist the possibility of creating a work that, simply by the clarity and precision of brilliant dark lines against white paper, is capable of arousing a great sensuous appreciation. Its appeal in this sense is markedly different from the equally sensuous appeal of the bolder but flatter woodcut. The raised lines of the engraving seem endowed with a particular power, perhaps because we sense the effort needed to create them. That the net of lines producing the engraved image has a strong decorative effect can be seen both in the Rosso print and in the very differently conceived engraving by Hayter (fig. 105). Here the decorative and expressive possibilities of the engraved lines both are exploited in such a way that the figure exists only in terms of the decorative pattern. In creating this image of a figure caught within the ornamental patterns of the engraved lines, Hayter combines both possibilities to give a succinct expression of death by water.

The print by James Ensor (fig. 106) immediately reveals to us the principal effect to be gained from the etching process. The rigid and precise line of the Hayter engraving is replaced in the etching by a fluid, active line, a line apparently made with great freedom of movement. The sense of resistance between the tool used by the artist and the metal plate is no longer present. Apparently, it was an effortless task for Ensor to fill his plate with innumerable figures of an inventiveness and immediacy we associate with a calligraphic line. It would appear that the process of making an etching resembles the use of pen or pencil in allowing the artist to transfer

105. STANLEY WILLIAM HAYTER. *Death by Water* (engraving). 1948

106. JAMES ENSOR. *Devils Battling the Angels and Archangels* (etching). 1888

the gesture of his hand to paper. The union between the print and the artist seems closer in this process because the physical effort of cutting into the metal to achieve a line is avoided.

Instead of removing the metal by sheer force, as the engraver does to make a line, the etcher employs an acid to act upon the metal plate. Using a very illustrative term, the etcher speaks of the "bite" made by the acid in the plate. To limit the bite to those areas that he wants removed, the etcher first covers his plate with a waxy substance called a ground. Then he draws the design on the wax, using a tool with a needle-like point that removes the wax wherever it touches, and thus exposes the metal underneath to eventual contact with the acid. The lines of the Ensor etching, which appear to have been made so freely and quickly, reflect the ease with which the artist could move his needle over the waxy surface. This method of working on the metal allowed Ensor to vary the direction and width of his line easily and so to describe for us a whirling, chaotic conflict of beasts whose forms are never the same. As we examine the character and actions of each figure in this mob, our impression constantly shifts from horror to humor—the same gamut of emotions that we might experience in a nightmare.

Ensor has kept our attention on the entire field of this demonic combat by avoiding the creation of a decorative light-and-dark pattern. The impression given by such a pattern could destroy the crucial formless and unorganized character of the print. But, as is obvious from the etching by Claude Lorrain (fig. 107), the contrast of light and dark is another quality inherent in the etching process. The method of achieving a scale of values in an etching is as effortless as the method of making a line, for the etcher can produce darker and lighter areas merely by varying the amount of time he allows the acid to work on particular lines or areas of the plate. He does so by exposing the plate to acid several times, being careful to protect from further contact with the acid those areas which he wishes to maintain at their present depth. Thus, the darkest areas in the Claude etching have been exposed to the acid more than once, whereas the single lines that stand out so clearly against the bright areas have been protected from further biting.

The brilliant areas which occur on either side of the figures—and which are so important for the movement of this group through the landscape—are made possible because of another characteristic of the etching process. For the contrast between light and dark areas also may be affected by the manner of inking the plate. Because the paper is forced into the grooves of the

107. CLAUDE LORRAIN. *The Flight into Egypt* (etching). 1630–33

108. J.-B. Camille Corot. *Sappho* (lithograph). 1872

plate by great pressure, it will pick up any trace of ink left on the smooth surface of the plate. By wiping the surface of the plate very clean in certain spots, highlights may be obtained in the print, for in those areas the whiteness of the paper will be strongest. Or, by leaving a slight film of ink over certain areas, grayed areas can be produced like those Claude has introduced in the sky. All these possibilities in creating light and dark areas are used by Claude, for whom the etching process has become the means of making a particular statement about a familiar Biblical subject. Through the contrast of dark and light areas, Claude creates a vista of an endless landscape under a vast sky, a scene through which the Holy Family travels. Although set within the most brilliantly lighted area of this scene, they nevertheless pass by almost unnoticed, as if a divine shadow had made them invisible. We, too, might not have noticed them had Claude not attracted our attention to them by setting off the arm and hand of the guiding angel against the most brilliant area of the etching.

Another process that offers the artist a great deal of flexibility in the use of line and of light and dark is lithography. In lithography the ink is transferred from the printing surface to the paper in a manner very different from that of the other three processes we have seen. For without being cut into, the special type of fine-grained stone or metal surface from which a lithograph is printed will retain the ink wherever the artist desires. The artist can simply draw his design upon the surface of the "stone," using a special kind of crayon, pencil, or ink that contains a certain amount of grease. Those areas of the stone touched by the crayon, more commonly used than the pencil or ink because of its natural grease-like feel, absorb the grease. Or the artist may use the even simpler method of drawing directly on a special greasy paper and then transferring the drawing to the stone. The stone is then chemically treated so that only the greasy areas will attract and hold the ink. In the actual inking process another step is taken that assures the separation of areas to be printed from areas to remain blank. The stone is kept moist with water, so that the non-greasy areas are made to repel the ink, and the greasy areas to attract it. The lithograph by Corot (fig. 108) was created through these simple means. The artist worked with a crayon on paper specially treated for transfer to the stone. The deep shadows and luminous areas of the landscape are reminiscent of the Claude etching, but here the values are muted and softened to make a gentler, more peaceful scene. The mood of reverie in which Corot envelops the figure of Sappho is quite different from the mood created by Claude. The impressions that the two artists wished to convey through their use of landscape were made possible not only by their ability to sense the visual quality of a scene but by their sensitivity to the inherent difference between the blunt-nosed, greasy lithographic crayon and the sharply pointed etching needle.

CHAPTER 11

The Flat Surface

109. HENRY H. RICHARDSON. Crane Library, Quincy, Massachusetts. 1880–83

THE MATERIAL OF WHICH A WORK OF ART IS MADE and the method of creating it have been seen to be important aspects of the creative process and to affect both what the artist chooses to express and how he expresses it. Regardless of whether these aspects manifest themselves as instinctive reactions or as conscious concerns of the artist, they are inevitably a part of what he is expressing, and so influence our experience of the work of art. Medium and technique are not the only factors, however, that determine the form given by the artist to a work of art. A less tangible, but no less influential, factor rests in what the artist sees as the inherent nature of the object he is creating.

The artist's concept of an object's inherent nature generally depends upon his understanding of its physical properties or of its purpose. Naturally, from either viewpoint, an object may possess many different potentialities; the artist's decision about which qualities to bring out affects the form of the work of art. Architects, for example, may conceive the inherent nature of a wall in different ways. To one, a wall's inherent nature may be defined primarily by the thickness or mass of the wall, and this concept is expressed by his treatment of the wall as a massive unit of contrasting solids and voids. Such a concept, for example, would seem to be expressed by Richardson in his design of the entrance wall of the Crane Library (fig. 109). Another architect may see a wall primarily as an unbroken plane, responding less to its thickness than to its surface property of flatness—a concept apparently embodied in the design by Sangallo for the entrance wall of the Gondi Palace (fig. 111). With respect to purpose, however, the two architects

110. HENRY H. RICHARDSON. Crane Library,
Quincy, Massachusetts. 1880–83

have both conceived the inherent nature of a wall in essentially the same way. Both Richardson and Sangallo have seen the wall primarily as a screen placed in front of the rest of the building. To another architect, the purpose of a wall may rest only in its role as one of the elements that give form to the entire structure he is creating—a concept that we may see expressed in the apartment buildings designed by Mies van der Rohe (fig. 112). All the different physical or functional qualities emphasized by these various architects can be included in any definition that we give to a wall as an object. In each case, the selection by the architect of one or more of these qualities as representative of the inherent nature of the wall affects the form of the building and our experience of it.

In making his choice, an artist may be guided or motivated by various factors. His concept of the object may be determined by his choice of material or technique, but these different aspects of the creative act are so interdependent that, from the object alone, we may not be able to distinguish the role that each part played in the creation of his work. In the buildings by Sangallo and Richardson, for example, although we can see how the type of stone used and the way in which it is laid both complement and help to define the architect's conception of the wall, we cannot say whether the material and technique gave rise to the conception or whether the conception governed their being chosen. In another instance, the artist may form his concept of the object he is creating on the basis of factors existing outside the object itself. He may see his work in a certain way because of a personal preference or belief rooted in an aesthetic creed or moral code.

111. GIULIANO DA SANGALLO
Gondi Palace, Florence. 1490

112. LUDWIG MIES VAN DER ROHE. Lake
Shore Drive Apartments, Chicago. 1949–51

With a work of art such as a painting, for example, the physical properties of the work are not necessarily those in which we seek its inherent nature. Yet its physical existence as a flat surface—a piece of canvas, paper, or wood—may be taken by one artist as the quality that he most desires to impart to his own work. For certain reasons, he sees this quality as one that must be preserved in his work. To him it is "wrong" to place upon this surface images that would destroy its integrity. To another artist such a concept of a painting may be of no importance. For him, the surface of a painting exists as a window through which the viewer is to see the world that he has created. For still another artist the physical surface of a painting does not derive from the material that it is painted upon, but comes into existence only through the actual texture of the paint he places upon the surface. All these concepts of the inherent nature of a painting result from different interpretations of its physical properties and purpose; and, in turn, these interpretations depend upon sets of attitudes acquired by the artist through experiences that need not be wholly visual. But whatever may be the source of the way in which an artist conceives an object, that he may exercise a choice is an aspect of the creative process of which we must be aware. For through this aspect we are introduced to still another way of seeing—a way that can make us see objects as being alike that, by definition, are different from each other.

The inherent nature that an artist sees as belonging to an object is the key to the similarity that we recognize in such diverse objects as a wall of a building, a page of a book, the inside surface of a bowl, a tapestry, a piece of furniture, a painting, a textile, an advertisement, a pottery jar. Although all these objects may be different with respect to size, material, technique, purpose, and form, all can be linked together visually if, when creating his work, each artist has been guided by the same basic concept. It is possible for each of the objects just enumerated, for example, to be conceived by its creator primarily as an object with a flat surface. In this sense it is unimportant whether that surface is of stone or paper or, indeed, whether it is actually flat, concave, or convex. And because all these objects were created principally in terms of surface, all the artists, whether painters, architects, or potters, worked in similar ways.

Any flat surface design presents to the artist considerations whose treatment inevitably leads him to follow an approach similar to that of other artists who have conceived their objects as flat surfaces. When seen as a flat surface, the design of a wall or of a book page involves each artist with identical principles. For example, because the architect of the Gondi Palace conceived its street façade as a flat surface, he necessarily relied primarily upon our reaction to the arrangement of the doors and windows on the surface of the wall for the visual effect of his building. In the same way, the book designer seeks to create an effect by the disposition of the printed text upon a page (fig. 113). The building and the page are both images whose form is a result of the artist's sensitivity to what happens when he divides this surface or when he introduces different shapes within the perimeter of the surface. The internal relationships of the shapes and areas and their relations to one another are concerns that naturally present themselves to both artists, for these are the principal means by which an artist creating a two-dimensional design can attain expressive power. No matter what the object he is designing may be, if he thinks of it primarily as a flat surface he cannot help being particularly conscious of the character of the shapes that he uses and of the pattern that results from their arrangement.

In the design of both the book page and the palace façade, each artist, by breaking up the major surface into smaller units, makes us see the whole in terms of the relationships of its parts. The thin lines on each of these pages, for example, divide the surface into vertical and horizontal areas of different sizes and shapes. Because of its size and tonal value, the larger and darker area that contains the text establishes a dominant relationship over the other areas, and they appear to frame it on the page. However, because the vertical lines do not extend to the upper edge of the page, an area is created here that does not enter into the same relationship as the others. The band at the top appears curiously empty and the text seems to push toward the bottom of the page. A visual image is created that tends to obliterate our sense of the original surface of the page.

LIVRE III.	LES AMOURS PASTORALES
Ce qu'il dit à Chloé	controuva qu'il avoit arraché des serres mêmes de l'aigle l'oison de Lycenion; puis, l'embrassant, la baisa comme Lycenion l'avoit baisé durant le déduit, car cela seul lui pouvoit-il, à son avis, faire sans danger; et Chloé lui mit sur la tête le chapelet qu'elle avoit fait, et en même temps lui baisoit les cheveux, comme sentant à son gré meilleur que les violettes, puis lui donna de sa panetière à repaître du raisin sec et quelques pains, et souventefois lui prenoit de la bouche un morceau, et le mangeoit elle, comme petits oiseaux prennent la becquée du bec de leur mère.
La chanson des mariniers	Ainsi qu'ils mangeoient ensemble, ayant moins de souci de manger que de s'entrebaiser, une barque de pêcheurs parut, qui voguoit au long de la côte. Il ne faisoit vent quelconque, et étoit la mer fort calme, au moyen de quoi ils alloient à rames; et ramoient à la plus grande diligence qu'ils pouvoient, pour porter en quelque riche maison de la ville leur poisson tout frais pêché; et ce que tous mariniers ont accoutumé de faire pour alléger leur travail, ceux-ci le faisoient alors; c'est que l'un d'eux chantoit une chanson marine, dont la cadence régloit le mouvement des rames, et les autres, de même qu'en un chœur de musique, unissoient par intervalles

104

DE DAPHNIS ET DE CHLOE	LIVRE III.
garderoient à leur propre fils. Car non-guères auparavant leur étoit né un petit garçon. Et Dryas lui-même quelquefois se laissoit aller à ces raisons; aussi que chacun lui faisoit des offres bien au-delà de ce que méritoit une simple bergère; mais considérant puis après que la fille n'étoit pas née pour s'allier en paysannerie, et que s'il arrivoit qu'un jour elle retrouvât sa famille, elle les feroit tous heureux, il différoit toujours d'en rendre certaine réponse, et les remettoit d'une saison à l'autre, dont lui venoit à lui cependant tout plein de présents qu'on lui faisoit.	invente des prétextes pour différer sa réponse
CE que Chloé entendant en étoit fort déplaisante, et toutefois fut long-temps sans vouloir dire à Daphnis la cause de son ennui. Mais voyant qu'il l'en pressoit et importunoit souvent, et s'ennuyoit plus de n'en rien savoir qu'il n'auroit pu faire après l'avoir su, elle lui conta tout: combien ils étoient de poursuivants qui la demandoient, combien riches! les paroles que disoit Napé à celle fin de la faire accorder, et comment Dryas n'y avoit point contredit, mais remettoit le tout aux prochaines vendanges. Daphnis oyant telles nouvelles, à peine qu'il ne perdît sens et entendement, et se séant à terre, se prit à pleurer, disant qu'il mourroit si Chloé	Chloé, ennuyée, dit tout à son amant,

109

113. ASHENDENE PRESS. Pages from *Les Amours Pastorales de Daphnis et Chloé*
Published in London, 1931

This effect disappears, however, when we look at the design in its entirety, for the page has been conceived not singly and independently, but in conjunction with the opposite page. Seen as a unit repeated on either side of the center of the book, the single page design becomes a part of a larger image. In this new context, the minor differences between the enframing elements now become more apparent, and the variety of their spacing and the contrast in values and shapes produce a rhythmic balance. This balance is not derived, however, simply from the repetition of identical units on either side of a central line, for the unbroken areas of white at the top of each page join to become a single unit within the over-all design. This unit brings together the other areas of the individual pages into a single visual image and, as a continuous white band stretching across the top of these and all succeeding pages, it carries the design from one set of pages to the next. Thus, it both binds the entire book into a uniform design and connotes the progression of the text.

Unlike our response to the book design, the feeling of balance and rhythm imparted by the palace façade (fig. 114) is achieved not by a division of its major surface area into smaller units but by the relationships that Sangallo establishes among the shapes that he places upon the surface. Although we are clearly aware of the three horizontal areas that divide the rectangular surface of the façade, our impression is stimulated more strongly by the arrangement of the

114. GIULIANO DA SANGALLO. Gondi Palace, Florence. 1490

doors and windows. Sangallo initiates our sensitivity to the arrangement of these elements by giving an identical shape to almost all of the windows and doors. By stressing their similarity of shape, he makes us less aware of the elements as individual units than of the way in which they are distributed over the surface.

Sangallo has arranged these shapes so that regardless of size, they are located at equal horizontal distances from one another (that is, if their distances are measured from a vertical dividing line represented here by the center line of the closed shutters). Thus, the distance between the centers of any two adjacent windows on the second or third floor is the same as the distance between the center of one of the doorways and the center of one of the rectangular windows. In addition, all these elements are arranged vertically so that their central dividing lines coincide. By these means, Sangallo makes us see the individual unit in terms of its contribution to the over-all design, and so creates for us a sharp sense of a precise pattern. Although this pattern is basically very simple, its effect is not the same as we might experience from any pattern established by the even spacing and regular alignment of similarly shaped units. The glimpse of a field dotted by the bales of hay left in the wake of a baling machine may produce a roughly similar effect, but it does not give us the sense of harmony that is our principal impression of this architectural design.

That we receive a sense of harmony from this design arises from the way in which the pattern of the shapes is related to the surface on which it is placed. Thus, we are aware not only of the relationship of the doors and windows with one another, but of their relations both to the surface areas surrounding them and to the entire rectangular surface of the façade. Shapes and surface both seem locked in a single, indivisible design of which the alteration of any one part would seem to invoke the destruction of the whole. The façade has this effect because Sangallo has linked all its parts together in a very specific way. The size of every door and window, as well as its location on the surface, has been determined in relation to a single unit of a certain size. Thus, all the parts of the façade design can be located and described in terms of the unit, or *module*, that Sangallo has chosen—the width of the small rectangular window. The width of the central doorway equals two such units; its height equals three. One unit defines the distance between this doorway and the closest side of the rectangular window, and one unit also equals the inside width of the windows on the second and third stories. The width of the cross-shaped stones between these windows is exactly one-half module. This modular unit, then, governs the entire design—a condition that could be expressed graphically by placing over the façade a grid made up of modular rectangles. The possibility of expressing the design of this façade by such a grid is, in part, responsible for the harmony that we sense in the design and for its appearing incapable of being altered. The use of a modular unit also accounts for the difference between the even spacing and alignments of the palace façade and those that occur in nature. In the case of the hay field, for example, although the space between bales and between rows may be constant, this distance is not necessarily related to the size of the bale.

The artist may make any one of the elements in his design into a module. He may determine his module by the nature of the material he works with, as a furniture designer does who takes as his module the piece of most readily available veneer, or an architect who utilizes a standard concrete block as a module. When the artist does use a module he creates, by necessity, a design in which proportional relationships play an important role. For, in using a consistent unit for determining height and width, he naturally becomes conscious of the way in which the relationship may be expressed arithmetically. For example, if a doorway is thought of as being one unit wide and three units high, the proportional relationship of 1 to 3 is more readily apparent than if the same doorway were described as being 2 feet 4 inches wide and 7 feet high. As the artist becomes aware of this means of expressing relationships between parts, he may consciously seek to achieve them—the possibility of creating such simply expressed arithmetical proportions

115. GIULIANO DA SANGALLO
Gondi Palace, Florence. 1490

becoming a controlling factor in his work. The instinctive feeling that he has for the relation-ships among the different parts of a flat surface design is transformed into the use of a method to achieve specific relationships.

The proportional relationships that an artist seeks to create in his work may be suggested by any number of factors, but the most attractive avenue for the artist often has led toward the theoretical world of "perfect" forms and "perfect" numbers. In this realm of philosophical and mathematical thought—to which men for centuries have attached so much meaning—are rooted various beliefs about "correct" systems of proportions. Architects particularly have laid stress on such beliefs as guides for their work. Francesco di Giorgio, like many other archi-tects of his time, used as a basis for his work a system of proportions derived from the human body (fig. 116). He did so because, for him, the human body, in being "God's handiwork," necessarily possessed divine proportions and, furthermore, reflected in miniature the order governing the entire universe. By following this example of a system of proportions, Fran-cesco believed his work could be perfect and, thus, as beautiful as the divine models. In his drawing Francesco illustrates this belief by showing us in the ground plan of a church how the proportions of the human body may be used to govern the width and length of the church, as well as all other relative dimensions and, also, to determine how the various areas within the church should be arranged. Other artists have developed proportional schemes using theories whose origins are less intellectual or more personal, but the very concept of a proportional system invites the artist to think in terms of some type of system.

We do not know what guided Sangallo in his selection of a proportional scheme, but such a scheme plays a governing role in determining our reaction to this palace façade. Our impression could not be produced solely by Sangallo's use of a module, for it is not the module that makes this particular pattern of doors and windows an organic part of this one façade. The module becomes an instrument of harmony only because of the system of proportion that Sangallo has adopted, for this system is what controls the actual number of modules used for the height or width of any one design element. His way of using these proportions is what makes this design more than a simple pattern that can be made on graph paper. Not only are the proportions that Sangallo chose for all the doors and windows related to the proportions of the entire surface, but each element has been given identical proportions. Height and width, in the major surface, are in the ratio of 2 to 3; in doorways and windows they are in the ratio of 3 to 2. Thus, in the major rectangle of the façade and the rectangular openings within it, the ratio of height to width is reversed, but the numerical values of this ratio are maintained. Since the arched shape of the entire doorway and window frame is also contained within a rectangle of these same proportions, the relationship between them and the façade's surface can be represented symbolically by two overlapping rectangles, a device that the architect introduces in the masonry pattern on the second floor. Thus all parts of this design are echoes of the largest form. By variation on a single theme—a single module and a single set of proportions—the harmony and seeming perfection of this design are created.

116. FRANCESCO DI GIORGIO. Proportion drawing from the *Codex Magliabechiano*. About 1480

Although the Ashendene Press book design and the Sangallo palace façade are different from each other in that the architectural design involves the introduction of shapes in addition to divisions of the surface, both designs are basically similar in that their individual parts are closely linked to the over-all shape of the surface itself. From the variations made on this relationship, our impressions of balance and harmony arise, a response whose nature is directly connected to the degree in which the artist varies this relationship. The sense of balance and harmony we receive from the design of the Café de Unie by Oud (fig. 117), for example, is quite a different emotion from that produced by the Sangallo design. Since the individual parts of its design are not so deliberately or consciously related to the over-all shape, we see them more as objects held in balance than as objects resting in balance. The total design provokes in us a sense of tension—a feeling similarly created by the two pages from a children's book (fig. 118) designed by Schwitters and Steinitz.

In this design, the separate parts do not appear to divide the page, but rather to bring it into being, as if it had not existed as a physical object prior to its being printed. Thus, the page appears less a carrier of the text and illustrations than an element that fits in between the shapes. We may even see these dark shapes as islands protruding from a flat body of water. But, despite the importance and independence of their various elements, the two pages are created to be parts of a unified design. By the character of the different shapes, as well as by the symbolic function of the arrows, there are created apparent paths of movement across the surface that bind the separate parts into a discernible constellation. And, although very different in appearance from

117. J. P. OUD. Café de Unie, Rotterdam. 1925

da kitzelte eines verkehrt, es wußte selbst nicht, wie und wo und warum, und wir wissen es auch nicht, warum es verkehrt war. Und plötzlich wurde er grasgrün, schrie furchtbar auf, sprang ein bißchen in die Luft und legte dabei ein schwarzes Ei. Und nun kitzelte jedes Kind einmal an der verkehrten Stelle. Und jedesmal legte der Hahnepeter ein schwarzes Ei. Und da es 13 Kinder waren, so legte er 13 Eier. Und dabei bemerkten es die Kinder, daß er hinten eine richtige Schraube hatte und einen richtigen

PROPELLER.

WENN WO NE
SCHRAUBE IST
MUSS MAN AUCH
DRAN DREHEN.

SO

drehte Hahnemann an der Schraube 3 MAL rum, nachdem er die Mutter gefragt hatte, wie rum man drehen müßte. Die Mutter aber sagte, man müßte rechtsrum drehen. Und als Hahnemann dreimal rumdrehte, tanzte der Hahnepeter wie

118. Kurt Schwitters and Kate T. Steinitz
Pages from *Die Märchen vom Paradies*. 1923

the other book design and from the palace façade, this design is also created in terms of the the over-all shape of the total surface. The various horizontal lines and the blocking of the type hint at the basic rectangular shape of the surface on which the smaller shapes are arranged, but this characteristic is made apparent principally by the balance of the two units of text. Of these two areas of type matter, the smaller one, on page 7, is made to appear heavier than its larger counterpart on page 6. Its presence in the lower section of the design automatically assures it a certain weight, further stressed by the darkness of both the bottom horizontal line and the solid rectangle along its side. By being extended to the absolute edge of the page, this rectangle gains in power and firmly anchors down this area of text. On the other page, the dark area formed by the large type of the word PROPELLER performs a similar function, but since it occurs beneath the area of text, it has the effect of making this area seem lighter in weight, almost floating. From this balance of opposing forces comes the impression of tension that we receive from this design. At the same time, it is also this balance that preserves a sense of the over-all shape of the surface, a quality that must be present if the functional demands of a book are to be satisfied.

119. MIMBRES INDIAN. Designs from the inside surface of pottery bowls found in the Swarts Ruin, New Mexico (after Cosgrove). About 800–1300

In all the examples we have seen, functional requirements have determined, to a greater or lesser degree, how the artist conceived his design. The architect had to work in terms of doors and windows, the book designer with words, sentences, paragraphs, and illustrations. Furthermore, these were only the individual parts of an over-all design necessarily conceived within the context of a page or a wall. But these functional demands, no matter how influential, do not alone account for the fact that of the designs we have seen, all have been conceived in relation to the over-all shape of the object. For, regardless of an object's function, an artist, when creating a design on a flat surface, may intuitively respond to the shape of that surface.

How the artist may be inspired by the kind of shape on which he is creating his design can be seen in a group of designs painted on the inside surface of pottery bowls by the Mimbres Indians (fig. 119). The series presented here is arranged to suggest a possible relationship between the various designs in terms of the different responses to the nature of a circular surface. The first design was created by simply dividing the circular surface into four equal parts and then applying an alternating pattern of horizontal and vertical lines to these wedge-shaped areas, which were thereby related diagonally across the surface, one area being the mirror image of the other. In the next design of our group, the same underlying concept prevails, but, because here the pairs of wedge-shaped units are differentiated from one another, both in size and in decorative pattern, they appear more like shapes than like surface divisions. As such, they seem to penetrate the circular surface from the outside rim—a direction emphasized by their points and by the location on the circumference of the darkest spots of the entire design. Yet, as we can see in the next design, only a slight change in the arrangement of these same areas can make us shift our attention to the area enframed by these wedge-shaped units. The adjacent design is an elaboration of the arrangement in which the central area appears to dominate. Here, the individual wedge shapes seem to have been designed in relation to the shape considered desirable for the central area. As this shift of emphasis takes place, the dark spots, which formerly tied the design to the circumference of the circle, disappear in favor of a dark outline around the central area.

As a possible next step in this sequence, we may select a design close to the preceding one with respect to the enframed central area but representing, because of a new feature, a significant change in the way in which the design was conceived. For, in this instance, the artist introduces a decorative motif at the center of the design, an act that has the effect not only of dividing the central area into two opposed areas but of suggesting that the design emanates from the center point. Although here only suggested by the curved lines that begin to encompass the angular shapes of the original wedges, in another design the central point of the circle has become the point that ties both shapes and areas together. The two animal forms placed within the white areas are mirror images of each other on either side of this point and, in a sense, seem to move about it. In three other bowls, we can also find designs that take a central point as their focal element. The central field is gradually expanded until, in the last example, the two figures exist alone in an area defined only by two circular lines; the controlling force of a central point is clearly indicated by the consistent use of mirror images. From this group of pottery designs we can see how the circular form

120. ROMANESQUE. *Dog, Acrobat, Siren*
Sainte-Madeleine, Vézelay, France. 12th century

of the bowl surface suggested to the artist the divisions of the surface and the character and arrangement of the shapes. In every case, the design grew out of an intuitive response to the circular surface—a response so varied that no repetitions occur among the more than seven hundred Mimbres designs known to us.

That the way in which an artist responds to a surface's over-all shape affects our experience of works of art can be seen if we contrast another of the Mimbres pottery designs (fig. 121) with a series of *roundels* made by a medieval sculptor (fig. 120). Compared with the Indian figures, whose body shapes are derived from the circular surface, the body shapes of the figures in this medieval design are not inspired by the circular shape of the medallion. The medieval figures retain their "normal" shapes, their bodies being affected only with respect to the positions in which the artist had arranged them in order to fit them within the circular format. Thus, although the acrobat on the French cathedral resembles the tumbling figure on the Indian bowl, the acrobat is a man fitted into a circle, not born of one.

Because of the way in which each artist saw his design in terms of the circular surface, we receive from their works correspondingly different impressions. The medieval sculpture impresses us because of the ingenuity it displays; we are fascinated and delighted by the artist's idea. Thus, our experience of the work, like the creative act that produced it, comes from a more conscious reaction to visual forms than occurs in our experience of the Indian design. Because of its relation to the circular surface, the Indian design appears to us to be inseparable from the surface. The design impresses us immediately as such a perfect, and perhaps inevitable, configuration that we feel the designer's sensitivity to the circular surface to be instinctive.

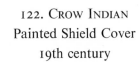

122. CROW INDIAN
Painted Shield Cover
19th century

121. MIMBRES INDIAN
Design from inside surface of pottery bowl
found in the Swarts Ruin, New Mexico
(after Cosgrove). About 800–1300

How subtly a design may be related to the total shape of its surface can be seen in the design of a Crow Indian shield (fig. 122). Again, a central point is the controlling force within this design, but no part mirrors another nor does any part correspond exactly to any basic division of a circle, although such divisions are suggested. The two wedge-shaped units of horizontal lines occupy almost exactly half the circle, but we are not so strongly aware of this aspect of the design as we are of the vertical line made by the edges of these areas across the surface—a line echoed by the boundary line of the area to the left. Of these three principal areas of the circle, none appears to us as a surface division, despite the fact that each is filled by a pattern of horizontal lines. The two wedge-shaped units appear to move toward each other, compressing the space between them as they do so—a movement induced by the dark vertical lines that point like radii toward the center of the circle. The center point of the circle is emphasized by the dark, rounded part of the bear, but the entire figure extends beyond this point, continuing a

123. CROW INDIAN. Painted Shield Cover. 19th century

movement to the left originated initially by the radius made by the bear tracks. The irregular shape of the area to the left, like the wavy lines within it, induces a movement toward the right-hand side.

In the various movements set up by the relationship of the parts with the entire surface lies the meaning of this design. For the apparent coming together of the two areas on the right is a movement that has forced the bear to move toward the center—his tracks clearly show us the path he has taken. The heavy radii serve to pinpoint the bear, to force him further toward the left-hand side of the shield, where he is met by the opposed movement generated by the wavy lines. This area becomes a force moving toward the bear, and, since the wavy lines represent bullets, the bear will be killed and the hunter protected. By virtue of the shield's design, success will be assured to the hunter who carries it. Thus, the shield is a subtle blend of the desired image and the inherent nature of a flat, circular surface.

CHAPTER 12

Shapes

124. SANTO DOMINGO INDIAN
Jar, from New Mexico
19th or early 20th century

HOW THE ARTIST CONCEIVES an object's inherent nature determines, to a large extent, the way in which he works. If, as we have seen, he chooses to see an object primarily as a flat surface, this decision has consequences that necessarily affect his work. When the surface is divided into smaller areas or different kinds of shapes are placed upon this surface, effects are produced with which he cannot help being involved.

The works that we have just seen have all reflected different ways in which an artist may respond to just one aspect of a flat surface design—the relation of its parts to its over-all shape. His concern was seen to take the form either of a conscious application of a system of proportions or simply of an intuitive response to the total surface. But, regardless of difference in approach or in the kind of object being created, the appearance of a work was, in great measure,

125. MESOPOTAMIAN. Goblet, from Susa
About 4000 B.C.

the result of the artist's concern with this one aspect. Thus, the Indian jar (fig. 124) and the palace façade are alike, and our experience of both is basically the same. By the division of the surface and the treatment of the decorative motifs, the Indian artist has intuitively created a surface design that echoes the jar's over-all shape in the same way that the different parts of the palace façade echo a total shape. Because both artists have worked in the same way, we are in both instances more conscious of the harmonious arrangement of the parts than we are of either the total outline shape or of any one decorative motif.

The different impression that we receive from the Mesopotamian vase (fig. 125) is directly related to the different conception its artist had of the object's inherent nature. The primary aspect of a flat surface design to which this artist responded was not the relationship of individual parts and the total form. For, although the surface divisions of the vase correspond to the nature of the entire object—the vertical panels stressing the rise of the body and the horizontal bands emphasizing the base and the rim—the ornamental motifs do not. The different shapes of the decorative elements placed within and between the panels are not derived from the total shape of the object. In creating these motifs, the artist has been concerned only with

SHAPES [173]

the individual character of their shapes; he has not created them with reference to a specific context. In this way, these motifs are quite unlike those found on the Indian jar, where the motifs are organic parts of the entire object and their shapes not independently conceived. Consequently, we do not find these particular shapes used on other kinds of Santo Domingo jars, whereas the shapes of the Mesopotamian piece are found repeated on many different kinds of vases and even on other kinds of objects. These shapes, because they are independent of the nature of the object on which we see them, exist apart from it—they have a life of their own.

The more our attention is drawn to the character of individual shapes, the less conscious we are of the work of art as a harmonious arrangement of parts. For the artist's concern for the surface as a pronounced part of his design decreases as he becomes more sensitive to the nature of the shapes that he places upon it. Progressively, the surface becomes considered only as a background serving to enhance the perception of the shape. One glance at the Zuni pottery drum (fig. 126) tells us that, for this artist, the surface existed only as a flat area to set off the shape that he has given to the deer. The artist, by isolating the figure on this otherwise undefined surface, calls our attention to it as a shape. The difference that this work implies about the artist's approach to the flat surface is made particularly obvious if we look at a Mimbres bowl (fig. 127) whose decoration also consists of only a single figure. In the context of the other

126. ZUNI INDIAN. Drum Jar, from New Mexico. 19th century

127. MIMBRES INDIAN
Design from inside surface of pottery bowl
found in the Swarts Ruin, New Mexico
(after Cosgrove). About 800–1300

128. EGYPTIAN
Inscription on the back of Queen
Hetep-Heres Carrying Chair
Dynasty IV, 2680–2565 B.C.

Mimbres designs that we have seen, this example stands out as one whose design obviously was determined according to a different concept of the flat surface. Neither the Zuni nor the Mimbres Indian work was conceived in relation to the surface's total form. The shape of neither figure echoes the larger form on which it is found; either shape could be placed on any flat surface.

Because of their contrast with the surrounding surface, the edges are the principal means by which we perceive the character of a shape. Therefore, when the artist works on a flat surface mainly in terms of shape, he becomes increasingly sensitive to the nature of these edges. As we may see in the two Indian designs and especially in the design of the Egyptian hieroglyphics (fig. 128), his concern over the edges of the shapes that he is creating often leads the artist to change the shape formed by the "natural" outline of a figure into a somewhat different and simpler shape; he offers our eye a more readily discernible shape, one whose character we sense clearly and immediately.

In this transformation, the shape becomes progressively independent of the natural object in somewhat the same way that a shadow exists as a thing apart from its subject. Its character

129. SCHOOL OF PISA. *Pietà* and *Deposition*,
details of a Crucifix. 13th century

depends not solely on the subject but, also, on the type of light that produces it and the kind of
surface on which it falls. Similarly, the artist, through concern for the edges of forms, converts
his figures into shapes which have an existence of their own and which may, in this process, even
gain a meaning of their own.

The artist, if he works in this way, tends to see and to express objects chiefly in terms of basic
shapes implicit in their structures. For example, the painter of the scenes from a crucifix (fig. 129)
has seen the three flying angels not as individual figures in the sky, but as a group forming
a single shape against the gold background. Although the number of figures remains discernible, the artist has merged the bodies, binding them together by a continuous line. This
line, in its movement about the figures, produces a single form that is so clear and strong that
we tend to see the angels as components of it rather than to see the form as a collection of
angels. The shape becomes a symbol of the angels' presence, not a description of them. In a
similar fashion, the artist has reduced the very complicated structure of a building with several
domes to a shape whose outline is easily comprehended, but which—in any naturalistic sense—
hopelessly merges the different parts of the structure. By its transformation into this shape, the
particular building the artist is representing—a temple—is made to exist for us not as an object, but as a symbol. As such, the shape acquires a greater meaning. It becomes "The Temple."

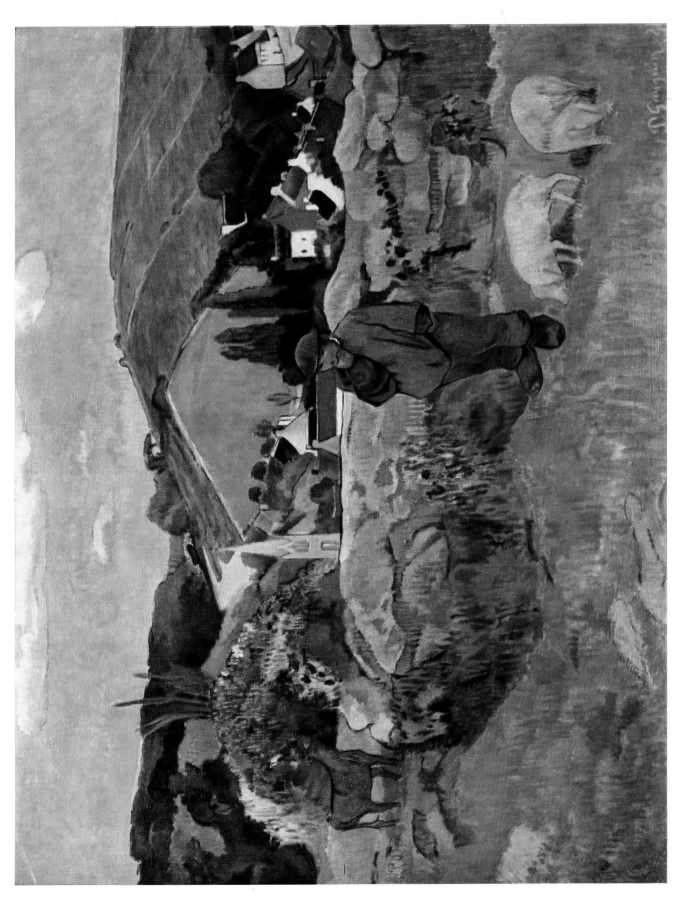

PAUL GAUGUIN. *The Swineherd.* 1888

BYZANTINE MOSAIC. *Emperor Justinian and Attendants* (detail). About 547 A.D.

PABLO PICASSO. *Three Musicians.* 1921

The artist has given a new meaning to these scenes by merging several figures or the different parts of a complicated building into a single shape. An opposite way of conceiving a form in terms of shape underlies the creation of the inlaid-enamel crucifix (page 180). For here the artist has brought the image into being by breaking up a single figure into individual shapes—shapes that, by virtue of their character and arrangement, create a form more meaningful than that of the figure itself. Unlike the artist of the previous paintings, this artist has not been conscious, while depicting the human figure on a flat surface, of its possible existence as a continuous outline shape—as we may see if we try to imagine only an outline drawing of this figure. As outline drawing, the figure not only loses its meaning as a form capable of evoking certain feelings, but also any meaning it may have as a description of an actual human body. For this figure exists as a human body only with respect to the character of the different shapes of which it is composed. Thus, we see the arm not because its outline is armlike, but because the different shapes within it correspond to our concept of the muscular structure of an arm. Our feeling for the character of these arms is evoked, not because the shapes describe in any accurate sense how the arm muscles are affected when placed in a certain position, but because their arrangement in a formal pattern makes us feel the lifeless quality of the arms.

Just as the meaning of the entire figure is independent of its continuous outline shape, so, too, the significant meaning of the shapes is independent of their existence as anatomical references. The statement that this artist makes to us about this figure comes through the nature of each shape and its relation to the other shapes. Because of the arrangement of the shapes of the chest, abdomen, and rib cage, for example, we sense acutely that this is a body suspended only at certain points. The pattern created by the shapes of the ribs emphasizes for us the relationship between the pear-shaped abdomen and the broad, stable shape of the chest. We are made particularly aware of the point at which these two shapes come together as the swirling form of the lower shape rises to a rounded lobe that fits within the curving indentation of the upper shape. Once we sense the quality of this relationship, we also see the lower shape as the heavier of the two. Through their relationship these two formal shapes forcefully express the suspension of the heavy body from the Cross. And, because this feeling is evoked by the character of the shapes and their arrangement, not by a description of a body in such a position, the form becomes a symbolic form just as the body of Christ was not simply a human body but a symbol.

The more an artist works in this manner, the more sensitive he becomes to the nature of shapes and to the effects produced by possible arrangements of them. He grows increasingly aware of the appearance of a shape as an isolated formal element, and of the influence that one

OPPOSITE PAGE

FRENCH ENAMELS
Cross, Chasse, and Reliquary
12th–13th centuries

SHAPES [181]

130. JEAN (HANS) ARP
Skeleton and Mustache (tapestry)
1958

shape may appear to exert upon another. We, too, respond to shapes in this way. For example, the tapestry design by Arp (fig. 130) appears to us to be made up of more than simply two individual shapes placed next to each other. Although these shapes do not in themselves imply movement, nor their arrangement suggest motion, they give us a sensation of their being drawn toward each other. We see them in this way because they are basically similar—both are shapes that spread out from the center—and because the top lobe of the lower shape appears capable of fitting into the rounded indentation of the upper shape. By these aspects of the shapes, as well as by their contrast with the surface, we are made to feel the force of their mutual attraction. Which shape exercises what attraction we cannot tell—each shape appears somehow to have determined the shape of the other. There is created for us, then, a total image whose meaning may be very different from the meaning of each individual shape—shapes to which Arp has given the names of "skeleton" and "mustache." Although the substitution of a word image for the shape image may hint to us of the derivation of the shapes, it does not elucidate the meaning of the total image. The combination of words is as curious and as provocative as that of the shapes, but the visual shapes are the more powerfully united, held together by the relationship we clearly see to exist between them.

Arrangements of isolated shapes, such as those of the Arp tapestry, appear to have meanings regardless of whether or not we can define such meanings precisely. Our everyday experience in a world of signs and symbols leads us to see such shapes as meaningful. We may even endow them with a significance that they do not necessarily possess, or with a meaning that the artist did not necessarily intend, for an artist may create such shapes spontaneously, without reference to a predetermined idea. But for us, such shapes still may have great visual impact and possess the power to evoke associations. Indeed, the very fact that such shapes may have emerged from his hand only in an unconscious gesture may make them seem to us even more mysteriously meaningful. This manner of seeing shapes governs our response to the group of painted pebbles dating from the prehistoric period of man (fig. 131). Their purpose unknown to us, we nevertheless are more apt to see them as symbols than as ornaments. These shapes are not decorative ones for us, but ones in which we sense meaning. This is a peculiarly visual experience—one that necessarily remains intensely personal, but one to which both we and artists are particularly sensitive.

When we see meaning in shapes like those painted on the pebbles, we do not do so because of any association we make between them and the shapes of natural objects. Their impact is a more purely visual phenomenon, the associations we make coming from our total visual experience. Our response does not originate in the recall of a particular visual experience with the shape of another object, but in the more comprehensive and personal vocabulary of shapes that we have created through an unconscious transformation of such individual experiences. Thus, our responses to shapes often seem to be instinctive; our sensitivity, to be intuitive.

When we are led to respond to a work in this manner what, if anything, it may represent is

131. PALEOLITHIC. Painted Pebbles,
from Mas d'Azil, France. About 12,000 B.C.

not a primary aspect of our experience. For example, because one part of the gold ceremonial knife from Colombia (fig. 132) is made to look like a face, we naturally can see all the other parts of it in terms of a human figure. This relationship is one the artist obviously intended us to perceive. But our impression of this piece does not rest chiefly in our being able to identify, for example, the crescent shape beneath the "head" as a pair of outstretched arms. The "arms" exist for us initially and primarily as a curved shape that echoes the shape of the blade, as well as a shape whose upward swing is the reverse of the downward curve of the "head." We are conscious of the interrelations of these shapes, not only because each contains a quality found in the other, but because the natural shape of each is sharply defined by its contrast with the open grillwork. Once we begin to sense these relationships, we are led to relate shapes that neither echo nor oppose one another, but simply recall the general character of one another's shape. The blade and the "head" are seen by us to relate to each other in this fashion, for the parts that make up the shape of the blade—a vertical unit from which a large arched shape is pulled out on either side to form narrow extensions that curve back toward the principal shape—these parts are similar to those of which the "head" shape is composed. Although these elements are put together differently in each case, we still sense an underlying similarity.

Because of these relations of shapes, this object exists for us as a work of art. The meaning of the form also rests solely in the arrangement of shapes that the artist has brought into being. The fact that it may also represent a human figure is an aspect of this object that follows, rather than precedes, our visual impression of it. And this is the context in which we must understand the "face" of the object: it is a comment by the artist on the arrangement of shapes that he has created, not an indication of an image that he wished the shapes to resemble. The "face" is a visual equivalent of the words "skeleton" and "mustache" that Arp assigned to the shapes on the tapestry. By these means, both artists have given us a glimpse into their own vocabulary of shapes; but, whether we see the object in the same way or in a more personal frame of reference, its meaning can be derived only from the shapes.

The meaning of the Colombian work exists on several different levels. It is, first of all, an object that was to be used in a ceremony as a symbol of a knife. Its total form and individual shapes are, therefore, originally derived from those that the artist saw to be implicit in a knife. As a work of art, however, it owes its existence to the sensitivity of the artist to the nature of these shapes and to the possible relationships between them as they were combined to create the form. In the course of this process there emerged for the artist another meaning, other than the symbolic one of the knife. The shapes took on for him the aspect of a human figure. Thus this work is simultaneously both a symbol of a knife and a symbol of a man, but its primary meaning rests in the shapes, for it is they that create the meaning of either symbol.

Shapes like those which make up the gold knife appear to us to have an existence apart from any particular use of them. We are apt to see them in this way because the more they become independent of a direct relation to natural objects, the more they become almost tangible objects in their own right. They constitute a set of basic shapes from which it is possible to form many

132. CHIBCHA INDIAN. Ceremonial Knife, from Colombia. Before 1500 A.D.

133. W. A. DWIGGINS. Specimen page of stencil shapes. About 1927

134. W. A. DWIGGINS
Ornamental design made up of
stenciled shapes shown in fig. 133
About 1927

quite different designs simply by putting them together in different ways. The specific appearance and possible meaning of a shape becomes dependent upon the context in which we find it. In this respect, shapes such as those created by Dwiggins (fig. 133) as component parts of stencil designs are not unlike letters of the alphabet.

The shapes that Dwiggins has created can be combined in many different ways, and the same shape can play different roles even within the same design. They are truly independent shapes that provide the artist with another formal, visual element and a rich source of expressive power. But, at the same time, the nature of the form that he can create with them necessarily depends upon the type of shape that he selects. For, like the letters of the alphabet, each shape, no matter how basic, possesses an individual quality that finally limits the possible range of effects that the artist can achieve through its use. For example, although the exact sound represented by "C" or "O" may vary according to the position of the letter in a word, or according to the way in which it is combined with other letters, the "C" or the "O" always represents a general type of sound. Ultimately, our language is limited by the 26 characters that we have

135. W. A. DWIGGINS
Ornamental design made up of
stenciled shapes shown in fig. 133
About 1927

136. JULIUS KLINKHARDT. Specimen page
of typographic ornament. About 1900

chosen to represent our speech. Similarly, the component shapes chosen by Dwiggins possess, by virtue of their selection, a circumscribed range of possible effect and meaning. A visual alphabet of shapes is far more extensive, however, than one of letters, as we can see by comparing the Dwiggins designs with the type ornaments by Klinkhardt (fig. 136), whose serpentine shapes contrast with the more geometrical shapes designed by Dwiggins in much the same way as the vowels of our alphabet contrast with the consonants. Artists who work primarily in terms of such shapes become as sensitive to the effects produced by their combination as poets to the sound of the words that they put together.

If an artist works almost solely in terms of these basic shapes, he is apt to think of them as if they were objects made out of some durable material. Similarly, such shapes may appear to us as if they were "ready made." The individual work of art in which we see them appears to result from the choice that the artist has made of such shapes from a kind of pre-existing stock, the work's particular form to be the result of the way in which the artist has assembled them. Because we are apt to see such shapes in this fashion, we are sensitive primarily to the way that

137. BYZANTINE MOSAIC
Justinian and Attendants
About 547 A.D.

the artist has fitted the different shapes together. For this reason, our experience of the Byzantine mosaic (page 178) is similar to our reaction to the painting by Picasso (page 179), but different from our experience with works like the Gondi palace façade or the Ashendene Press book page. We see the mosaic and the painting, not in terms of a harmonious arrangement of parts, but in terms of how the work is built up from different shapes. The sensation we have of how the work was constructed is ultimately influential for us in determining the meaning that we find in the created forms.

In this mosaic, it is the way in which the shapes are joined together that is the primary factor for our impression, not the character of the individual shapes being assembled. For the actual shape of the piece of glass used to make up the mosaic is relatively unimportant; its effect would not be greatly dissimilar if, instead of the square piece of glass, the artist had used one that was rectangular, or even triangular. The appearance of the figures results primarily from the way in which it was necessary to fit the smaller parts together to produce the image. As we can see, the artist used different means of putting the shapes together to achieve the character he wished to give to any one part of the entire mosaic. With the bowl, for example, he placed the squares in rows that repeated the curvature of the object. Thus, the character of the total image does not grow out of the actual shape of the individual mosaic square, but out of the way in which the squares are combined. Because we sense so strongly that they were created in this way, the figures become for us not figures on a surface but figures that are the surface. Form and work of art are one entity for us, and the forms become not representations of figures but actual figures which, because they exist in a world of colored glass, are necessarily supernatural. To understand them rationally, we see them as symbols.

In the painting *Three Musicians* by Picasso, the individual shapes are more important for our impression, not only because they are larger but because they interlock in a certain way. On the one hand, the individual figures emerge because of the way the shapes are brought together; on the other, the shapes interlock with one another in such a way that the single figures are simultaneously obscured. For the colors and patterns that Picasso gives to the different shapes make them flow into one another, in such a way that it is impossible for us to differentiate the figures precisely. The shapes create a screen of color and pattern between us and what we feel to be the real figures of the musicians. They seem to be somewhere beyond our grasp, the interlocking shapes turning all the figures into a façade that seems, despite its gaiety of color and frivolity of subject, to mask a more sinister image. Because these figures are bound together in this fashion, we are apt to see the hound stretched out along the floor, and the hooded figure to the right, as objects whose presence is somehow ominous. That the hooded figure is the one who holds the music that the others must play becomes a fact that gives a new meaning to the flat, cardboard cut-out scene before us. But, whatever meaning we may eventually see in these images—and their meaning is probably not precise but a matter of mood—the effect of the painting rests in our sensitivity to shapes and to their possible combinations on a flat surface.

Although Picasso uses interlocking shapes to knit the individual figures into a screen of color and simulated texture, he also creates for the figures a setting separate from the surface of the painting itself. We see the figures against a dark background. In the painting *The Swineherd* (page 177), however, Gauguin uses flat shapes of strong hues and contrasting textures not only to define the individual objects but to unite them with the setting itself. The entire surface of the

138. PABLO PICASSO. *Three Musicians.* 1921

139. PAUL GAUGUIN. *The Swineherd.* 1888

painting is made up of these interlocking shapes in such a way that there no longer exists any distinction between objects and setting. By this union of shapes, Gauguin creates an image that seems timeless and unchanging. We do not have any sense of the distance that separates the objects from one another, nor do we feel that the objects in the scene are palpable. The painting resembles a scene glimpsed from a quickly moving train, a scene which, for some unknown reason, remains stored in our memory until, at an unexpected moment, it suddenly presents itself with startling clarity to our inner eye. Because of this combination of shapes, the images remain forever locked in place.

As we can see in the paintings by Picasso and Gauguin, when the artist works with shapes, he tends to distinguish among them through the use of different colors and different textures. As he does so, the individual shape loses its importance in favor of a new sense for the entire surface. In the painting by Gauguin, for example, although we are conscious of the particular combination of shapes, we also begin to see the surface as having much the same appearance as a textile—one in which the design has grown out of the actual weaving process itself. In these instances, the shapes are imbedded in the surface in the same manner that the decorative motifs of a carpet exist only in the thick texture and rich color of the material. This is true in the painting by Vuillard (page 232) of a scene in the Tuileries Gardens; it is only by virtue of their contrasts in a simulated texture that the shapes of the various objects take form. The shapes of the foliage and the shadows on the ground are painted upon the canvas to appear as if they were woven out of a material. The various figures within the setting seem to be made out of the same material, the edges of their shapes blurred by being caught inside this light-reflecting surface. Because we are encouraged to see these shapes primarily in terms of their simulated texture, the blue dress of the girl in the foreground stands out against the melting colors of the rest of the surface as though appliquéd upon a textile; the light-green branches extend across the upper part as though they had been embroidered upon the surface.

In the painting by Vuillard, the artist's interest in texture begins to displace the importance of the individual shapes and their combinations in favor of the appearance of the entire surface. But the Vuillard work is only a step in this direction; in contrast to the painting of a similar scene by Klimt (fig. 140), the areas of texture in the Vuillard still exist as clearly discernible shapes. Klimt's dominant interest in the texture of oil paint itself has led to a painting in which the areas of color have no easily perceptible shapes. In blending with one another, the areas create on the canvas a surface that is a thick, rich mass of color. The texture of the paint casts a unity over the whole scene that never allows us to be conscious of anything but the entire surface. Thus, Klimt makes us experience the work in a manner essentially different from our experience with the Vuillard painting. In the latter case we were conscious of the play between textured surfaces, colors, and shapes of different kinds, as well as the play between a world of nature and one of paint. Klimt, on the other hand, is consciously attempting to make us aware of the whole of his painting, to have us enjoy it directly as a painted world which refers to the world of nature only through such associations as our visual experience with color and texture

140. GUSTAV KLIMT. *The Park.* 1910

will conjure up for us. For this reason, Klimt avoids creating shapes, in the same way that he avoids an illusion of space or depth, and avoids, as far as possible, any direct description of objects we might easily associate with a park. He does so because he is not painting a description of a real, or even an imaginary, park. He is creating a park in the texture and color of oil paint. The surface of the work of art itself *is* the park.

The work by Klimt reveals a concept of a painting as a flat surface that is essentially different from that held by the artists whose works we recently have seen. However, if we accept the painting by Vuillard as representing a step in the direction of Klimt's concept of the flat surface,

141. THEO VAN DOESBURG. *Composition: The Cardplayers.* 1916–17

we may see how a concern of the artist for shapes might actually lead to the point where the chief impression of his work is in terms of its entire surface area. Such is the case with the work by Van Doesburg called *The Cardplayers* (fig. 141). Here, the artist has not only reduced the possible figures of whose existence the title of the painting hints, to a series of shapes of color and light, but has limited the shapes to a single type. It is as if Picasso's *Three Musicians* or Gauguin's *The Swineherd* had come apart before our eyes, leaving only a surface in which the shapes, and the areas that separate them, are of equal importance. The forms that result are the accidental groupings that we ourselves make of the basic shapes; the exact configuration that the artist intended is not necessarily what we shall create. For the total complex of shapes has become so much more important than any individual one, that we cannot absolutely distinguish, in any rational sense, the total form from the shapes that make it up. A similar dissolution of individual shapes into an over-all design can be seen in the beaded collar designed by a Tlingit Indian (fig. 142). As an object on which is represented a shark that has devoured a seal, the collar is almost unintelligible to us. It exists primarily as a decorative surface on which the contrast between light and dark creates a pattern that does not delineate the individual shapes but defines the entire form of the collar. The black-and-white design that decorates the Indian jar (fig. 143) affects us in a similar fashion. Because the decoration is too intricate for our eye to readily distinguish the individual motifs of which it is composed, we sense the movement of the entire design across the surface. In doing so, we are made aware of the total shape of the jar. By stressing, in this way, the surface of the object, the artist has made us conscious of the actual three-dimensional character of the vessel instead of the flat surface design which adorns it.

142. TLINGIT INDIAN. Beaded Collar,
from Klukwan, Alaska
19th or early 20th century

143. ACOMA INDIAN
Jar, from New Mexico
About 1910

CHAPTER 13

Physical Space

144. MOCHICA INDIAN. Jar, from the
Central Andes. I A.D.–1000 A.D.

THE MORE EMPHASIS THE ARTIST PLACES on the entire surface of the work of art, the more likely he is to think of it as a physical, palpable object. In both the painting by Klimt and the Tlingit beaded collar, such a conception is reflected in the important role that the material itself—paint or glass beads—plays in our impression of these works. Because we are conscious of the painted or beaded surface, we are more aware of the painting and the collar as actual objects. Similarly, the over-all pattern of shapes covering the surface of the Acoma Pueblo jar (fig. 143) intensifies our awareness of the jar as a three-dimensional object.

However, in this case our comprehension of this three-dimensional object differs from what we have experienced with other three-dimensional works of art. Not only do we see this Indian jar as a three-dimensional object of a particular shape, but we sense its interior as well. We do so because the flat surface design, by appearing as if it were wrapped around the jar, stresses the fact that the jar is a container. We see the jar as a shape that encloses something. Naturally, our impression is based partly on our prior knowledge that the jar *is*, in fact, a container, but the degree to which we are aware of the space-containing properties of an object depends largely upon how the artist treats the surface.

145. HOHOKAM INDIAN
Shell Pendant, from Arizona
About 1000 A.D.

146. NAZCA INDIAN. Jar, from Peru
About 300–600 A.D.

In the case of the group of objects shown here, for example, although each one encloses space, we are particularly conscious of this aspect in one instance only. Despite our knowledge that the Mochican Indian frog jar (fig. 144) is a container it does not give us any impression of the space that it actually encloses. Inspired by the plastically modeled character of a frog's body, this artist has added to, and molded together, the basic surface of this jar in such a way that if it were not for the handle we would see the jar simply as a piece of sculpture. If the Mochican jar arouses in us an impression like that received from the sculpture by Reg Butler (fig. 96), the Hohokam shell ornament (fig. 145) has an effect like the sculpture by Brancusi (fig. 93). Incising the surface so that he barely disturbs its natural form, the Hohokam artist has made the shell's rounded, compact form suggest the body of a frog pressed flat upon the ground. We see the shell ornament as a solid object, even though, structurally, it is a hollow, space-enclosing object.

In the Nazca jar (fig. 146), on the other hand, the suggested animal image does serve to define the jar as a container, for the simple indications of legs and eyes painted upon the surface emphasize the swelling shape of the jar. The artist saw in the swollen body of a frog a shape and character that corresponded to the basic nature of the enclosed shape of the jar. The jar's smooth, unbroken surface, in combination with the reference to an animal form, helps us to sense—more acutely than in any of the other instances—that the jar contains interior space.

147. Louis Sullivan (with Dankmar Adler)
Guaranty Building, Buffalo. 1894–95

Sullivan faced problems quite different from those of the Nazca Indian, but the architect's concept of the basic nature of the skyscraper (fig. 147) was like the Indian's way of seeing the jar. Both the building and the jar present to us, by virtue of the treatment of their surfaces, a clear indication of the space that they contain. Sullivan does not permit one detail to distract our attention from the total surface of the wall. Each element of the design contributes to produce the effect of a rising, shell-like structure. The necessarily numerous windows are arranged to pierce the plane of the wall in a way that makes us see the wall as a single sheet of material. Set within shallow, arched panels that rise the entire height of the building, the windows carry our eye up quickly over the surface to the top, where the walls bend out to form a cornice that resembles the flared rim of a vase. This analogy is strengthened further by the circular windows which, in their placement at the top of the building, operate much like a band of decoration about the rim of a vase. If Sullivan's building reminds us of a vase, it is because he has designed it in the same spirit as the potter who builds up the walls of his vase in a continuous movement and, in decorating it, does not disturb its smooth surface by projecting ornament, but through a flat surface design gives emphasis to its basic form.

The simplest articulation of such a rising surface may be sufficient, however, to make us see the work more as a modeled, plastically conceived object than as one that encloses space. The bronze Chinese wine vessel is an example (fig. 148). Although we are particularly sensitive to this vessel's gradually rising curve—from a narrow base to a broader top—we are equally aware of the delicate balance in which its different parts are held, for the decorative flanges at the base, and the protruding ring slightly above, interrupt the continuity of the rising curve. Along with the judiciously placed areas of engraved ornament, these simple additions of protruding decoration have the effect of focusing our attention upon the articulation of the vessel. We become aware of the interrelationship of rim and base, as well as the role of the rising curve in keeping them in balance. As a result, the vessel appears to us primarily as a beautiful arrangement of solid shapes in tension—not unlike the architectural unit of base, column, and capital. By being conceived in this fashion, the Chinese vessel—despite its actual function—does not convey the impression of being a container of space.

In those instances where we are simultaneously aware both of an object's external shape and of the space that the object encloses, the character of that space begins to play an important part in our impression of the object. Similarly, when the artist creates such a work, he is conscious that at the same time he is giving form to the physical material, he is molding or shaping space. From the interplay between these two elements emerges the character of the work of art.

Pevsner, for example, has conceived his work of sculpture in terms of a spatial relationship that is as visible and comprehensible as the material form itself (fig. 149). The space whose

148. CHINESE. Ku (wine vessel)
Shang Dynasty, about 1400 B.C.

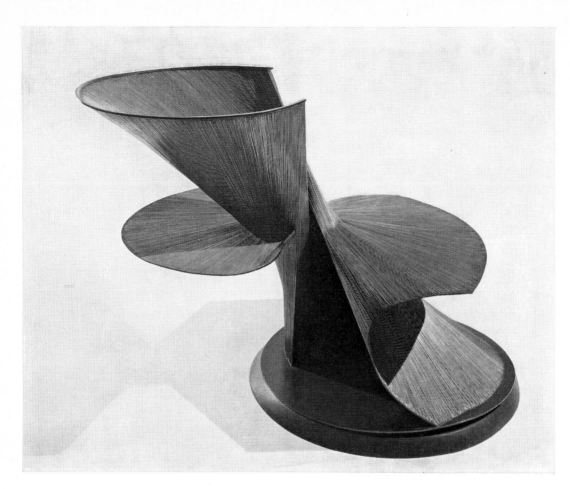

149. ANTOINE PEVSNER
Developable Column. 1942

presence within the Nazca jar or the Sullivan skyscraper was only indicated to us by the treatment of the surface has become, in this instance, a perceptible substance. It is as if the Chinese bronze vessel had been twisted apart—split open to reveal the space within. The feeling of movement that the Pevsner work imparts arises from the tension between solid and void. This feeling does not result solely from the spiral form of the piece, but is produced by our awareness of the space caught within it. This space, by making us feel the power of the walls wrapping around it, transforms the metal object into a living, organic form. And the balance of space and solid material gives the piece a stability that assures it the possibility of continuing to grow, to envelop more space. We see it here at what appears to be a momentary stage of its growth.

The importance of space for determining this work's character is obvious if we try to imagine what this sculpture would look like as a completely enclosed shape. As a solid, spiral form, the sculpture might be seen as a symbol of motion, but no longer as an object in motion. The tension between solid and void, which generates the sculpture's moving force, would be dissipated.

Between the Pevsner sculpture and an imaginary solid version of it lies a difference much like that between the reclining figures by Arnolfo di Cambio and Matisse (figs. 150 and 151). Obviously, there are many differences between these two works—one is carved out of stone, the other modeled in a pliable material; the limbs of the one figure are set at rest, those of the other in tension. But our comprehension of these aspects of the two figures is heightened by the

ABOVE

150. ARNOLFO DI CAMBIO
Virgin of the Nativity. 1296–1302

LEFT

151. HENRI MATISSE
Reclining Nude. 1907

factor of space—by its respective absence or presence. The monumentality of the figure by Arnolfo is the result not only of its size, but of its massiveness. This impression of mass is due both to the simplicity of the piece's outline and to the exclusion of any space that might normally be expected between various parts of the figure. Consequently, we sense keenly the figure's weight and the downward force that holds it firmly in place. This impression does not encourage us to think of this figure as capable of movement; but, if we should imagine that it could change its position, we would expect its movements to be slow and ponderous, the weight of the massive limbs demanding a tremendous exertion of force to move them.

The limbs of Matisse's figure, however, convey a strong feeling of capacity for movement, despite their heavy, massive appearance. What muscular tension we associate with the figure because of its position is intensified by the interplay of space and solid that it exhibits. The spaces surrounded and defined by its arms are not merely empty holes in solid material but openings that make us aware of the space enveloping the figure. By channeling a portion of this space, they make us sense its flow about the entire sculpture. As a result, the figure lays claim to a greater amount of space than it actually occupies—an area defined by the movements that we feel the figure is capable of making. From this interplay between solid and void comes the figure's surprising vitality.

The relationship between space and solid material in the sculpture by Matisse is the reverse

152. HENRY MOORE
Reclining Figure. 1957

of what we found in the piece by Pevsner, where the solid material moves about to encompass the space. In the Matisse, the space, by flowing about and in and out of the figure, encompasses the solid form. In contrast to either one of these pieces, however, the reclining figure by Henry Moore (fig. 152) possesses a relationship between solid and void more difficult to define precisely. On the one hand, the solid material appears to encompass the pockets of space, but these, in turn, seem to create a different form out of the same material. We are in doubt about whether the material creates the space or whether the shape of the space molds the solid material. This ambiguous relation between the sculpture's interior and exterior form is further compounded by the discovery that, if we move from one side to the other, the sculpture is capable of transforming itself into a completely new form. Particularly important for our experience of the sculpture is the space that moves completely through the piece. In doing so, this void appears to unite the different parts in such a way that we see the piece not as an object with two different sides, but as a form in motion. As a result, we feel that, as we move from one side of the sculpture to the other, the form moves also. The image suggested by the forms—a reclining woman—shifts position so as always to be facing us.

In the sculpture by Moore, space is a virtual solid whose shape and character are as great a concern of the artist as the shape and character of the physical material itself. Moore is able to see the object clearly with respect to both its interior space and its external shape. For us, these two aspects of an object and the relationship between them are not always easy to grasp.

To aid in our comprehension of these aspects, as well as to clarify their own, artists sometimes employ diagrammatic means to describe these relationships. Peruzzi uses such a method to indicate the spatial significance of a proposed ground plan for St. Peter's in Rome (fig. 153). To illustrate the consequences that the various parts of the plan imply, Peruzzi represents them in a sequential order. We see represented (beginning in the lower portion of the drawing) first the form of the exterior walls as well as the outline shape of the different columns and piers that are to encompass the interior space of the building. All of these elements are then shown to us in successive degrees of completeness until, finally, we are shown the appearance of the entire column or pier and the vaults that they will support. Peruzzi clarifies for us the shape and nature of the space that will be modeled by the solid masses, and enables us to visualize simultaneously both the exterior and interior form of the building.

What Peruzzi has accomplished by a cutaway drawing, in which he breaks down a complex structure of solids and voids into its component parts, Uccello has accomplished by depicting the material form of a metal vessel as if it were transparent (fig. 154). Because Uccello sees the body of this chalice to be made up of a series of interlocking planes, he is able to represent through a single network of lines both the exterior form and the interior space of the object. By ignoring the surface appearance of the chalice in favor of depicting what might be called the object's underlying structure, Uccello gives us, not a description of the vessel, but a graphic definition of the ideal form of a chalice as a three-dimensional object. By his approach, Uccello makes us aware of the chalice's simultaneous existence as a material object within which there is a space and as a shape of space around which there is a material form.

153. BALDASSARE PERUZZI. Plan for St. Peter's, Rome
About 1520

154. PAOLO UCCELLO. *Chalice*
About 1440

155. Naum Gabo
Spiral Theme. 1941

To achieve in sculpture an effect like that of Uccello's network of graphic lines, Gabo makes use of pieces of transparent plastic (fig. 155). The sculpture, however, does not describe space by defining elements that might confine it, but seems to be a crystallization of space itself. The plastic spiral is a record of one of the possible shapes in which the intangible element of space may occur, as ice is a record of the shape of water. In both the plastic and the ice, we are enabled to visualize an element that previously seemed to be without an actual shape of its own. Gabo's transparent plastic structure gives us a hint of the possible shapes of space, just as a photomicrograph may make the crystalline, mathematical structure of a mass of soap bubbles seem as real and tangible as brick and mortar. By saying something similar about the world of space, Gabo makes us more conscious of the existence of space as a physical element.

The architects of this suspended ramp (fig. 156) have worked with space in a similar way, for the aluminium rods that support the ramp make us conscious of the form of the space in which the ribbon of concrete floats. However, at the same time that the rods define a cylindrical

156. PEREIRA AND LUCKMAN. Spiral Ramp,
Convair-Astronautics Plant, San Diego. 1958

form, they also permit the space of the room in which we see the ramp to pass completely through the form. Space, in this instance, becomes for us a physical entity which can assume several shapes simultaneously but which cannot be restricted to one. Because of this, we feel the space to be continuously in motion, an impression that makes real a movement that the shape of the ramp alone could only symbolize.

The spatial feeling suggested by the appearance of this ramp is made even more explicit if,

157. PEREIRA AND LUCKMAN. Spiral Ramp,
Convair-Astronautics Plant, San Diego. 1958

as in this case, we can experience the space directly. For, unlike the other works, where we have had to look from the outside, here we actually can penetrate into the interior of the object. When we walk up and down the ramp, the ambiguous, transitory nature of the space is made evident, for a precise conception of the space in any part of the structure eludes us. Because the space is continuous between the room and the ramp, the space in which we know ourselves to be is not markedly different from the space in which we are not present. Our only means of locating ourselves is by physical contact with the concrete ramp. Since the ramp is suspended, our identity with its physical properties leads us also to feel suspended—a feeling intensified by the fact that the entire ramp rises from, or descends to, a basin of water.

If, while we were on this ramp, a solid wall should suddenly be wrapped around it, we should immediately be aware of being within a vastly different kind of space. By shutting us off from the space within the rest of the room, such a wall would, of course, define the entire cylinder of space that the ramp occupies. But, at the same time, the wall would also effectively break up the space within the cylinder into smaller units. For the wall's role as a vertical plane connecting the horizontal planes of the ramp would make us feel that a part of the space had been trapped between the various levels of the ramp, while another part in the center remained free. The previously shifting forms of a single, continuous space would, therefore, be translated into seemingly more tangible, volumetric shapes.

The spatial effects that would be produced if this ramp were to be enclosed are similar to those which we experience when we ascend the ramp designed by Bramante (fig. 159). Here, too, we encounter both trapped and free space. As we walk up Bramante's ramp, we are conscious of moving through a channel of compact space that coils about a central core of open space into which we cannot enter. Although we know that both areas of space are physically continuous, we, nevertheless, see the central core of space as if it were a hole or void that cuts through the total space of the ramp. As we continue to ascend, however, the screen of columns that goes around this central void helps to make us aware that the central space also has a tangible, single shape. Seen from the darker, and seemingly more dense, pocket of space in which we stand, the shape and nature of the central space are given tangible form by the light that streams through it from above. It becomes a column of space around which is wrapped the continuous ribbon of ramp columns. The more sensitive we grow to these spatial forms, the more we realize that their shape and character have determined the material form of the ramp. Apparently, Bramante conceived his work primarily in terms of the possible relations among different clearly defined shapes of volumetric space. Because of the play of movement between these two shapes—we sense the space both to flow about and also to rise directly from top to bottom—the spiral described by the solid ramp is put into a continuous motion. In this respect, the ramp by Bramante is the antithesis of the previous example, where the ramp is a frozen spiral that floats in the vacuum of the continuous space.

158. ANONYMOUS. Cross section of
Bramante's Spiral Ramp. About 1550

159. BRAMANTE. Spiral Ramp,
The Vatican. About 1503

Because we have just been looking at the Bramante ramp, we may be reminded of it by our first view of the screen of piers and columns set within the Royal Chapel at Versailles (fig. 162). We may even see the central space of the chapel as if it were an elongated version of the central space of the ramp. If we do see the chapel in this way, we miss the sharp impact that the space within the ramp had upon us. But the longer we remain within the chapel, the more we realize that, although its spatial effect is comparatively less immediate and less intense, its space is equally tangible. We come to realize that the relationships that we see among the different parts of this building are determined essentially by the shape and nature of its interior space.

This church, because it is a royal chapel, is necessarily divided into two major areas: a lower level, where the service was conducted and where members of the court congregated, and a gallery level, where the king and his immediate circle attended the service. Each area, therefore, has its own focal point—the altar on the ground level, the person of the king himself on the gallery level. Each of these focal points had to be maintained in its role as a distinctive element within the chapel while, at the same time, being made to serve as only one of the several parts that are necessary to the larger meaning of the entire building. These relationships Mansart achieves through his careful planning of the chapel's spatial effect.

The first step taken toward the control of this space was to establish a viewpoint from which the space of the chapel was intended to be seen, for the effect of the chapel was planned principally for the benefit of the king sitting in the royal tribune (the same area of the gallery from which our view of the chapel is presented). Seen from this point, the basic areas of space within the chapel are the central area of free space and the bands of more enclosed space curving about it. We are conscious of the central space as a volumetric shape with two principal directions—one directed horizontally toward the curve of the apse, the other directed vertically toward the curve of the ceiling vaults. But the basic relationships among the different areas of space are expressed by Mansart in a gentler, subtler fashion through the use of light.

160. Cross section of the Royal Chapel
of the Palace at Versailles

161. Exterior view of the Royal Chapel
of the Palace at Versailles (engraving by J. Rigaud)

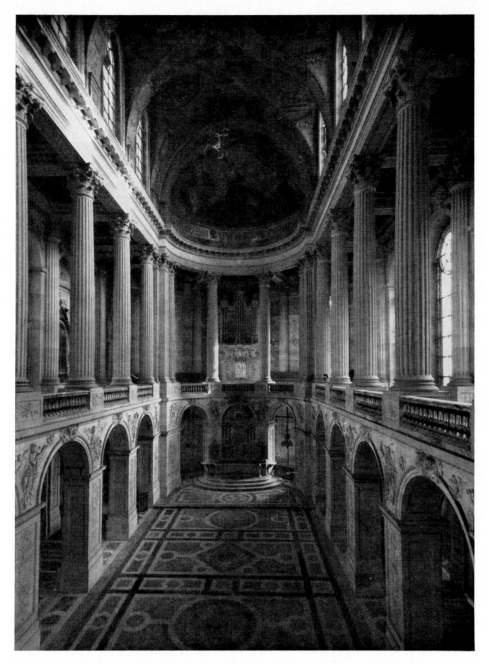

162. JULES HARDOUIN-MANSART. Royal Chapel (view from the Royal Loge),
Palace at Versailles. 1691–1710

The vast amount of light entering this chapel from the three rows of large windows on either side is used by the architect to heighten our feeling of the presence of space throughout the entire chapel. Mansart makes light produce this effect by controlling the nature of the surfaces on which it falls. Because of the very pale color of the stone, the lowness of the relief carving, the shallow fluting of the columns, and the gilding of the balustrades, strong shadows are eliminated, and the light appears to be absorbed by the surfaces rather than to be reflected from them. We

163. Plan of the Royal Chapel
of the Palace at Versailles

164. JULES HARDOUIN-MANSART
Royal Chapel (view of the Royal Loge),
Palace at Versailles. 1691–1710

feel that light does not pierce but permeates the space within the chapel. Consequently, in every part of the chapel, we are aware of the space. It seems to have filled the building shell, as rising water fills the hollows and recesses of any object in its path. The light so softens and blurs the edges of the separate shapes of space that they tend to melt together into a single, amorphous spatial shape.

At the same time, however, Mansart continues to keep us aware of the separate shapes of space that exist within the total space. Again, he uses light as his means of emphasizing space. By cutting off from our direct view the window openings in the curved end of the chapel, Mansart avoids throwing the piers and columns in this area into flat relief. Instead of creating a silhouette that would define the space too sharply, the diffused light reveals and emphasizes the space behind the piers and columns. So conscious are we of the presence of space, here, that it becomes easy to imagine that if we were to touch it, it would feel like velvet. Because the presence of this space is so evident to us, we tend to think of it as a substance that has penetrated into this part of the building from somewhere else; we see it as a continuous part of that space which is along the side walls. Thus, the bands of space appear to flow through the curved area and their motion to continue back along either side toward the royal tribune. And, since this tribune is the other dark area within the chapel (it opens directly off the royal suite), the current of space seems, upon approaching this point, to have made a complete circuit of the chapel. The two darker areas become, in effect, anchor points for the two rings of space. And because, within a total space that is soft and fragile in its effect, these rings are separated from each other, they appear to be held in a state of suspension. The gallery band of space seems to float above the lower ring.

Both of these rings gently grasp the central area of space, as if to keep it from rising too rapidly. But their presence also enhances our feeling for the rising movement of the central space, by making us conscious of its ascent through them. The gallery columns echo this effect,

165. ANTOINE COYPEL. Ceiling painting the Royal Chapel, Palace at Versailles. 1708

for their directional force is not primarily horizontal, as might result from their repetition around the chapel, but vertical. The inherent verticality of their solid form is stressed by the almost palpable quality of the space in which we see them. It makes us conscious, foremost, of their rising movement through it. But when their ascent is halted by the strongly accented cornice, the central space continues to mount. Free from the encircling bands of space, it moves higher, in contact now for the first time with the window openings and the direct light, until it seems about to escape through the openings in the vault. And in a sense it does, for as it reaches this point, it is transformed into a space that is no longer tangible. Through the illusion of the ceiling paintings (fig. 165) it becomes an undefined celestial space that both extends and culminates the space of the chapel.

Through all of these spatial effects, Mansart turns the symbolic form of the royal chapel into a real presence. The three levels of being—mortal, divine-king, and celestial—are all seen to exist in a hierarchical order. The connecting link between these levels is the continuous, central space around which they move—the space in which stands the altar where the act of faith that binds them all together is performed.

If, from the Versailles chapel, we could move directly into the church of Sant' Apollinare in Classe (fig. 166), we would have the feeling that a complicated spatial structure had been transformed into one whose effect is simple and immediate. It would seem as if the soft, quietly moving space of the chapel suddenly had been clapped into a single, firmly defined space. Upon entering the Ravenna church, our sense of an intricately achieved balance of space would disappear, for here we are conscious only of the central nave space. Although, physically, the screens of columns open up the pockets of space along either side, because of the effect of the brilliant light within the nave the columns visually blot out these flanking areas of space. The lustrous marble shafts of the columns and the essentially bare, light-colored walls reflect the light so strongly that the windows and the spaces between the columns stand out like shapes outlined on a flat surface. The even distribution of the intense light makes us see the nave walls as flat, precisely cut planes of little thickness; they seem to drop into place about us like curtains, abruptly shutting off the space without. And, as the exposed beams and rafters of the roof fill and darken the upper space of the church, we are also conscious that a horizontal and equally flat plane is being drawn over our heads.

The space in which we find ourselves is so precisely defined—its shape and character so strongly accented by the contrast between the dark ceiling and the light walls—that we unconsciously seek a relief from it. We are led to the only area within this forceful space that provides a point of rest—the apse. Its curved wall seems to soften the otherwise angular shape of the

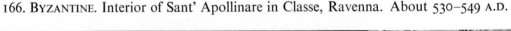

166. BYZANTINE. Interior of Sant' Apollinare in Classe, Ravenna. About 530–549 A.D.

168. Byzantine
Sanctuary of Sant' Apollinare in Classe,
Ravenna. About 530–549 A.D.

167. Byzantine. Aerial view
and plan of Sant' Apollinare in Classe,
Ravenna. About 530–549 A.D.

nave space, and the warm glow of its light, which is made to enter here through translucent sheets of marble, seems to change the quality of the space as well. Naturally, our eye is led to this area also by the two rows of columns, arches, and roundels (a movement more apparent in the wide-angle lens of the camera than in what we see when inside the church), but what actually makes the apse into the focal point of the church is our feeling for its existence as a space that is different and somehow isolated from the rest. By the steps that raise it above the level of the nave and by the mosaics that decorate it, this section of the church is physically described and labeled as a sanctuary, but these elements only record in symbolic form a presence of which the spatial effects of the building have already made us aware.

It is only after we have been inside the Versailles chapel or the Ravenna church that we can read into their external form the specific nature of the space within. We must wait until we enter

169. GIANLORENZO BERNINI
Façade and plan of Sant' Andrea al Quirinale,
Rome. 1658–70

these buildings before we are engaged by their spatial effect. From the moment, however, that we come upon the Roman church by Bernini (fig. 169), we are caught up in an interplay between shapes of space. As we approach this church, the street before it breaks back on one side, giving way to an area of space shaped by two low, curving walls. Our eye immediately is led to the tall and narrow façade of the church which, because of its proportions, dominates and occupies the space before it, much like a statue standing in a niche. But, as we look up at the façade towering above us, the emphasis that Bernini has placed on its flat, angular qualities makes us see it as a sharp plane that cuts into the arc of the niche of space. And we become aware at the same time that the columns and curved entablature of the porch do not appear to be built onto the façade but to protrude through it from the inside—an impression suggested to us by our glimpse of the church's side walls moving forward on either side to meet the flat plane of the façade. This oval curve being continued by the curve of the porch, we feel that the porch has been pushed into the outside space by the force of the interior space as it meets both the flat plane of the façade and the countermovement of the arc-shaped exterior space—an impact whose strength is reflected in the successively broadening arc of the steps. All of these implied movements of curved forms make us conscious of the almost tangible quality of both the exterior and the interior space, in the same way that the waves made by a pebble tossed into a quiet pool make us aware that what seems like a transparent sheet of water is actually made up of a physical substance of a particular density.

The countermovements of these two spaces are interrupted by the façade, which in being placed at the point of intersection of these two arcs heightens our sense of passing from one space to the other. We see the entire façade as a single, monumental doorway. The instant that we pass through it, going from the brilliant outdoor light to the darker interior, the interior space seems to reverse its forward movement, as if our opening the door had allowed the exterior space to force the interior space back. The walls, curving away from us on either side, seem to sweep around quickly to catch the space before it can escape from its oval container. They meet—directly across from where we have entered—at a porch-like structure similar to what we have seen on the exterior. But rather than to project into the space, this structure seems to yield to the force of the space now moving in its direction. Through it the space escapes into the sanctuary and, in doing so, is transformed into light. Within the ring of dimly lit chapels, the sanctuary shines so brilliantly that it seems to have been caught in a ray of light

170. GIANLORENZO BERNINI. Interior of Sant' Andrea al Quirinale, Rome. 1658–70

171. GIANLORENZO BERNINI. Interior of
Sant' Andrea al Quirinale, Rome. 1658–70

coming from above. And, as we look up, our eye swept by the curve of the pediment, we discover the statue of St. Andrew, who seems to be carried up by the ray of light to the space
above. All of our impressions of this space follow upon one another so quickly that our
experience seems instantaneous—we feel that we have entered the church just at the moment
that Andrew has been lifted to the realm of saints. An aura of light, entering from the windows
which ring the lightly colored dome, separates our darker space from the heavenly sphere into
which St. Andrew is taken up. The space that fills the dome seems to remain suspended, an
almost motionless bowl of space floating above us.

Like Mansart, Bernini has used space to make visible to us the relations among the different
levels of being which exist according to the beliefs of the Church. The difference between our
experience in these two buildings rests in the way in which each artist conceived of space as an
almost palpable substance—the one creating a space held in balance for us to see, the other
creating a dynamic sequence of spatial effects for us to experience. Bernini makes the space so
real for us that, as in our experience with the sculpture by Henry Moore, we are not sure whether
the solid structure has shaped the space, or the space has shaped and modeled the solid form.

CHAPTER 14

Time and Motion

FROM THE SUCCESSION OF EXPERIENCES that we undergo when we approach, enter, and move within Sant' Andrea comes our final impression of this church. The character and meaning of the building as a whole are disclosed to us only after we have encountered, one by one, all the parts of what obviously was a planned succession of effects. To create such an impression was Bernini's intention. He conceived the church in relation to a moving spectator—a conception to which the building's physical elements primarily owe their forms. The interchange between exterior and interior space—the ebb and flow of space through the portal—makes us conscious of our own movement through this space. We are also made aware of experiencing the different parts of the building in an ordered sequence, for by giving the major units forms that are similar but slightly different Bernini has caused our experience of one unit to be conditioned by our memory and experience of another. The repeated oval curves of the low screening walls, steps, and main walls of the church; the uniform columns and pediments of the exterior porch and the altar chapel, are impressed upon our consciousness like variations on a musical theme. Bernini, then, has not only worked with space as though it were a tangible substance but, by controlling our movement through it, has also worked with the still more intangible element of time.

Naturally, time and motion are involved in our experience of any architectural complex, but the artist need not make them the positive, determining factors in a building's form. For example, neither the amount of time we might need to look at the church at Ravenna nor the movements necessary for us to explore it were taken into account by the architect. Even if the architect should think of his work in relation to a moving spectator, our experience of his work need not be the same as it is within the complex designed by Bernini. Our experience within the city square designed by Gabriel is quite different (fig. 172), although here, too, the physical form of the work of art has been determined to a large extent by the effect that Gabriel intended us to experience as we move within it.

172. Jacques Gabriel. Original design for Place Louis XV
(now Place de la Concorde), Paris

In Gabriel's city square, our movements are deliberately left unchanneled, and we arrive at our comprehension of the total work after a series of progressive discoveries. Gabriel enables us to see all parts of this complex without moving in any one direction or leaving the main area of the square. The only element that might attract us, either as a visual focal point, or as a point toward which we might move, is the church at the far end of the street leading off to the right. But this building has been so carefully related to the rest of the complex that there is no possibility of its becoming an object of our attention or movement. Gabriel establishes this relationship in two ways. By gradually widening the street as it recedes toward the church, he avoids turning it into a tunnel of space that would invite us to leave the open space of the square. And by controlling the proportions of the parts of the church he keeps it from appearing either significantly larger or smaller than the two buildings between which we see it, although, in fact, it is both farther away and a great deal larger. As a result, we see the church in relation to the rest of the complex just as in Perugino's painting, *The Marriage of the Virgin* (fig. 72), we saw the temple in relation to the event taking place in the foreground. The church is established as a part of this complex—its presence is clearly felt—but it does not contend for attention with the equestrian statue of Louis XV, the object for which this entire complex was designed to serve as the setting.

Ultimately our wanderings within the vast space of the square lead us to the statue of the king, if for no other reason than a desire to inspect it at closer range. The moment that we arrive at this point, however, the seemingly amorphous character of the space that we have been in is transformed unexpectedly into a clearly discernible order. No matter in what direction we look—up the sloping hill of the Champs-Elysées, across the river to the left, into the alley of trees in the Tuileries Gardens, or off to the church on our right—we feel the space moving away from us toward the horizon. Because, up to now, Gabriel has made us aware that our movements through the vast space of this square have been incidental—not directed by the design of the complex—we now feel that the statue of the king controls and organizes the space we see opening around us. The different parts of the complex are brought into a unity whose existence we had not previously suspected—a design is disclosed to us, in its entirety, at one particular moment in time.

Both Bernini and Gabriel, by controlling our movements through space, are able to determine how we will comprehend their work. Although in these instances we actually move through a physical space during a specific length of time, even our experience with works of art whose space cannot be penetrated physically is equally involved with time and motion. For an artist may introduce these conceptions into his work simply by controlling the relationships

173. JACQUES GABRIEL. Original plan for Place Louis XV
(now Place de la Concorde), Paris

174. German
The Journey and Adoration of the Wise Men,
leaf in the Berthold Missal. 13th century

that he allows us to see among the various parts of his work. The artist of the medieval miniature (fig. 174), for example, makes us associate one specific area of the picture plane with one
particular moment in time by making the first figure to enter the doorway be the last to leave
it. By the device of giving different positions and directions to the same figures in the top and
bottom bands, the artist—without needing to depict it—is able to inform us of a movement in
which the figures must have been engaged. Our knowledge of this motion combines the three
rigidly separated bands of space into a linked chain of events.

In the painting by Sassetta (fig. 175), time is defined for us as something more than a factor
separating a series of steps in space. Within a spatially continuous landscape, Sassetta represents
events that occur at different moments of time. Here, space and time are unified in the sense that
the farther away an object is seen to be, the further removed it is in time. The city barely visible at
the top of the painting is the point from which St. Anthony started a journey that will ultimately
end with his discovery of St. Paul. Between these two points—points that serve as the top and
bottom of the picture plane, the foreground and background of the illusionary space, as well as
the beginning and end of the story—we can trace the zigzag direction of his journey as he
approaches the wilderness, encounters the centaur, and emerges from the forest into the

clearing. Although at times the saint disappears from our view during this journey, we sense an uninterrupted flow of movement, just as in watching a car descend a curving mountain road, we are aware primarily of its continuous motion, not simply its motion during the brief periods in which it is visible. Whereas in the previous work we connected, one by one, three isolated moments of time, here time becomes a continuous path moving through the landscape and passing in and out of the picture plane.

Both Sassetta and the medieval artist convey a concept of time and motion in their works by representing the same object at different points in space. Because of our experience in our own world, we see the relationship between these repeated objects in terms of time and motion.

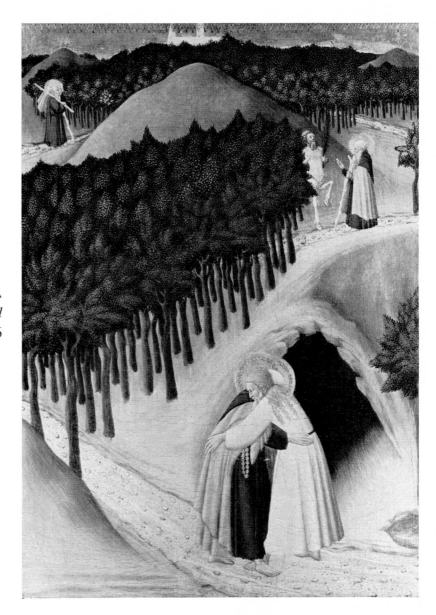

175. SASSETTA
The Meeting of St. Anthony and St. Paul
About 1432–36

The sculpture by Giacometti (fig. 176) is also composed, basically, of similar objects repeated at different points in space. Here, however, because the figures are pointed in different directions within an undivided space, the relationship that we see among them is one of an implied movement that will take place at a certain time. Rather than conveying to us a story of what has happened within a span of time, Giacometti makes us sense what is going to happen at a particular moment.

By the contrast between the light, wiry, rigid figures and the heavy slab of their base, Giacometti makes the figures appear to be held fast in place. The state of tension that this contrast creates is strained further by the directional force that each object suggests by its stance. This directional force that is exerted between figure and figure is seen by us as clearly as if inscribed like a path across the base. Each figure becomes for us not passively stationary but verging on movement. At some given moment, each will start along its own path. We feel that if there were a key for us to turn, all of the figures would begin to move like those of a mechanical wind-up toy, with movements so timed and controlled that they can cross one another's paths without colliding. We are made to sense time as an actuating force that will set the figures into motion—a force by which the ebb-and-flow motion of the city is controlled.

Through the implied directional forces that criss-cross the base of the sculpture, Giacometti links a group of fixed objects into an arrangement that suggests a future motion. But a group of equally stationary objects is arranged by Cotan (fig. 177), in a way that makes us sense the relations among them as an actually moving force. Here, the individual parts are related, not by a past or future movement, but by an already existing one. We see them woven together in the same way that musical notes are strung together for us when we hear sounds from an instrument move up or down the scale. For the position of each object in this painting has been determined

176. ALBERTO GIACOMETTI. *City Square.* 1948

177. Juan Sanchez Cotan. *Quince, Cabbage, Melon, and Cucumber.* About 1602

in relation to its possible existence as a step in an evolutionary development of forms. There is a clear, organic movement among the compact, shiny ball of the quince, the heavier, unfolding head of cabbage, the melon from whose sphere a section has been removed, the segment of the melon, and the elongated form of the cucumber. The difference between the two extremes of this scale of forms—the quince and the cucumber—is softened and transposed by the changes that take place in the objects separating them. The transformation of form suggested in this sequence is more important for our impression, and for the meaning of the work, than the nature of the individual object within the arrangement. But, because these objects are, at the same time, arranged in a scale of tension—from suspended to resting—we are made particularly aware of the individuality of each of the objects. Consequently, we clearly feel the various steps by which we see this development take place, and the time spent in doing so.

The sensation induced by the Cotan painting of a progressive movement from one object to

178. WASSILY KANDINSKY
Isolated Objects. 1934

another vanished abruptly when we look at the Kandinsky watercolor (fig. 178). None of these objects appears to have an affinity for another, nor does there seem to be anything in the nature of the objects that determines the particular arrangement in which we now see them. What Kandinsky has created, through slight variations in their shape, color, value, and size, is an arrangement of similar objects in which each is isolated from every other. Each object remains fixed in its place, appearing as sharp and individual as the letters on an eye chart. No movement, present or future, is implied between the objects. Instead, because the different objects stand out so clearly against the brilliantly white field of the paper, each seems to vibrate with a motion of its own. Because of this tension between object and field, each object appears to pulsate as our glance moves from one to another. The entire arrangement seems to come to life in the same way that an instrument panel seems to have a life of its own as we watch its lights flash on and off.

If the figures in the work by Giacometti actually were set into motion, or the tension were broken that holds the objects in the Kandinsky watercolor apart, we should be surprised if the resulting movements turned out to be the same as the movement that we sense the shapes of the Miró painting to be engaged in (fig. 179). Our impression of the Giacometti piece leads us to expect a sudden start of purposefully directed movement; we should expect the objects in the Kandinsky work, if they were set free, to come together with a clash in the center of the picture.

Both such actions are quite different from the ambling, drifting, and even somewhat chaotic-appearing motion that Miró creates by gradations of value and modulation of shapes within a vaguely mysterious space. The longer we watch this painting—watching, not seeing—the more infinitely varied its movements seem to become. Miró, by repeating different types of shapes in both outline and solid form, induces us to see the shapes as moving in space, bumping or by-passing one another and occasionally merging. Accompanying this floating motion is another, with a jerkier, faster rhythm coming from the changes that we see taking place among some of the shapes, such as the interchanges occurring among the three horseshoe-like shapes in the top central portion of the canvas. One shape is seen rising uneasily from a darker shape, its cousin is seen to be caught on a wire, and the third shape is seen sinking down near a larger outline shape. These different impressions constitute a witty play on shapes that is not unlike the play on words in a poem by Odgen Nash, in which the sound and meaning of the words fuse and blur, so that the essence of the poem rests solely in the shifting sequence of images provoked as we read it.

179. JOAN MIRO. *Composition.* 1933

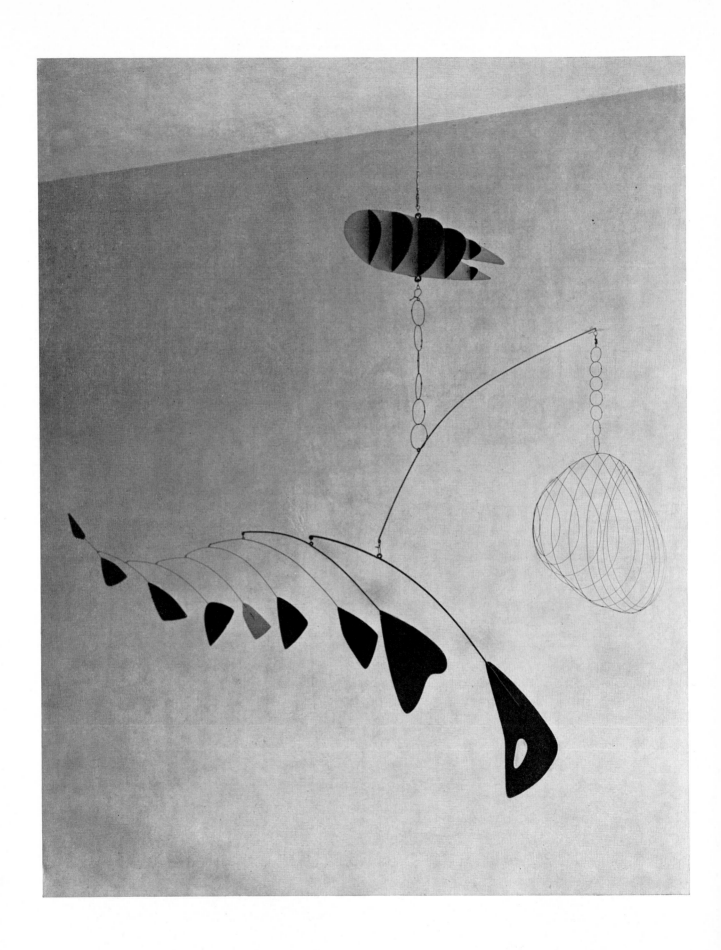

But, unlike the poem which comes to an end and which may be read again, the painting by Miró seems to elude a conclusion. We see it only at a certain moment in its existence, and feel that we never will see it in exactly the same way again. Time, here, is like a gentle but constant current of air that keeps the shapes in motion and that creates with them an ever-changing pattern.

Immediately to shift our attention from the painting by Miró to the mobile by Calder (fig. 180) is to make us feel that these painted shapes have suddenly been taken captive. Their previously free motion now seems controlled and directed. The identity of space-time-motion which existed for us in the painting has necessarily disappeared, as what were painted shapes have now become metal shapes existing in the physical world and subject to its mechanical laws. But, as we continue to watch the mobile, we realize that with these shapes Calder has created a work of art whose meaning and existence are embodied almost solely in its motion. For the necessity of physically connecting each individual part of the mobile to another part, and of suspending the entire network from a fixed point in space, becomes for Calder the means of achieving a specific type of actual motion. He is able to control precisely the number and type of movements that the work will perform, as well as to determine the span of time during which it will move, once it is set in motion. The material parts of the mobile owe their nature solely to Calder's concept of the motion that he wished to create. Like the individual dancers in a ballet, each part of the mobile is assigned specific movements to execute. As we watch these being successively and simultaneously performed, they are woven together into a form whose sole substance is a motion developed between a beginning and an end.

Because we can see the mobile at the very moment at which it starts to move as well as at the moment it comes to a stop, this object can be said to have a dual state of existence. Between different points in time—from start to stop to start again—the mobile is alternately in a state of motion and a state of rest. These two states are unified, held together for us, because we are able to see the metal shapes of the mobile during both states. The metal shapes are our points of reference for comprehending the motion of the mobile and for giving a form to the mobile while it is at rest. To see such a tie between the form of an object at rest and that of the same object in motion is denied us when we watch in action the object that Duchamp calls "a rotary, optical precision apparatus" (fig. 181). Duchamp destroys our points of reference between the two states in order to make us see motion itself. This artist wishes to show us motion as a visual form that exists at a certain moment in time, to show us the immaterial form of motion which

OPPOSITE PAGE

180. ALEXANDER CALDER
Lobster Trap and Fish Tail. 1939

181. MARCEL DUCHAMP. *Revolving Glass*
(left: shown at rest; right: shown in motion). 1920

Calder builds up for us over a period of time but which he can never show us as a whole. Duchamp creates this effect by arranging a series of painted glass panels on a shaft in such a way that, when they are set in motion, the individual form of each panel will disappear as the rate of speed increases. Visually, the individual forms no longer exist. We see in their place a new and single form—a visual form of motion.

Duchamp has stressed, both by the materials that he has employed and by the forthright way in which he has used them, the character of this object as an apparatus—as a collection of parts that work together to achieve a common function. The title that he has given to the work— one that might have been taken from the catalogue of a machine-tool plant—also emphasizes its resemblance to an instrument used for some scientific purpose. Both of these aspects of the work are means by which Duchamp attempts to transfer the work from the realm of illusion into one of reality. By making this work appear so purposeful—so serious in intent—Duchamp succeeds in impressing upon us that what we see happen when the work actually is put into motion is a convincing demonstration of the validity of some physical law.

In creating a work that is a precise, concrete demonstration of the visual form acquired by a physical object as it is engaged in motion, Duchamp poses a philosophical question concerning the true state of being. He is concerned not with the effect that motion may have on the appearance of a physical object, but with the form actually possessed by an object that can put itself into motion. In some ways the Duchamp apparatus is similar to the Calder mobile. It, too, goes from a state of rest to a state of motion only through the intervention of an outside force and it also can move only in a rotary direction about a fixed point in space. But, whereas Calder creates in the mobile a work that gives an illusion of possessing an inner source of motion because of its sensitivity to the slightest amount of pressure, Duchamp actually embodies in the apparatus the same principles as those found in a self-propelled object. Because its parts, in fact, move in relation to an inner motion—the spinning shaft—and because in attaining speed, they disappear from view, the machine re-creates in a work of art the essential aspects of an object that can generate its own motion from within itself. When we watch the mobile move, we see the effect of motion upon the visual form of an object that is inherently stationary, even though its form may have been determined with respect to the motion in which it will be engaged—like a ball that is to be thrown through the air. Its visual form during its flight is acquired only incidentally, by reason of its having been put into motion. When we watch the apparatus by Duchamp, however, we see the visual form inherent in any object that can put itself into motion—like a bird that flies through the air. Its visual form during its flight is actually a part of its true form.

The apparatus by Duchamp represents one solution to the problem of conveying in a work of art the total form of a self-propelled object. His painting *Nude Descending a Staircase* (fig. 182) represents another. In this instance, Duchamp defines the total form of such an object through suggestion rather than demonstration. He does so by giving us only a momentary glimpse of a moving figure—a view that is similar to what, when watching the apparatus, we see at the moment that the visual forms of the glass panels begin to blur and almost melt together. The painting represents only one stage of what, in the apparatus, is a whole cycle of changing form. We comprehend the decomposition that has taken place in the individual forms of the figure because of our previous knowledge of what these forms look like when at rest. Our experience of situations similar to that in which the figure is placed makes us realize that we are seeing the figure in only one moment of its continuous descent around the spiral staircase.

182. MARCEL DUCHAMP
Nude Descending a Staircase, No. 2. 1912

183. MARCEL DUCHAMP
Nude Descending a Staircase, No. 1. 1911

From the differences that we can see between the first (fig. 183) and second versions of this painting, such a solution appears to have been the result of a growing realization on Duchamp's part of the actual nature of a moving human figure. All the revisions that Duchamp makes in the second version have the effect of making us more fully aware of the human body as a form whose definition is relative to its motion at one particular moment.

These revisions affect almost all aspects of the painting. When we see these two works together, our impression that the figure is moving faster in the later version is due only in part to the fact that Duchamp has increased the fragmentation of the figure. That the figure in the first painting appears more to have paused during its descent down the spiral stairway than to have been moving past us is due primarily to the change in the relation of the figure to its setting. For, in the earlier painting, Duchamp indicates so much of the space and structure of the spiral stairway that the setting in which the figure is placed is not dissimilar from the space-time landscape in which Sassetta places the figure of St. Anthony. The view that Duchamp gives us of the stairway in the later painting is quite different. Here, the steps also have become fragmented, as if our previously precise view of them had been blurred by the moving figure. The picture plane has, in fact, become a much smaller opening. We now seem to see the figure as if we were watching it from a point outside one small opening in the wall enclosing the entire ramp by Bramante. By restricting our view of the stairway, Duchamp suggests to us that we are seeing this figure in three stages: coming down the stairway toward us, increasing in size as it passes directly in

MARCEL DUCHAMP. *Nude Descending a Staircase, No. 2.* 1912

JACKSON POLLOCK. *One* (detail). 1950

WASSILY KANDINSKY. *Tempered Elan.* 1944

EDOUARD VUILLARD. *Under the Trees.* 1894

front of the opening, and about to move out of sight down the rest of the stairway. The figure is a moving object that enters and leaves our sight, creating for us an experience similar to our seeing a train at close range come into view, pass us by, and disappear.

At the moment in which this happens, we are conscious of the train only as an object moving at high speed under its own power. Because we are not aware of either its starting or ending point, its form for us, visually, is solely one of motion. Similarly, we see the figure in the second painting not as an object being moved from one point in space to another, like the figure of St. Anthony in the Sassetta painting, but wholly as a figure in motion. In the same way that a rush of air or the sound of a whistle may symbolize the power of a train for us, Duchamp uses a simple graphic symbol to indicate the source of power of the moving figure—the circular, dotted lines painted near the center of the figure, in the only bright color on the canvas. Like the white circles that he painted onto the hub of the rotating shaft of the apparatus, they indicate clearly the source of the object's power.

Boccioni, like Duchamp, has also chosen to convey the form of a moving figure by isolating it in one particular moment of time (fig. 184). But he shows us—in the solid material of sculpture—an even briefer glimpse of the total visual form of an object that can put itself into motion. This figure has this particular form only between the two points in space defined and emphasized

184. UMBERTO BOCCIONI. *Unique Forms of Continuity in Space.* 1913

by the separate bases of this piece of sculpture. A moment earlier in its motion it had a different form, and in a future moment it will have yet another. By showing us this unique form of the figure, Boccioni makes us realize that, in reality, an object that has the ability to move does not have a single visual form by which it can be defined. We realize that the figure of a man walking actually has a continuously changing form that cannot be represented totally. Either we are given its form in one split second, as in this sculpture, or we are given only an illusion of its actual form.

Duchamp and Boccioni have been led to conceive their works in this way not because they wish simply to convey motion for its own sake, but because, for them, motion is the principal aspect of the human figure. For these artists, the reality of the human body is its ability to move; the reality of its visual form is its capacity for constantly decomposing and recomposing itself. Because their intention is to convey this reality, both artists have attempted to create a work of art that does not depend upon illusion to achieve its effect. Instead of describing the effect of motion or of creating the illusion of motion, these artists seek to re-create, in the work of art, the reality of the visual form of a moving figure. Thus, they reject devices such as those used by Sassetta or Giacometti to persuade us that the various figures repeated in different sections of the picture plane or on the base of the sculpture are actually related through time and motion. Boccioni and Duchamp do not wish to *inform* us that motion has taken or will take place, but to persuade us that what we see in the painting or sculpture *is* the visual form of a moving figure.

Because their intention is to diminish the role that illusion plays in the relationship between us and the work of art, both Boccioni and Duchamp attempt by various means to make their works appear less like painted or sculptured images. Boccioni, for example, polishes certain areas of the bronze so that the physical outlines of the statue appear to be dissolved in light. And, by employing two separate blocks for a base, he keeps the figure from being easily seen as a piece of sculpture. Duchamp gives his painting the appearance of somehow embodying a mechanistic truth by virtue of the metallic-like shapes that describe the parts of the human figure and by use of a palette that reduces the possible sensuous appeal inherent in the color and texture of paint. Just as he endows the apparatus with the appearance of an object illustrating a scientific truth, Duchamp makes his painting appear to be a simple statement of scientific fact by painting the title on the surface of the canvas (page 229). His making the title a physical part of the painting leads us to see the work as a frank, direct expression of identity, in the same way that we see the labeled animals in a zoo. We tend to see the painting as simply the embodiment of what its title says it is.

These attempts, however, to make our experience of the works direct and immediate are only partially successful. In actuality, we are aware of either piece first as a specific type of work of art—as a painting or as a piece of sculpture. Our experience can only be secondary to this act of recognition. As long as both works exist for us as art objects with certain formal characteristics, our experience of them is less immediate than with the apparatus by Duchamp. This object has no specific form of which we are conscious beyond what gives it existence as an apparatus. In

186. ISAMU NOGUCHI
Kouros. 1944

185. GREEK
Kouros, from Melos
About 575–550 B.C.

this case Duchamp succeeds in creating an object that we experience directly only because the work of art in itself is not "artlike." All the formal qualities of a work of art, as well as illusory devices, have been destroyed.

The piece by Noguchi entitled *Kouros* (fig. 186) illustrates precisely the difference between a work of art whose form can be described in terms of certain formal characteristics and one whose form can only be defined in terms of our experience when viewing it. For the work by Noguchi is the re-creation of all the characteristics implied or described in the type of ancient Greek statue of a male standing nude called a kouros. As we look at this piece by Noguchi, the different shapes seem to vibrate and to move together in the same way that the shapes in the painting by Miró seem to be engaged in a constantly changing motion. Noguchi, by denying us the possibility of seeing a single, complete form, makes it impossible for us to comprehend the work as a piece of sculpture with a specific form, as we do the Greek work (fig. 185). But, from the constantly shifting image, we experience all of the characteristics that we find in the Greek statue—rigidity of stance, tautness of muscular tension, articulation of the body, suggestion of a forward stride. But we do so directly, without first being aware of the form as a work of art, for the formal qualities by which the Greek artist conveyed these characteristics—the symmetry of the figure, the planar definition of its anatomy—are absent.

When we see the work by Noguchi we inevitably sense the existence of some kind of motion. By emphasizing the way in which the different shapes are related to one another, he makes us conscious, primarily, of how they are held together. Because we see how one shape fits into another, and because the positions of some shapes appear to depend upon the existence of others, we are more aware of the acts of balance and counterbalance that the shapes perform than we are of their material form. Our experience when seeing the sculpture by Noguchi is similar to what we experience in that brief moment during a high dive when we see the parts of the diver's body brought together in a certain way. His body before and after this moment is not the primary factor in our experience, even though it makes the experience possible. In the same way, the marble shapes appear to come together to make this piece of sculpture at the moment that we first see it; we are not aware of its previous existence as a material object. Thus, the work is unlike the Greek sculpture, of whose material form as a piece of stone we are particularly conscious, which exists as a work of sculpture whether or not we are looking at it. As we walk about the Noguchi piece we discover that its parts do not move together to make up an object with a front, back, or sides, but seem, instead, to move in relation to the center area—an area which is similar to the hub of the apparatus or the graphic symbol on the Duchamp painting, but which, because it is invisible, makes us feel rather than see the presence of an inner source of power.

Although we are more directly involved with the work by Noguchi than we are with the Duchamp painting or the Boccioni sculpture, here, too, our involvement is still less than total. For the nature of our experience with the work by Noguchi is in part dependent upon our degree of familiarity with Greek sculpture, in the same way that our experience with the works by Duchamp or Boccioni is related to our knowledge of the visual form of the human body at rest. In each of these works our experience must proceed by means of the comparison that we make between what we see and the mental image that we must provide from our memory. The extent to which we must be involved in such a comparison makes our experience to that extent less real and less immediate. Only with the Miró painting, the Duchamp apparatus, or the Kandinsky watercolor, for example, does our relationship with the work of art reach a level at which our experience is shaped only by what we can actually see at a particular moment.

Yet, even with these works, our experience is still not completely direct and immediate, for a part of our reaction is due to the "artlike" qualities that they exhibit. The Miró painting, for example, contains an illusion of physical space. The shapes in the Kandinsky watercolor are defined so precisely that we are conscious of them as belonging to the world of art forms to the same degree that we recognize the vegetables and fruit in the Cotan painting as belonging to the natural world. And the constructed, mechanical qualities of the Duchamp apparatus make it appear a work created for such a single, specific purpose that we wait to be informed by it—to be given a demonstration—rather than become directly involved with it.

187. Jackson Pollock. *One.* 1950

All of these aspects of a work of art are done away with in *One*, 1950, by Jackson Pollock (page 230 and fig. 187). In this painting we are given no illusion of physical space, no precisely defined shapes, no sense of purposeful construction. We see only a canvas of a certain size (9′ × 17′ 10″) on which occurs different kinds of paint of varied colors and textures in seemingly accidental and unrelated forms. Nowhere in this work are we given a key by which any specific previous emotion or experience will serve us as a guide for our reaction. Our reaction can come only from what we see while we look at the painting. As we become involved with this work, we see the areas of different colors and textures of paint begin to converge, pull together, suddenly fly apart, or remain isolated from the others. The whole surface comes alive with movement: forms appear and disappear. At one moment, we are conscious of the shimmering current of brown and black that moves across the canvas; at another, of the cascade of blue from the top; or we are caught up in the quicker, darting movements of the white, only to be stopped by a blob of gray or white that suddenly brings us back to the surface of the painting. The longer we look, the more we become aware that such possible movements and relationships are infinite in number. Visually, we are experiencing a situation that might be paralleled musically by our being given, simultaneously, a series of chords, crescendos, melodic passages, and fugal interchanges. While we listened, our ear would be caught by different parts of the sound at different times, and we would begin to build our own piece of music rather than search for some predetermined form or development. We begin to do the same with this painting. We stop seeking any one image, we stop searching for a specific impression. At the moment we do so, our experience becomes our own—a personal experience that is new and, therefore, real to us.

Unique though we feel our experience to be as we enter into this new world of paint, we soon realize that we are sharing an experience. From the way in which the paint occurs on the canvas we receive a clear impression of the act of painting that created it. Because we feel the motions through which he went, we sense in the work the presence of the artist himself. We recognize that the painting is literally the record of the experience in which Pollock was involved at the moment that he poured the paint upon the canvas. And, because he did so without thinking of illusory devices and without using a set vocabulary of art forms, the experience is recorded in no other form but the actual paint and the actual dimensions of the canvas. (For this reason a Pollock painting cannot be "reproduced"—seen in a different size and in a different material it becomes something other than the work itself.) Thus, the pictorial reality of this painting is the physical reality of the painting—a work that results from Pollock's involvement solely with the experience of the moment and his direct expression of it.

We are able to share in this experience to the degree that we are able to share all human experiences. The extent to which we take part depends both on our visual sensitivity and on our willingness to become involved. But, although we may share in this experience, our experience necessarily is never the same as was that of the artist. What is real for us at the moment at which we see it is not what was real for the artist at the moment that he painted it. And, even for the artist, the experience of seeing the finished painting is not the same as the experience that the painting records, for the painting *is* what the artist *was* at the time that he painted it. As a record of his experience at that moment in time in which he was impelled to engage in some type of motion to express himself, the painting by Pollock is neither more nor less than the embodiment, in a work of art, of the artist himself. The complete equating of artist and work is an ultimate phase in the artist's concept of a work of art—a concept in which material, technique, form, and artist are one. Beyond this point, we deal no longer with a work of art but with the mind of the artist.

PART THREE *The Critic*

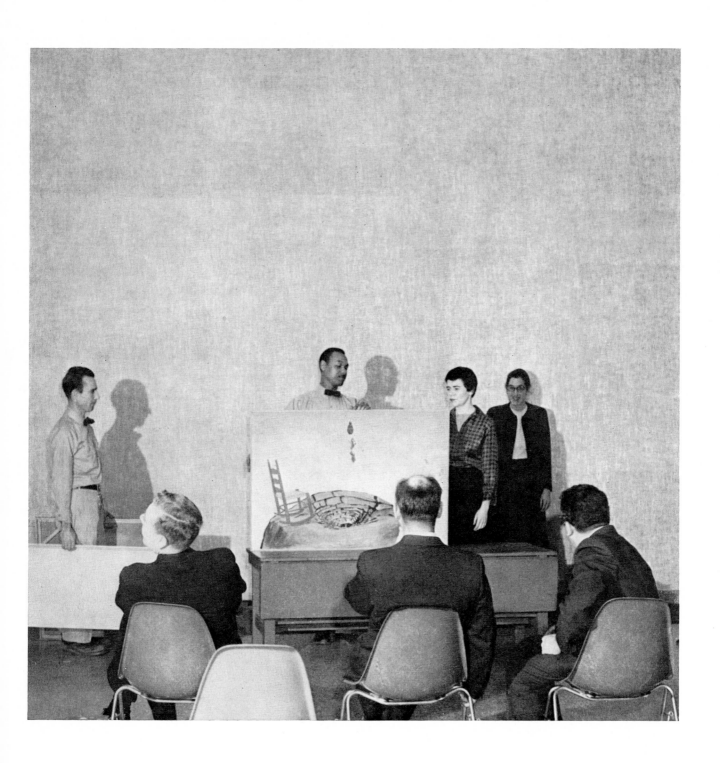

CHAPTER 15

Style

188. Giovanni Bellini
The Flight into Egypt
About 1480

THROUGH BECOMING MORE AWARE of how we respond to different visual elements, and by recognizing some of the different ways in which artists approach their work, we have come to see a work of art principally in terms of the meaning expressed in its visual forms. However, as we come into contact with greater numbers of works of art and our familiarity with the visual world increases, we discover that we begin to see a work of art in still another way.

In our initial stages of seeing works of art, each new work we met offered us such a completely different experience that we tended to think of it as an isolated phenomenon. For example, when we first encountered the painting by Bellini (fig. 188), we saw it as the product of Bellini's unique, personal use of the elements of line and volume. Now, however, we have reached the stage at which our response to such elements is more intuitive and our impression of new works is likely to be affected by our memory of others. Our visual memory expands our experience of the work of art immediately before us to include awareness of relationships between this work and others. Thus, when we encounter the painting by Cima (fig. 189), we are quick to sense in it a use of line, volume, and light and dark similar to what we have already seen in the work by Bellini. Progressively, such relationships—the differences and similarities we detect among works of art—begin to play a part in the way we see an individual work.

As we become aware of the similarities and differences among works of art we are encouraged to see an individual work as a part of something larger. Recognizing, for example, the similarities between the paintings by Bellini and Cima induces us to see both of them as belonging to some common order. This link between the two works becomes even more sharply defined if we now encounter a work like the painting by the Mondsee Master (fig. 190), which is so vastly different from both the Cima and Bellini paintings in its use of line and volume. By virtue of this strong contrast, the similarities between the other works seem to justify more than ever the suggestion that the two are somehow the same, and that a polarity can be set up among all three works. From the moment that we are aware of it, the greater grows the probability that our visual memory will lead us to see the other works that we encounter in terms of this possible polarity. To the work of Cima and Bellini will be added those paintings which seem to exhibit similar characteristics; to the work by the Mondsee Master will be added those other paintings which seem similar to it. We begin to see works of art in terms of their similarities and contrasts with others.

189. CIMA DA CONEGLIANO
The Virgin and Child with a Goldfinch
About 1509

190. MASTER OF MONDSEE
The Flight into Egypt
About 1490

As our visual memory progressively makes us more aware of the characteristics shared by various works, our way of seeing undergoes a change. The emphasis that we place on similarities among works of art leads us to become aware principally of those similarities which occur the most frequently. From these common features we form in our mind a model work of art—a mental image that comes to represent for us what we call the "style" of a work of art. The more firmly implanted this image becomes in our memory, the more we tend to see a new work of art in relation to it—to see in terms of style.

We may first become aware that we are seeing works of art in this way when we discover that we recognize the style of an individual artist. We have come to know the way in which this artist works and to identify his other works through this knowledge. For example, from our knowledge of how Bellini uses line, volume, or color in various ways, we form an idea of how he most frequently uses these elements. This observation, after having been sufficiently confirmed, leads us to expect to find something of this idea reflected in other works of his. Thus, we begin to see his work in terms of what we have distilled as his style.

In the process of reaching this stage, however, we also have been struck by similarities such as those between the two paintings by Bellini and Cima, and, in turn, by the combined differences that these two paintings share with the work by the Mondsee Master. And, at the same time, we have become aware of other factors by which these groupings can be described or catalogued in our mind—a process that is the natural result of the ever-increasing number of works of art coming into our consciousness. Because the works that appear to bear a certain likeness to one another are also those which were created at the same time or in the same place, we commonly associate style with the time or place in which the artists worked. Thus, the similarities between the paintings by Bellini and Cima would be recognized by us to be related to a period of time covering roughly the latter part of the fifteenth century and the beginning of the sixteenth; and, because the different-appearing work by the Master of Mondsee belongs to this same period, we would recognize further the distinction that exists among them with respect to place of origin—Italy as against Austria, Northern Europe as against Southern. If we should then encounter the works of Perugino and Raphael, their similarities to the Bellini-Cima paintings would only enforce for us our concept of an Italian style of that time that was different from the style of the Mondsee Master. The differences that we originally saw between the paintings come to be defined or labeled with reference to geographical facts. Thus, our concept of style, as we formulate it from what we see in the works we encounter and from what we remember of other works, begins to be associated by us with factors that exist outside the work of art, and begins to enable us to give a name to what we see as similar and common.

By encouraging us to see in terms of style, our visual memory acts as a kind of drug that can stimulate our sensitivity to the character of an individual work and heighten our perception of the entire visual world. But it is also a drug that can dull our perceptivity and induce us to confuse an intellectual with a visual experience. Which experience takes place depends upon whether we allow our visual memory to supplement or to supplant our eyes; whether our visual

191. PERUGINO
The Marriage of the Virgin. About 1500

192. RAPHAEL
The Marriage of the Virgin. 1504

memory continues to be formed out of a succession of individual visual experiences or begins to be shaped artificially from seeing works of art as examples of style. If, for example, we had looked at the painting by Perugino (fig. 191) only as an example of the Italian Renaissance style, had seen it only with respect to the qualities that it shares with other works of the same period, our understanding of it could lead us to see the painting by Raphael (fig. 192) only as similar to it. The differences between the two—and the essential meaning of each work rests in the differences—would have escaped us. Our sole relationship with either painting would have consisted merely of our ability to identify one as being of the same period as the other. Although this pursuit provides us with a certain intellectual pleasure—not unlike the pleasure derived from solving a crossword puzzle—it is a substitute for the visual experience, not an extension of it. Seeing in terms of style will increase our pleasure and expand our understanding of the individual work of art only if we recognize that style is a result of the creative process, not a factor that determines it.

If seeing in terms of style is to expand rather than to dilute our visual experience it must provide us with something in addition to what we can gain solely from seeing the individual work but without, at the same time, providing us with anything that is not implied in the work of art itself. To achieve this end, we must continually refine our concept of style by our understanding of the way in which the creator of a particular work of art has expressed himself. Under these conditions, seeing in terms of style is to reverse but not to abandon the pair of analytic binoculars through which we have been looking at works of art. Our close-up view of isolated, individual works of art is transformed by our concept of style into a broad view of many objects in a specific setting. From this view we become aware of an additional meaning of the work of art that, although always present, had not previously been apparent.

193. ANONYMOUS FRENCH
Inkstand. About 1900

194. PERCY STAMP
Hatpin. 1908

When, for example, we encounter, one by one, a number of contemporaneous objects—the desk by Guimard, the glass by Tiffany, the inkstand by an anonymous French artist, the silver pin by Stamp, and the candelabrum by Van de Velde (figs. 193–197)—their obvious similarities of linear shape produce for us a concept of the style of the period around 1900. Despite the differences of size, material, and purpose, the differences among the artists and even among their places of origin, the concept that we have built up on the basis of their visual similarity makes us recognize that all of these artists approached the creation of their work in the same way. By virtue of seeing these objects in terms of a style, we come to understand the individual work in a way that would not necessarily be apparent from seeing only the one object. For from seeing all of these objects together we realize that the artists have used sinuous line as a moving force to transform metal, paper, or wood into objects that, although different in purpose, exist for us, visually, principally as arrangements of shapes. Seen in this context, we understand more readily that the desk by Guimard exists primarily as an arrangement of these formal elements, only secondarily as a desk.

Seeing works such as the objects from the period around 1900 in terms of their similarities can, therefore, make us understand more clearly the individual artist's intention. But, at the same time, because we have also become aware that these artists share a common approach to their work, we recognize that the work of each artist is in part the result of factors that exist outside of the artist himself. Once we realize that the appearance of such works as the glass by Tiffany or the silver pin by Stamp is due to the fact that these artists lived and worked in a particular period, the more pertinent it becomes to determine what these factors are which have shaped the artists.

Seeing in terms of style makes us consider, then, why the artist expresses himself as he does. What has led, for example, the artists from around 1900 to have a common approach to their

195. LOUIS C. TIFFANY
Glass. About 1900

196. HENRY VAN DE VELDE
Candelabrum. About 1902

197. HECTOR GUIMARD
Desk. About 1903

work becomes a question whose answer promises to give an additional meaning to each of the works. If we take this further step in the development of our visual experience we are led to see the work of art not only in relation to others but in relation to all of man's creative activity and to his total experience. The meaning of the individual work of art comes to be understood in terms of its relation to basic ideas and concepts that govern more than man's visual expression. Although aware that the possibilities for expression offered by the visual world are distinctive and unique, we begin to realize that these possibilities exist for the artist because they are rooted in man's attempt to define himself. A concern for understanding the relationship between the whole of man's experience and the visual world brings us directly into contact with the particular interest of the art critic, art historian, and aesthetician.

Our realization that there are factors outside both the work of art and its artist that affect its appearance leads us to try to define more completely the style that has been responsible for making this apparent to us. In doing so, we find that we must supplement our own experience of works of art with the information about this style that the art historian can give us. Because of his familiarity with a greater number of works of art and because his synthesis of his observations of them proceeds according to method, he is able to provide us with a more precise definition of a style. To do so, he first examines the single object in all of its aspects—considering

199. JACQUES CAFFIERI. Firedogs. 1752

198. TORII KIYONAGA
Three Young Women and a Fan Vendor
(woodcut) Japanese, about 1789

200. GERMAN. Baptismal Font
(detai). 1467

201. VICTOR HORTA. Entry Hall,
Tassel House, Brussels. 1892–93

its authorship and date, its subject matter and purpose, as well as the character of the artist who created it. He weighs the role that each of these factors may play in determining the appearance of the work. While doing so, he also ascertains in just what way the single work is related to his initial concept of the style. By examining many contemporary works and using such a system of checks and balances, he refines his concept of a given period's style to the point where he may reasonably assume that it accurately reflects all of the major attitudes expressed in the works of that time. The amount of his knowledge about the creation of the work and the extent of his sensitivity to the visual statement made by the work determine the accuracy and pertinence of the definition of style that he eventually will provide for us.

If, like the art historian, we should seek to define more precisely the style of the period around 1900, we would discover that among the many works related to it are several that we had seen previously only as isolated objects—works, for example, like the painting by Klimt (fig. 140), the type ornament by Klinkhardt (fig. 136), the woodcuts by Schmidt-Rottluff (fig. 98) and Munch (fig. 102), and the painting by Vuillard (page 232). And, too, we would come to see that Gauguin's concept of the visual image as a combination of shapes, his two-dimensional rendering of space, as well as his concern for the surface appearance of the canvas (page 177) are not only ways of seeing that he shares with other artists of this time, but ways that he may, to some extent, be credited with originating. Examining such works from this era also would reveal to us the influence exerted on these artists not only by the Japanese woodcut (fig. 198) but by the works of earlier artists of such diverse periods as the eighteenth century in France (fig. 199) and the fifteenth century in Germany (fig. 200). From the works like the entry hall designed

202. MAURICE DENIS
Easter Morning. 1891

by Horta (fig. 201) we would learn that these artists strongly desired to make their work appear as if it were a growing, organic structure of the botanical world. And we would also come to learn, from paintings like the one by Denis (fig. 202), of these artists' inclination to express themselves through symbols. Our knowledge about the art of this period is expanded by all of these diverse observations and, in the process, our mental image of the style takes on, progressively, a more specific form. We begin to see it as a developed unity with a beginning and an end—a way of thinking that is manifested in part simply by the fact that we begin to call this style by name—choosing, from among the many names that this period gave to its art, the name *Art Nouveau.*

The more clearly this style begins to emerge in our mind as an independent identity—a kind of phenomenon of the visual world—the more we begin to see the possible interrelations among the many diverse qualities that we have discerned in it. Consequently, we find ourselves defining the Art Nouveau style in progressively broader terms; formulating a definition of the style that is not only pertinent for the individual work but, at the same time, is sufficiently comprehensive to include all of the works that we have discovered to belong to the style. Viewing the style as a whole leads us to see, for example, that the similarity between the work by Guimard and those of the French eighteenth century is not significant because of any specific relationship between the Art Nouveau period and the eighteenth century, but that it is significant only in that it is a particular manifestation of a general tendency of many of Guimard's contemporaries to return for inspiration to earlier works of art that show an insistence on the use of curved forms and sinuous line. Continually evaluating in this way the particular example in relation to what we know of other works eventually transforms our image of the style as a consistent, self-contained but abstract concept into one in which it is envisaged as a living force. We feel its power, for example, when we recognize that in some of their works created long after the Art Nouveau style had subsided, both Picasso (page 179) and Kandinsky (page 231) still reveal the influence that this style had upon them in their youth. The moment that style becomes alive for us marks the beginning of our understanding of it as the visual embodiment of man's thought and of our valuing it for the glimpse that it gives us into the creative mind.

If we wish to take advantage of this flash of perception to acquire a greater understanding of the creative mind, an even further synthesis of the style is necessary. We must seek to determine the significance that each observation acquires when it is seen in relation to the others. For example, we must see what we have learned of the Art Nouveau artist's interest in nature in conjunction with his marked preference for expressing this interest in materials like iron, glass, exotic woods, and gems. When plant forms are seen in this context, the artist's fascination with them no longer seems, as it otherwise might, to indicate delight in nature for its own sake, but seems to suggest a different attitude. The stalk, leaf, and bud—when cast in these favorite materials, imbedded in the flat mosaic wall, or held taut upon the surface of the painting—appear to be used as foils in a conflict between the man-made and the organic worlds. By virtue of this insight we come to recognize that by his preference for materials that carry the connotation of artificiality; by his inclination toward forms of art that call attention to themselves as artifacts (mosaics, embroideries, stained glass, and stenciled wallpapers); and by the premium that both of these preferences place upon the art of the maker and the skill of the creator, the artist consistently states that a work of art is a thing apart from either what it may represent—such as the park in the painting by Klimt—or even from what, in a functional sense, it actually may be—such as the desk by Guimard. Similarly, we may now see that a conscious contrast between form and representation also underlies the Art Nouveau artist's predilection to use a symbolic rather than a descriptive statement in his work, for a symbolic presentation basically gives precedence to the form of the symbol over what actually is symbolized. The more sharply our attention is focused on this aspect of the Art Nouveau style, the more we realize that line and shape are not an end in themselves, but the means by which the artist is able to assert the priority of the work of art's formal arrangement over the material out of which it is made, as well as over the function that it may perform or the object that it may represent. Progressively we come to understand that this style's hallmark of the sinuous line and curved shape is the visual expression of a creative attitude which has as its primary goal a work of art whose principal meaning rests in its physical, tangible self.

By such a formulation of a style something is revealed to us of the common attitude that underlies the similarities of its visual expression. It also offers us a basis for a comparison among all the creative arts of this period—a possibility which in turn provides us with a means of further verifying or expanding our synthesis of the style. We can discover by these means, for example, whether similar characteristics appear in the works of writers or composers of the Art Nouveau period which indicate that they share the approach to the work of art that we found to exist on the part of the painter, the cabinet maker, or the architect. Within at least the music of Debussy and Strauss, the poetry of Verlaine and Mallarmé, and the plays of Ibsen and Hofmannsthal, there exist sufficient similarities to suggest that in these areas also the artist preferred a symbolic statement, presented his work within a very consciously determined formal arrangement, frequently chose a subject whose nature contradicted the form into which he placed it, and tended to stress in his work those elements that were most unique to his particular art form. Such a comparison would also serve to make us more conscious of another aspect of this period's creative attitude—one which perhaps by being the most obvious, in that it was called "new art," does not, nevertheless, immediately appear to us as significant. But, recognizing within the music of Debussy, or the poetry of Mallarmé, the importance to these artists of presenting their work in a form other than the traditional, gives a renewed emphasis to the existence of this similar tendency in the visual arts. Here, too, the artists invent new forms rather than reinterpret the traditional ones. This further insight into their creative attitude gives an additional significance to our formulation of this style, for not only did these artists apparently desire to create a work of art in which form and meaning were synonymous, but to do so in a new language of art forms.

Our discernment of the significance of the Art Nouveau's principal characteristics as reflections of the artists' intentions leads us to sense more acutely its vitality as a complex of creative ideas and convictions. When we reach this point we begin to see those formal similarities that may exist among works of art in a way that brings us closer to understanding the factors which, although they may help shape an artist's approach, are not necessarily evident from the individual work. For example, in the painting *Tempered Elan* (page 231) Kandinsky's arrangement of clearly separated areas of color and curved shapes upon the surface of the canvas is in itself reminiscent of Art Nouveau forms that appear in his work of the early 1900s (fig. 203). On the basis of such purely formal similarities, however, the significance of this relationship between Kandinsky and the Art Nouveau style is not apparent. But, if we conceive the Art Nouveau as a style whose artists sought to establish the primacy of the world of art forms and consciously to separate it from the world of nature, then Kandinsky's relationship with it becomes meaningful in that it gives us an insight into what may have led him to create paintings like *Tempered Elan* or *Summer* (fig. 204). Kandinsky's invention of the painter's non-objective world and his belief in it as the only possible means of expression for the creative artist is now put into a context by this relationship, which allows us to perceive more readily his intention and to see even the single work with an increased understanding. And, in a less specific sense, understanding the Art Nouveau style in terms of the primacy it gives to the artist and to the world he creates may also suggest to us something of the creative attitude that underlies a work of art like the painting *One* (page 230) by Jackson Pollock. In these last two instances we have

203. WASSILY KANDINSKY
Summer (woodcut). 1903

204. WASSILY KANDINSKY
Summer: Composition 3. 1914

started to think of the Art Nouveau style as representing a cohesive body of artistic thought, which by its occurrence is responsible for determining the art that followed it. Now that we can see this style as the expression of a specific aesthetic attitude, it emerges for us as a creative force in its own right.

To think of Art Nouveau as representing, or being the product of, a specific creative attitude enables us to see it within the framework of the whole series of such attitudes that constitutes the history of man's creative activity. We can understand more exactly the connotation of this particular attitude by comparing it with the ways in which artists had previously conceived their work. We try to see, for example, whether, within the numerous recognizable styles of the Western visual arts, there is a parallel to the Art Nouveau style. We have already noted that in terms of certain formal characteristics—particularly with respect to the use of line—some Art Nouveau artists were inspired by the art of the French eighteenth century, and others by the art of the Late Medieval period. If we now seek, however, to relate our concept of the total Art Nouveau style to one of the past styles, we should have to determine whether there existed greater similarities between these two styles than merely a similarity of visual appearance. It is, however, the existence of such formal similarities that guides us in our analysis. In the same way that we have proceeded in building up that concept of the individual style, we must proceed in our evaluation of its relationship with any other style.

205. FRANCO-BURGUNDIAN
The Trinity Morse (ecclesiastical brooch)
About 1400

206. LORENZO GHIBERTI
St. John the Baptist. 1412–16

What we would discover about the Art Nouveau style in this process is that it bears a striking affinity to a style that existed in Europe around 1400, called the *International Style.* In the formal sense, the International Style is characterized by a predominantly flat, linear expression and a use of curved, streamlined shapes that tend to transform whatever is represented into an exquisite pattern of colors and textures. The powerful fascination that a rhythmical line, used for its own sake, held for these artists can be seen, for example, in the statue by Ghiberti or the French manuscript painting (figs. 206 and 207). And the artists' pleasure in creating a work as an arrangement of interesting shapes can be seen in Pisanello's painting of St. Eustace (fig. 208). They, too, seem to prefer to work with metallic and precious materials, which they wrought into objects of intricate detail, such as the brooch (fig. 205) made by a French goldsmith for a clerical vestment, with its minute rendering of leaves, branches, and figures. The high esteem in which these objects were held by artist and patron alike indicates to us their admiration and preference for works that revealed the art of a skilled craftsman. The elegant and the sophisticated, the artificial and the sensuous, the symbolic and the exotic, are all characteristic of this style, as is an interest in nature that expresses itself in the landscapes of the paintings and the thickly intertwined foliage that flourished on the manuscript borders and around the arches of of their buildings. And—as in the Art Nouveau work—here, too, there seems to be a sense of willful contradiction between subject and object. A vast panorama of a landscape is held flat on the surface by the use of color and shape, or allowed to expand into depth only within the confines of an area that is microscopically measurable. An extremely realistic object is painted side by side with one that is consciously mannered and artificial. By the very lushness of the manuscript borders, teeming with many kinds of leaves, flowers, and insects, the work of nature is translated into a work that is, first of all, the work of the artist. Similarly, the wealth of recorded detail that the painter shows us of the buildings and costumes gives precedence to a pictorial reality over the observably possible. In all of these aspects this style seems to represent an attitude of its artists toward the work of art based on an awareness of the difference between the visual and the natural world that, although not as clearly stated, is certainly akin to the attitude of the Art Nouveau artist.

ABOVE

208. PISANELLO. *The Vision of St. Eustace.*
About 1438

LEFT

207. FRENCH. Leaf in an
Hours of the Virgin. About 1430

209. PIERO DELLA FRANCESCA
The Flagellation of Christ. About 1456

Once alerted to the possibility that there may exist various periods in the history of art whose artists used similar formal means, and that these similar formal characteristics reflect a similar creative attitude, we start to think of the work of art more specifically in terms of its meaning as a visual embodiment of the direction of man's thought. We now see the individual painting or the piece of goldsmith's art in a context that makes apparent a motivation of the artist of which he, himself, was not necessarily conscious. For comparing and contrasting styles gives us a hint that a pattern may be discerned in man's past artistic activity, that could guide us to a more complete understanding, not only of the style itself, but of the nature of the creative act as well. To determine this pattern more clearly, we seek out in greater detail the circumstances surrounding the creation of these styles. For example, we should like to know more about the art immediately preceding and immediately following the International and the Art Nouveau styles. From what we would learn about the works of art prior to either of these two styles, it would appear that there was a general tendency among these artists to work increasingly in the manner of descriptive realism. We would also learn that each of these styles comes at the end of a long period during which the artist's concept of his work would seem to have undergone little change. Using the terms in their broadest possible sense, we can refer to these long periods as the Medieval and the Renaissance traditions. Those differences that exist between works of art created at different times within either one of these traditions are relatively minor contrasted with the differences that we can see between a work of the Medieval tradition and one of the Renaissance tradition. For example, the difference between the sixteenth-century painting by Bellini (fig. 188) and the eighteenth-century painting by David (fig. 60) is less than the difference between Bellini and the thirteenth-century German artist (fig. 174). An equally large difference would seem to separate the work of the twentieth century from that of the Renaissance tradition, and thus it becomes apparent that both the International Style and Art Nouveau occur immediately before the time when artists began to see in such a new way that their work became radically different from what had preceded it. Both of these moments coincide with a deliberate intellectual and quasi-scientific investigation of the pictorial means by which the physical object is represented. The "invention" of perspective and the "invention" of Cubism are equally decisive events in the history of Western art, for they symbolize a new concept of the relationship between the object being represented, the visual representation of it, and the viewer. The paintings of both Piero and Picasso (figs. 209 and 210)—two of the artists most directly associated with these investigations—are products of a systematized application of a new way of seeing, although the pictorial reality is different for each case, as is the illusion that it asks us to engage in.

Whether coincidental or truly parallel, such similarities are strongly suggestive that both the International and Art Nouveau styles reflect a creative attitude that—by deliberately sharpening the contrast between the pictorial and the natural worlds—was in part responsible for a subsequent formulation that set out precisely what would be the relationship between the two. In one instance a finite, static world was organized behind the picture plane, a result that we see in Piero's painting; in another, a timeless, constantly shifting world of multiple views embedded in the picture plane resulted. With Piero, the artist's desire to fix the interrelations of the objects within the world he created behind the picture plane gave, in essence, priority to describing the physical form of the single object. With Picasso, the artist's interest in making the picture plane itself the pictorial reality gave in essence priority to describing the relative form of the single object. In both cases these investigations brought forth a way of seeing and

210. PABLO PICASSO
Ambroise Vollard. 1910

comprehending physical reality that previously had not found expression in the visual arts and that corresponded to the emergence of an equally new approach to the comprehension of the physical world in science and philosophy. That these important steps in the development of man's thought should have occurred in conjunction with the creative attitude that characterizes the Art Nouveau and the International Style encourages us to see the art of these two periods in a different light and to be better able to evaluate the forces that produced them.

To see these forces we must take into consideration the conditions in which the artist existed. For the Art Nouveau period, for example, we should now view more clearly the significance of the political, sociological, or economic conditions of the artist's life in determining his creative attitude. We should see in a new light the artists' reaction against the industrial society that had grown up during the nineteenth century; against a code of morals that suffered rather than encouraged individual freedom; and against the dominance of the traditional historic styles of art that had persisted throughout the century. In this light we can understand more clearly why the artist of the Art Nouveau drew his inspiration from whatever was unlike the commonly held concept of what it should be like. We begin to understand why, in works of art, what had been symmetrical was now assymetrical, what had been straight was now curved, what had been still was now charged with movement. We are likely to see even more significance in the circumstance that he also transforms even the symbols he spoke with—the lily of purity becoming a symbol of suggestive sensuality. And because of what we already have learned from the work of art itself about this artist's attitude, we would realize that these actions do not amount merely to a revolt against the accepted. For we know that in this process the artist created a basis for a totally new language of pure form. What the artist succeeded in creating, by his attempt to express himself in a work of art that recognized no authority other than its own, was not only a new art style but an entirely new concept of the creative artist. The line drawn between the world of nature and the world of art was, in itself, only a symbol of the line that was being drawn between the creative artist and the world of mechanization, administration, and conformity. Opposed to it, the artist brought forth a new world that both preserves and continues man's creative and spiritual expression.

From our attempts to determine the phenomenon of style we gain an ever-expanding concept of the nature of the creative act. How instructive this way of seeing becomes for us depends upon the degree to which we remain flexible in our use of it. We must continue to be aware that, starting with other similarities as a base for our seeing in terms of style, we might ultimately discern other patterns and other cycles within the history of art. If we work with style in this manner, then, by the process of formulation, rejection, or refinement, we constantly increase our visual perceptivity and comprehension.

CHAPTER 16

On Judging Quality

TO SEE A PAINTING, a piece of sculpture, or a chair in the broad context provided by our concept of its style is, ultimately, to focus our attention all the more sharply on its unique character. From viewing the individual object within the framework of its similarities with other works we are led inevitably to be as sensitive to its differences. For example, the similarities that link the paintings by Cima and Bellini serve to impress on us not only the common approach of the two artists but, as well, the separate way in which each of these artists works within that common approach. We come to sense more keenly the individuality of each painting; we appreciate each one for the unique experience that it offers us. To the extent that style affords us the possibility of perceiving these differences is measured its value to us as observers, for unlike the historian or philosopher of art our primary concern is with our response to the work itself.

The more we are aware of the uniqueness of the experience that each offers us, the more we are drawn into forming qualitative judgments about all of the works of art that we encounter. Our tendency to make such judgments, born of our now more intimate relationship with works of art, is strengthened by the growing immediacy of our response to them. A significant part of our past experience merges in our mind to form on an unconscious level the basis for a response that we consciously identify as a more intuitive apperception of works of art. Our past observations of art have coalesced to orient us toward expectations of what works of art are or ought to be.

On the basis of what we have observed to be possible, we expect that a certain level of ability will underlie any work of art that we encounter. A work, if it does not meet our expectations, is unsatisfying for us, and, therefore, a poor work of art. The very least that we expect from any work, for example, is that it be made by someone whose expressive intent is not defeated by lack of skill. If a painter is concerned with making the objects represented in his work appear natural, we expect that we shall be able to recognize what he is representing. An image painted to be recognized as an orange but looking more like a lemon or a ball does not

211. CIRCLE OF CARAVAGGIO
The Fruit Vendor (Man Selling Melons)
17th century

satisfy us, because we know that images can be painted that do resemble oranges. Or, because we have seen paintings in which spatial relations among objects are conveyed clearly, we expect similar clarity in paintings by other artists who desire to suggest such relations. In this sense, the painting by a Caravaggio follower (fig. 211) does not come up to our expectations: a confusion about whose hand is whose disappoints our expectations of what the artist's ability should be within his chosen area of performance.

Our past experience also leads us to hold other expectations beyond a minimal criterion of skill. In accordance with our observations of the use of line, color, and shape in widely different works of art, we have formed some idea of the expressive possibilities that these elements offer artists. We come to judge an artist's work in relation to how well he takes advantage of these expressive possibilities. Our idea of its quality is determined by our grasp of the artist's feeling for the particular visual essence of what he uses to create an image. If, for example, there are shapes within a painting, our idea of the painting's quality depends on the degree of sensitivity this artist displays for a shape as a visual element. In a line drawing of a dancer, we expect that the expressive power of the work will depend upon the quality of the drawn line. If it does not, we consider the work to be a poor drawing even though the artist may have had sufficient skill to place on the paper a representation of a figure in the act of dancing. As a drawing the representation would not embody what we have come to recognize as the mark of the artist who works with line.

In all of these instances, our judgment of what we may call the artistic ability of the artist is obviously related directly to our own visual sensitivity. Like its meaning, the quality of a work of art emerges for us only through our response to its particular visual characteristics— not through our application of some predetermined standard. The expectations that we bring to the work from our past experience must be flexible enough to allow us to recognize and accept new possibilities. We must be able to extend our expectations—not to be limited by them. Judging the level of artistic ability in a Cubist painting by Picasso or a painting by Jackson Pollock according to expectations derived from seeing Italian Renaissance paintings imposes a standard upon such works that limits our understanding of them. Clearly, this area of our judgment is circumscribed by the extent of our sympathy for what the artist is doing. We must be sympathetic to the work—not in the sense of being prejudiced in its favor, but of under-standing what the artist wishes to express. In fact, to use artistic ability as a criterion is not possible at all, unless we can first infer from the object itself that the artist knew and accepted what he had to do in order to achieve what he wanted to do. The quality, for example, that we find in a work of folk art such as the painting by an anonymous American artist (fig. 212) lies precisely in the naïve, innocent character that we believe it to possess. The extent of our appreci-ation of it depends largely upon our recognizing that the artist disregarded or did not know the means of visual expression that we have come to expect works of art to possess. To judge whether artistic ability is positively absent or negatively present in a work depends upon whether or not we can discern the intention of the artist.

Evaluating artistic ability implies an awareness on our part of the obstacles to expression inherent in the means that the artist has chosen. In addition, it implies an appreciation of the way in which the artist overcomes these obstacles. We judge the quality of a work of art not only by whether the artist has succeeded but, also, by how well he has succeeded. Because the extent of our appreciation is relative to what we have come to know is possible, the quality

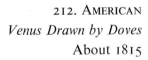

212. AMERICAN
Venus Drawn by Doves
About 1815

213. GERRIT VAN HONTHORST. *The Supper at Emmaus.* About 1630

that we attribute to a work depends upon the context in which we see it. For example, familiarity with many works by one artist leads us to form a concept of his general artistic ability. Accordingly, we begin to evaluate the individual work in the light of what we have seen the artist is capable of achieving. If a work fails to meet our standard for this artist, we are apt to speak of his having had a "bad day." On the other hand, we also come to recognize those works in which the artist has achieved his intention to a degree that surpasses all his other attempts. If such a work stands out too sharply from the rest, we are likely to speak of his having been "lucky," but if, instead, the work appears to extend rather than to exceed our expectations, we are likely to speak of it as his masterpiece. Within what we know of the artist's intentions and his ability, this one work appears to overcome the obstacles inherent in his chosen means of expression to such an extent that we feel that nothing could be changed without destroying this perfection. Naturally, by such a statement we do not literally mean that not one line or shape could be altered. We express ourselves in this way because we recognize how rare such an accomplishment is, and are disinclined to believe that it could be achieved in any other way.

Critical judgments such as these imply a new relationship between ourselves and the individual work of art. We have become conscious of the work of art as an accomplishment of its artist as well as an object to be experienced in its own right. We come to appreciate the work of art in relation not only to how well the artist succeeds but to the kind of obstacles that he sets for himself. The more difficult we know his attempt to be, the more highly we value the work that results. Similarly, we have less regard for a work in which the obstacles set by the artist had previously been attempted by others and whose solutions are but little different. Such a work does not satisfy our expectations to the same degree as the work of the artist who originally conceived his intention in this fashion. Thus, although we should judge the level of artistic ability in the painting by Honthorst (fig. 213) to be very high, our experience of it, nevertheless, is tempered by our knowledge that the means by which the artist has sought to create this experience were originally conceived by Caravaggio. When we see it in relation to the painting by Caravaggio (fig. 215), we value the painting by Honthorst less highly because his intention does not seem wholly of his own invention. This factor of originality is an ultimate measure of quality within the area of artistic ability. Its presence or absence within a work directly affects whatever final determination of quality we might choose to make among works of art otherwise similar in their level of artistic ability. If we continuously appraise this ability in a work of art—and we may do so either in an unconscious preference for some works over others or in a carefully determined, critical choice—we are also drawn into making an evaluation of the work of art in terms of the experience that we receive.

In judging the quality of a work of art on the basis of the type of experience that it offers us, we leave the relatively objective area of judgment that we have defined as artistic ability and enter the more subjective area in which we evaluate the significance of the artist's intention. In this area our judgment of the work of art does not proceed from what our past visual experience has led us to know is possible, nor from the degree to which our expectations are fulfilled. It arises, instead, from what we feel that the work of art reveals to us. In this sense, no matter how high we may judge the artistic ability of a work to be, regardless of our degree of admiration for the way in which the artist achieved his intention, such a work seems to us to be lacking in quality if our imagination is not in some way stimulated.

To evaluate a work of art in terms of our experience of it is necessarily a very personal and subjective act. Precisely because of this, such a judgment is also the one which has the greatest meaning for us and the one which provides us with our strongest convictions. Naturally, then, this aspect of our relation with the work of art can color our judgment of any other aspect of the work. It can be responsible, for example, for making us award a high value to works of low artistic ability. For this reason, we must be alert to recognize what part of our judgment is due to an objective appraisal of a work's artistic ability and what part to a more purely subjective response. And, within the latter, we must, if we wish to be responsible critics, try to determine further why for us one artist's intention seems more significant than another's.

In this area of judgment, the quality that we attribute to a work of art is relative not only to our visual sensitivity but to our capacity for understanding a work of art in terms of human experience. Any work that stimulates our imagination or otherwise makes us aware of its having revealed something to us adds to our own experience by giving us an insight into some aspect of life. Our judgment, in this instance, is necessarily relative to the extent of our framework of reference for evaluating human experience. Our judgment depends upon our level of intellectual and emotional maturity—upon our ability and inclination to comprehend reality. What level

214. REMBRANDT. *The Supper at Emmaus.* 1648

of quality we see in a work of art—and in a sense this level is a measure of the greatness of a work of art—relates, then, to our discernment of its meaning in these terms and to how this meaning accords with our personal philosophy.

If we prefer, for example, the painting by Rembrandt (fig. 214) to the painting by Caravaggio (fig. 215), our inference of its superior quality is based on such an accord. For us, apparently, the painting by Rembrandt clarifies and intensifies, or newly interprets some aspect of human experience for which we have sensitivity, sympathy, and concern. In taking account of our reaction, we might describe the painting as having a "meaning beyond itself," indicating that this work makes us aware of a content beyond the visual forms themselves. To say "beyond," however, is not to imply "apart from": for whatever insight we receive comes from the visual forms. In fact, our preference for the Rembrandt is based not only upon an accord with its meaning but upon our sympathy with the way in which this insight is conveyed. Thus, the painting's quality—its depth of meaning for us—depends upon how tellingly it becomes a link for us between its visual self and our fund of grasped, felt, and understood human experience.

If we prefer the painting by Rembrandt it is not, then, because it possesses a greater insight than the Caravaggio, but, rather, because we are more receptive to the way Rembrandt communicates the insight.

Comparison of the two paintings may provide a clue to the relation between our preference for a particular presentation and our judgment of the depth of meaning in a work. Both the Rembrandt and the Caravaggio are works of great technical skill and artistic ability, and both use similar visual means to depict the same event, yet each artist chooses to stimulate our imagination in a different way and each work is an object that encourages a different process of apperception. In both paintings we are attracted immediately by the way the paint appears: spread and molded by Rembrandt's brush, smoothed and polished by Caravaggio's. We respond with similar emphasis to Caravaggio's constricted stage of violent gesture and to the hushed and atmospheric realm of the Rembrandt. We feel with equal intensity the impact of the harsh spotlighting in the Caravaggio and the quasi-physical, quasi-divine lighting of the Rembrandt.

In the Rembrandt each one of these aspects works to increase our feeling for the tangibility, physical as well as psychological, of the figures depicted. The minimized description and the

215. CARAVAGGIO. *The Supper at Emmaus*. About 1598

216. J.-B. SIMEON CHARDIN. *Still Life*. About 1755

calm, restricted gestures intensify our impression of the individuality and emotion of the persons involved in this drama. Because of the powerful suggestion of the personality of each of the figures and his reactions within a particular situation, we can immediately respond to this painting in terms of a meaning related to human experience.

Caravaggio speaks to us less directly. The contrast between his visual means and Rembrandt's only reflects the two men's basically different ways of appealing to our imagination. Here, each of the visual elements builds persistently toward creating a work of less immediate emotional involvement. We no longer are seeing a work in which we have a direct feeling for the figures as human beings, but a work from which we draw our inspiration through a symbolic statement. The exaggeration of gesture is a symbol of emotion rather than an expression or suggestion of it. The specific and explicit facial descriptions of the figures limit our ability to become emotionally involved with them as human beings. The still-life objects, too, are exaggerated. By virtue of their simplified form and their luminosity they become painted symbols far more beautiful than their natural counterparts. Less mysterious in immediate appearance but no less mystic in its insight, the work of Caravaggio suggests its meaning to us only through an association of the ideas generated by the painted objects, not, as in the Rembrandt, through an immediate human understanding generated by the figures represented. The Caravaggio painting is a tableau that hints of a meaning whose revelation depends upon our contemplation of it. In contrast, the Rembrandt painting is a play that expresses its meaning directly through the words and actions of its characters. Which of these two works has the greater meaning for us will depend upon which we prefer of these two equally possible ways of communicating insight.

Quite clearly, in both the Rembrandt and Caravaggio paintings the instrument by which our imagination is first aroused is physical beauty. Through all the visual means with which we have come to be familiar, each artist brings us to the point where our engagement with the painting continually increases. But of the two, the work by Caravaggio more constantly enforces upon our experience the sensuous beauty of the forms with which we are involved. As a result, what the painting by Caravaggio reveals to us is more unique, less a part of our general experience, than what we gain from the painting by Rembrandt. The direct insight that Rembrandt gives us into human personality allows us to endow his painting with such a breadth of meanings that our experience of it as a unique phenomenon is, in fact, diminished. On the other hand, the uniqueness of our experience with the work by Caravaggio does not thereby limit the depth of meaning we may see in it. Indeed, because we are conscious that its meaning is revealed to us by virtue of its physical particularities, our experience of it is intensified and more readily extended. Whatever insight we receive from the Caravaggio we receive more sharply and with a feeling of greater penetration because it is more specifically concentrated in this one work.

The power and incisiveness that this sense of the beauty of a work of art can lend to our feeling of the uniqueness of our experience can also transform our comprehension of the meaning of a work of art into an intuitive apperception of it. In the Chardin still life (fig. 216), for example, the impact of physical beauty through colors, shapes, and their arrangement can so stimulate our imagination that we feel that we have suddenly gained an insight into something very meaningful. The fact that we may not be able to describe exactly the nature of that insight does not reduce the meaning it has for us but enhances it. The reality for us of this moment of intuitive and seemingly total comprehension adds to our experience as a human being in a direct rather than a conceptual manner. This glimpse of truth confirms the fact that other experiences—whether with works of art or in any area—are indeed possible and meaningful for us.

Regardless of whether our preference in the way in which an artist adds to our experience is for that of Rembrandt, Caravaggio, or Chardin, the extent of experience possible in these works is a measure of their greatness. In each case our imagination is stimulated because we have been able to share directly in the vision of the artist. This is our initial and ultimate purpose in looking at works of art: to be able to benefit from the imagination of the creative artist who, by impulse or by unconscious generosity, provides us with one of the few means that we have for finding meaning and significance in what we do.

LIST OF ILLUSTRATIONS

The publisher and author wish to thank the museums, galleries, and private collectors for granting permission to reproduce the works of art in their collections. Photographs have been supplied by the owners or custodians of the works reproduced; those instances where photographs were supplied by other sources are gratefully acknowledged.

80. PICASSO. Detail of *Four Ballet Dancers*

81. PABLO PICASSO. *Four Ballet Dancers*. 1925. Pen. The Museum of Modern Art, New York (Gift of Mrs. John D. Rockefeller, Jr.)

82. GEORGE ROMNEY. *Dancing Figures*. About 1775. Pen. The Metropolitan Museum of Art, New York (Rogers Fund, 1911)

83. JEAN-AUGUSTE DOMINIQUE INGRES. *The Golden Age* (study for the fresco in the Château de Dampierre). About 1845. Pencil. Musée Ingres, Montauban, France (Photo: Ressequié, Montauban)

84. JEAN-AUGUSTE DOMINIQUE INGRES. *The Golden Age* (detail). 1862. The Fogg Art Museum, Harvard University, Cambridge, Massachusetts (Grenville L. Winthrop Bequest)

85. VINCENT VAN GOGH. *Night Café* (and detail). 1888. Yale University Art Gallery, New Haven (The Stephen C. Clark Collection) (Photo: The Museum of Modern Art, New York)

86. GEORGES DE LA TOUR (?). *The Ecstasy of St. Francis* (and detail). 1640–45. Wadsworth Atheneum, Hartford (Photo: E. I. Blomstrann, New Britain, Connecticut)

87. ANDREA MANTEGNA. *St. Jerome* (and detail). About 1470. Museu de Arte, São Paulo

88. JOHN SELL COTMAN. *Greta Bridge* (and detail). 1805. Watercolor. British Museum, London

89. KURT SCHWITTERS. *"Merz" Drawing*. 1924. Collage of cut colored papers and a button. The Museum of Modern Art, New York (Katherine S. Dreier Bequest)

90. ARISTIDE MAILLOL. *Study for "Summer."* 1910–11. Bronze. Collection Mr. and Mrs. Alan Wurtzburger, Baltimore

91. ERNST BARLACH. *Man Drawing a Sword*. 1911. Wood. Galleries of the Cranbrook Academy of Art, Bloomfield Hills, Michigan (Photo: Adolph Studly, New York)

92. MICHELANGELO. *Pietà*. About 1550–56 Marble. Cathedral, Florence (Photo: Alinari)

93. CONSTANTIN BRANCUSI. *Fish*. 1930. Marble. The Museum of Modern Art, New York (Acquired through the Lillie P. Bliss Bequest)

94. SIENESE. *Adam*. About 1485. Bronze. The Cleveland Museum of Art (John L. Severance Collection)

95. DAVID HAYES. *Woman Dressing*. 1958. Welded steel. Private collection, New York (Photo: The Museum of Modern Art, New York)

96. REGINALD BUTLER. *Girl*. 1956–57. Bronze. Collection Pierre Matisse, New York (Photo: Pierre Matisse Gallery)

97. RICHARD STANKIEWICZ. *Bird Lover in the Grass*. 1957. Welded steel and iron. Courtesy of the Stable Gallery, New York

98. KARL SCHMIDT-ROTTLUFF. *Woman with Hat*. 1905. Woodcut (Photo: Kohlhammer Verlag, Stuttgart)

99. ERICH HECKEL. *Woman on the Shore*. 1914. Woodcut. Pomona College Gallery, Claremont, California (Photo: Robert C. Frampton, Claremont, California)

100. CHRISTOFFEL JEGHER (after Rubens). *Hercules Fighting Envy and Deception*. About 1635. Woodcut. The Metropolitan Museum of Art, New York (Rogers Fund, 1918)

101. Detail of *Hercules Fighting Envy and Deception*

102. EDVARD MUNCH. *The Kiss*. 1902. Woodcut. The Museum of Modern Art, New York (Gift of Mrs. John D. Rockefeller, Jr.)

103. PIERRE MILLAN (after Rosso Fiorentino). *Dance of the Dryads*. About 1550. Engraving. The Metropolitan Museum of Art, New York (Gift of Miss Georgiana W. Sargent in memory of John Osborne Sargent)

104. Detail of *Dance of the Dryads*

105. STANLEY WILLIAM HAYTER. *Death by Water*. 1948. Engraving. National Gallery of Art, Washington, D.C. (Rosenwald Collection)

106. JAMES ENSOR. *Devils Battling the Angels and Archangels*. 1888. Etching. The Museum of Modern Art, New York (Gift of Mrs. John D. Rockefeller, Jr.)

107. CLAUDE LORRAIN. *The Flight into Egypt*. 1630–33. Etching. The Metropolitan Museum of Art, New York (Dick Fund, 1946)

108. J.-B. CAMILLE COROT. *Sappho*. 1872. Lithograph. National Gallery of Art, Washington, D.C. (Rosenwald Collection)

109. HENRY H. RICHARDSON. Crane Library. 1880–83. Quincy, Massachusetts (Photo: Wayne Andrews, New York)

110. HENRY H. RICHARDSON. Crane Library. 1880–83. Quincy, Massachusetts (Photo: Wayne Andrews, New York)

111. GIULIANO DA SANGALLO. Gondi Palace. 1490. Florence (Photo: Alinari)

112. LUDWIG MIES VAN DER ROHE. Lake Shore Drive Apartments. 1949–51. Chicago (Photo: Hedrich-Blessing, Chicago)

113. ASHENDENE PRESS. Pages from *Les Amours Pastorales de Daphnis et Chloé*. Published in London, 1931 (Photo: Robert C. Frampton, Claremont, California)

114. GIULIANO DA SANGALLO. Gondi Palace. 1490. Florence (Photo: Alinari)

115. GIULIANO DA SANGALLO. Gondi Palace. 1490. Florence (Photo: Alinari)

116. FRANCESCO DI GIORGIO. Proportion drawing from the *Codex Magliabechiano*. About 1480. Biblioteca Nazionale, Florence (Photo: Robert C. Frampton, Claremont, California)

117. J. P. OUD. Café de Unie. 1925. Rotterdam (Photo: E. M. van Ojen, The Hague)

118. KURT SCHWITTERS and KATE T. STEINITZ. Pages from *Die Märchen vom Paradies*. 1923. Published by the Apossverlag, Hanover, Germany (Photo: Robert C. Frampton, Claremont, California)

119. MIMBRES INDIAN. Designs from the inside surface of pottery bowls found in the Swarts Ruin, New Mexico (after Cosgrove). About 800–1300. Peabody Museum of Harvard University, Cambridge, Massachusetts

120. ROMANESQUE. *Dog, Acrobat, Siren*. 12th century. Sainte-Madeleine, Vézelay, France (Photo: Archives photographiques)

121. MIMBRES INDIAN. Design from inside surface of pottery bowl found in the Swarts Ruin, New Mexico (after Cosgrove). About 800–1300. Peabody Museum of Harvard University, Cambridge, Massachusetts

122. CROW INDIAN. Painted Shield Cover. 19th century. Smithsonian Institution, Washington, D.C.

123. CROW INDIAN. Painted Shield Cover. 19th century. Smithsonian Institution, Washington, D.C.

124. SANTO DOMINGO INDIAN. Jar, from New Mexico. 19th or early 20th century. Whereabouts unknown (Photo: Courtesy Denver Art Museum)

125. MESOPOTAMIAN. Pottery Goblet, from Susa. About 4000 B.C. British Museum, London

174. GERMAN. *The Journey and Adoration of the Wise Men*, leaf in the Berthold Missal. 13th century. The Pierpont Morgan Library, New York

175. SASSETTA. *The Meeting of St. Anthony and St. Paul.* About 1432–36. National Gallery of Art, Washington, D.C. (Kress Collection)

176. ALBERTO GIACOMETTI. *City Square.* 1948. Bronze. The Museum of Modern Art, New York (Purchase)

177. JUAN SANCHEZ COTAN. *Quince, Cabbage, Melon, and Cucumber.* About 1602. The Fine Arts Gallery of San Diego

178. WASSILY KANDINSKY. *Isolated Objects.* 1934. Philadelphia Museum of Art (Louise and Walter Arensberg Collection)

179. JOAN MIRO. *Composition.* 1933. The Museum of Modern Art, New York (Gift of the Advisory Committee)

180. ALEXANDER CALDER. *Lobster Trap and Fish Tail.* 1939. The Museum of Modern Art, New York (Gift of the Advisory Committee)

181. MARCEL DUCHAMP. *Revolving Glass* (left: shown at rest; right: shown in motion). 1920. Yale University Art Gallery, New Haven (Collection Société Anonyme)

182. MARCEL DUCHAMP. *Nude Descending a Staircase, No. 2.* 1912. Philadelphia Museum of Art (Louise and Walter Arensberg Collection)

183. MARCEL DUCHAMP. *Nude Descending a Staircase, No. 1.* 1911. Philadelphia Museum of Art (Louise and Walter Arensberg Collection)

184. UMBERTO BOCCIONI. *Unique Forms of Continuity in Space.* 1913. Bronze. The Museum of Modern Art, New York (Acquired through the Lillie P. Bliss Bequest)

185. GREEK. *Kouros*, from Melos. About 575–550 B.C. Marble. National Museum, Athens (Photo: Hirmer Verlag, Munich)

186. ISAMU NOGUCHI. *Kouros.* 1944. Marble. The Metropolitan Museum of Art, New York (Fletcher Fund, 1953)

187. JACKSON POLLOCK. *One.* 1950. 9′ × 17′10″. Collection Mr. and Mrs. Ben Heller, New York (Photo: The Museum of Modern Art, New York)

188. GIOVANNI BELLINI. *The Flight into Egypt.* About 1480. National Gallery of Art, Washington, D.C. (Mellon Collection)

189. CIMA DA CONEGLIANO. *The Virgin and Child with a Goldfinch.* About 1509. Reproduced by courtesy of the Trustees of the National Gallery, London

190. MASTER OF MONDSEE. *The Flight into Egypt.* About 1490. Kunsthistorisches Museum, Vienna

191. PERUGINO. *The Marriage of the Virgin.* About 1500. Musée des Beaux-Arts, Caen, France (Photo: Giraudon)

192. RAPHAEL. *The Marriage of the Virgin.* 1504. Brera Gallery, Milan (Photo: Anderson)

193. ANONYMOUS FRENCH. Inkstand. About 1900. Bronze. The Museum of Modern Art, New York (Phyllis B. Lambert Fund)

194. PERCY STAMP. Hatpin. 1908. Silver. Private collection, New York (Photo: George Barrows, New York)

195. LOUIS C. TIFFANY. Glass. About 1900. Favrile glass and silver-plated bronze. The Museum of Modern Art, New York (Phyllis B. Lambert Fund)

196. HENRY VAN DE VELDE. Candelabrum. About 1902. Silver. Nordenfjeldske Kunstindustrimuseum, Trondheim, Norway (Photo: Fachklasse für Fotografie, Kunstgewerbeschule, Zurich)

197. HECTOR GUIMARD. Desk. About 1903. The Museum of Modern Art, New York (Gift of Mme. Hector Guimard)

198. TORII KIYONAGA. *Three Young Women and a Fan Vendor.* Japanese, about 1789. Woodcut. The Metropolitan Museum of Art, New York (Howard Mansfield Collection, Rogers Fund, 1936)

199. JACQUES CAFFIERI. Firedogs. 1752. Ormolu. The Cleveland Museum of Art (John L. Severance Collection)

200. GERMAN. Baptismal Font (detail). 1467. Church of St. Severus, Erfurt, Germany (Photo: Dr. Franz Stoedtner, Düsseldorf)

201. VICTOR HORTA. Entry Hall, Tassel House, 6 Rue Paul-Emile Janson, Brussels. 1892–93 (Photo: Dr. Franz Stoedtner, Düsseldorf)

202. MAURICE DENIS. *Easter Morning.* 1891. Collection Dr. Jean-Baptiste Denis, Rouen

203. WASSILY KANDINSKY. *Summer.* 1903. Woodcut (Photo: Courtesy Professor Will Grohmann, Berlin)

204. WASSILY KANDINSKY *Summer: Composition 3.* 1914. The Museum of Modern Art, New York (Mrs. Simon Guggenheim Fund)

205. FRANCO-BURGUNDIAN. *The Trinity Morse* (ecclesiastical brooch). About 1400. Gold and enamel. National Gallery of Art, Washington, D.C. (Widener Collection)

206. LORENZO GHIBERTI. *St. John the Baptist.* 1412–16. Or San Michele, Florence (Photo: Alinari)

207. FRENCH. *David, Uriah, and Bathsheba: the Virtues and Vices*, leaf in an Hours of the Virgin. About 1430. The Pierpont Morgan Library, New York

208. PISANELLO. *The Vision of St. Eustace.* About 1438. Reproduced by courtesy of the Trustees of the National Gallery, London

209. PIERO DELLA FRANCESCA. *The Flagellation of Christ.* About 1456. Gallery of the Marches, Ducal Palace, Urbino (Photo: Alinari)

210. PABLO PICASSO. *Ambroise Vollard.* 1910. Pushkin Museum, Moscow (Photo: Courtesy Editions Cercle d'Art, Paris)

211. CIRCLE OF CARAVAGGIO. *The Fruit Vendor (Man Selling Melons).* 17th century. The Detroit Institute of Arts

212. AMERICAN. *Venus Drawn by Doves.* About 1815. Watercolor on silk. Abby Aldrich Rockefeller Folk Art Collection, Williamsburg, Virginia

213. GERRIT VAN HONTHORST. *The Supper at Emmaus.* About 1630. Wadsworth Atheneum, Hartford (Ellen Gallup Sumner and Mary Catlin Sumner Collection)

214. REMBRANDT. *The Supper at Emmaus.* 1648. National Art Museum, Copenhagen

215. CARAVAGGIO. *The Supper at Emmaus.* About 1598. Reproduced by courtesy of the Trustees of the National Gallery, London

216. J.-B. SIMEON CHARDIN. *Still Life.* About 1755. National Gallery of Art, Washington, D.C. (Chester Dale Collection, Gift)

page 9. Photographed at the Museum of Modern Art, New York, by Rollie McKenna

page 123. Alexander Calder in his studio, photographed by Rollie McKenna

page 239. Photographed at the Cleveland Museum of Art

INDEX

All text references are to page numbers. A numeral followed by an asterisk (*) indicates the number of a page on which a colorplate appears. Numbers set in italic type indicate the figure numbers of black-and-white illustrations.